CLEVELAND COUNTY
Pride of the Promised Land

The Norman–Cleveland County Historical House, located at 508 North Peters, was built in 1899 on "Silk Stocking Row," by William S. Moore. The Harry Lindsay family bought the house in 1908 and made it their home for many years. Courtesy Gil Jain, University of Oklahoma.

CLEVELAND COUNTY
Pride of the Promised Land
An Illustrated History

By Bonnie Speer

Who's Who, Past and Present Editor: Micah P. Smith
Partners in Progress Editor: Jerri Culpepper

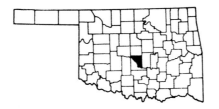

An Oklahoma Centennial Project

Sponsored by
Norman Galaxy of Writers
Published by Traditional Publishers, Norman, OK

Books by Bonnie Speer:
Errat's Garden
The Father of Gold Dredging, Benjamin Stanley Revett
Heck Thomas, My Papa
Moments in Oklahoma History, a Book of Trivia
Cleveland County, Pride of the Promised Land

FIRST EDITION: December 1988

Copyright © 1988
Bonnie Speer
Norman, Oklahoma

All rights reserved. No part of this book may be reproduced or utilized in any form or by any means, electronic or mechanical, including photocopying and recording or by any informational storage and retrieval system, without the expressed permission from the author.

Design:	Bob Buford, Norman, OK
Dust Jacket Painting:	G. N. Taylor, Durant, OK
Typography:	Type Traditional, Norman, OK
Published:	Traditional Publishers, Norman, OK
Printing:	Transcript Press, Norman, OK
Binding:	Motter Bookbinding Co., Muskogee, OK

ISBN: 0-943087-02-3

CLEVELAND COUNTY
Pride of the Promised Land
An Illustrated History

Dedicated to
JOHN WOMACK
whose passion for history left
Cleveland County with a wealth
of historical material.

TABLE OF CONTENTS

Page

Preface...ix
Introduction xi
Chapter One: The Virgin Land...............................1
Chapter Two: Claiming the Land.............................11
Chapter Three: The Struggle For Survival.....................21
Chapter Four: Norman, A Territorial Town....................33
Chapter Five: Transportation and Communication..............53
Chapter Six: Other Towns In Cleveland County...............71
Chapter Seven: A University Town.............................91
Chapter Eight: War Clouds and the Depression.................107
Chapter Nine: The Later Years...............................123
Chapter Ten: OU Football...................................137
Who's Who, Past and Present....................................149
    Presidents of The University of Oklahoma 150
    M. C. Runyan 150
    James H. Felgar 150
    Carl W. Kuwitzky 150
    H. H. Herbert 151
    Julia Beeler Smith 151
    John T. Washburn 151
    Dr. Joseph A. Rieger 151
    Garner G. Collums 152
    Abe T. Johnston 152
    Edna M. Couch 152
    Ruth Foreman Updegraff 152
    Horace H. Bliss 153
    George L. Cross 153
    Odies L. Primrose 153
    Cleo Sikkink Cross 153
    Paul W. Updegraff 154
    Savoie Lottinville 154
    Joseph R. Taylor 154
    James O. Hood 154
    Horace B. Brown 155
    John Womack 155
    Roy Valouch 155
    Ida Sloan Snyder 155
    Micah P. Smith 156
    Viola Hatfield Smith 156
    Edward F. Montgomery 156
    Wayne S. Wallace 156
    Henry C. Easterling 157
    Arrell M. Gibson 157
    Patricia Toothaker Donahue 157
    Richard C. Luttrell 157
    Robert J. Buford 158
    Bonnie Lue Speer 158
    Charles W. Bert 158
    Shiro Takemura 158
    Jim Miller 159

Donald Mayes 159
James G. Harlow, Jr. 159
Harold R. Belknap, Jr. 159
Franklin S. Coulter 160
Bill Williams 160
Carl M. Rose 160
Larry B. McDade 160
Kenneth R. Johnston 160
Tommy J. Bishop 161
G. Neal Taylor 161
Bob Usry 161
Nathan Glen Veal 162
Jerri Culpepper 162
Partners in Progress 163
Allard Cleaners 164
Cleveland County Record 164
Central Pharmacy 164
Gordon's Specialty 165
Hitachi Computer Products 166
Interurban Restaurant 167
IOOF Cemetery 168
Don James Co. 168
Mayes Funeral Directors 169
McDade Studios 169
Moore-Norman Vo-Tech 170
Norman Chamber of Commerce 170
Norman Regional Hospital 171
The Norman Transcript 172
Oklahoma Electric Co-operative 173
Oklahoma Gas & Electric Co. 174
Pab Personnel 175
Primrose Funeral Home 175
Shaklee Corporation 176
Sooner Fashion Mall 177
Transcript Press 178
Tarver Construction Co. 179
Type Traditional 179
The University of Oklahoma 180
Bob Usry Plumbing, Inc. 181
Valouch Electric Co. 181
Wright's IGA 182
Bibliography 183
Index 184

PREFACE

History is a record of significant human achievement affecting a nation or place, and a pictorial history is a visual record of that achievement. Though Cleveland County is young compared with many other areas in the United States, it still has had time to develop a proud heritage.

Most of us simply think of Cleveland County as our home, but famous people have lived here, the county has hosted presidents, and it is a cultural site.

The county has changed greatly over the years. Originally an empty prairie with a railroad line running through it, settlement occurred with a bang on the day of the run, April 22, 1889. The county has progressed steadily ever since. Today, while retaining some of its rural characteristics, Cleveland County has adapted to urban growth.

But through all of these changes, Cleveland County remains a special place for many people, a place where people's priorities still revolve around their schools, churches, neighbors, and families.

These varied and common activities form the basis of this illustrated history, which was seven years in the making. The photos have been chosen to tell the story of hometown life.

I wish to thank a number of people who helped me collect the material for this book. John Womack generously shared his knowledge of Norman and offered unlimited use of the photos and other material in his collection, and he proofread early copy for errors. My thanks also to Dr. Arrell Gibson who reviewed the first five chapters of this book for accuracy shortly before his death, to Dr. George Cross who read chapters six through eight, to Harold Keith and Jim Weeks for reading chapter ten, and to Joan Laughlin, Wynona Rennie, and Jack Dreesen each of whom read portions of chapter six. Ford Michael spent hours copying the majority of the old photos in this book with his camera.

Jane Bryant, managing editor of *The Norman Transcript*, generously contributed use of *The Norman Transcript* photo collection without which my work would have been much harder. Barbara Vanderburg assisted me in finding these photos. *The Transcript* photos form the backbone of Cleveland County's illustrated history. Many duplicates of this collection are also housed in the Pioneer Multi-County Library in Norman, to which William H. Lowry, director, gave me access, as well as other resource material.

Jan Burton, associate director of the University of Oklahoma Sports Information Office, gave me unqualified access to that department's picture file. "Chuck" House, editorial supervisor, *The Oklahoma Daily*, student newspaper of the Journalism Department of the University of Oklahoma, granted similar permission, as did Rodney M. Heisberger of the University of Oklahoma Drama Library.

Joyce Rex at McClain County Historical Society, John Lovett, Western History Collections, University of Oklahoma, and the staff of the Oklahoma Historical Society were always eager to help.

Other Cleveland County residents provided individual pictures which were greatly appreciated. Bob Blackburn, of the Oklahoma Historical Society, gave me advice and encouragement. Jack Black helped me obtain the picture for the dust jacket.

A special thanks to Edna Mae Couch for first suggesting this project to me, and for supplying me with books and old newspaper clippings as resource materials.

—Bonnie Speer

INTRODUCTION

Bonnie Speer's pictorial essay depicts the stages in Cleveland County's transformation from wilderness to rapidly enlarging small cities; from an Indian-pioneer frontier to a recent rush for modernity. Her illustrations disclose the Cleveland County area as a part of the Indian Territory, originally assigned to immigrant Creeks and Seminoles following their agonizing "Trail of Tears." Because these Indians participated on the side of the Confederacy in the Civil War, the federal government took their land with the intent of colonizing tribes from other parts.

Scenes copied from frontier photographers' glass plate negatives document Cleveland County's pioneer period. This portion of Indian Territory came to be called the Unassigned Lands because no Indians were re-settled here, and as cattlemen from Texas and Kansas grazed their herds over its rich grasslands, it served as the ranchmen's last frontier. Pressure from homeseekers and railroads led Congress to open the Unassigned Lands to settlement in 1889. Thus, Cleveland County was the scene of the great land run of that year and became one of the first counties established in Oklahoma Territory. However, Oklahoma City, only twenty miles away and soon to become the state capital and largest city in the state, confronted Cleveland County civic leaders with the continuing problem of establishing meaningful identities for their towns. For many years, Cleveland County functioned as a ranching and farming area, and as the home of the University of Oklahoma, educational center for the state and region.

In World War II, the county's role became international in scope when military authorities established two huge bases in Norman for training naval air personnel. In recent times, Norman, Noble, and Moore have become enlarging industrial centers, their plants served by the north-south mainline of the Santa Fe Railway and Interstate 35, and as residential centers for many thousands of daily commuters to Oklahoma City. Also, Lake Thunderbird, which provides water for the growing cities, has become a popular recreational center for water sports, fishing, and camping. Most important of all, the University of Oklahoma has enlarged its outreach through its programs in general education, petroleum geology, engineering, certain of the arts, publications of the University of Oklahoma Press, and intercollegiate athletics, focusing on football. These provide Cleveland County the identity and acceptance long sought by civic leaders.

Arrell Morgan Gibson
George Lynn Cross Professor of History
University of Oklahoma
November 20, 1987

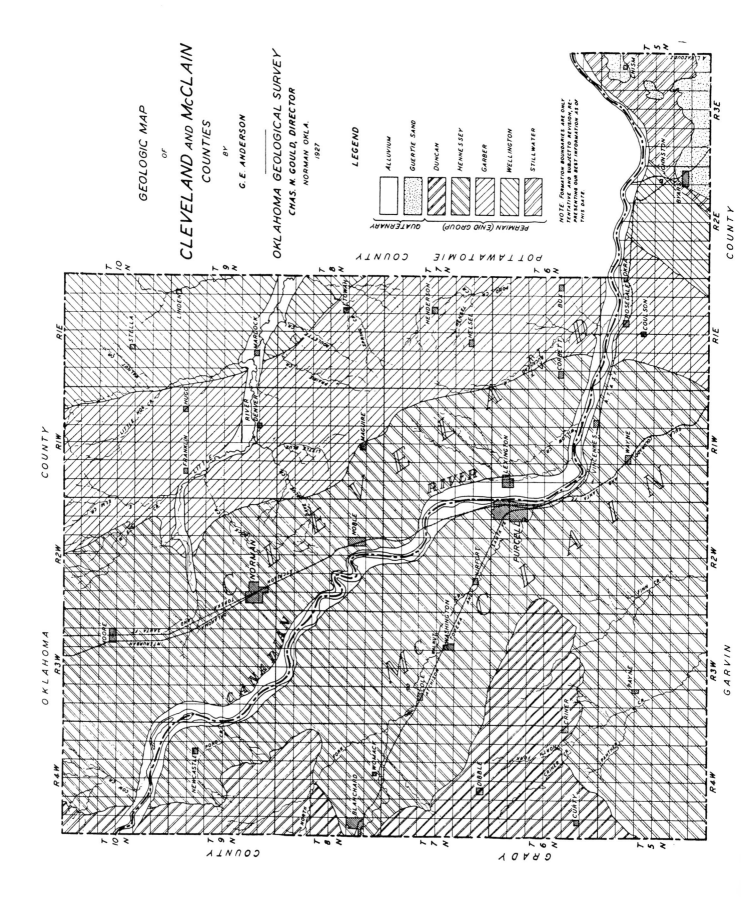

GEOLOGIC MAP
OF
CLEVELAND AND McCLAIN
COUNTIES
BY
G. E. ANDERSON

OKLAHOMA GEOLOGICAL SURVEY
CHAS. N. GOULD, DIRECTOR
NORMAN OKLA.
1927

LEGEND

Alluvium
Guertie Sand
Duncan
Hennessey
Garber
Wellington
Stillwater

QUATERNARY
PERMIAN (ENID GROUP)

NOTE: FORMATION BOUNDARIES ARE ONLY
TENTATIVE AND SUBJECT TO REVISION, RE-
PRESENTING OUR BEST INFORMATION AS OF
THIS DATE.

CHAPTER 1

The Virgin Land

That portion of central Oklahoma, where Cleveland County is now located, rested in the bottom of a shallow sea 250 million years ago. When the sea dried up, it left a series of high terraces created by mud and silt deposits. The area was drained by two major rivers, which we have come to know as the Canadian River and Little River, in addition to a number of smaller streams.

Large mammoths and other prehistoric animals roamed the area. Big game hunters began to wander into the region about 12,000 years ago. During the next 11,000 years, these cave dwellers became sedentary and planted corn, beans, and squash. They learned to use the bow and arrow and to make pottery.

On the eve of European discovery, Caddoan-speaking cultures from the east had established farming communities in eastern Oklahoma near Spiro. These people learned to use metals, established an art form, and developed a wide trade area that included central Oklahoma and extended to the Mississippi River, and Gulf Coast.

Plains tribes roamed the region to the west of the Spiro people. A natural boundary divided these two cultures. It extended from southern Kansas across eastern Cleveland County and into northern Texas. Called the Cross Timbers, this heavily wooded section, varying in width from five to thirty miles, separated the hardwoods of the eastern lowland forests and the western prairie grasslands.

So striking was this boundary that legend claimed the Cross

Large mastodons, such as this one exhibited in the Oklahoma Museum of Natural History on the University of Oklahoma campus, once roamed the Cleveland County area. Courtesy Bonnie Speer.

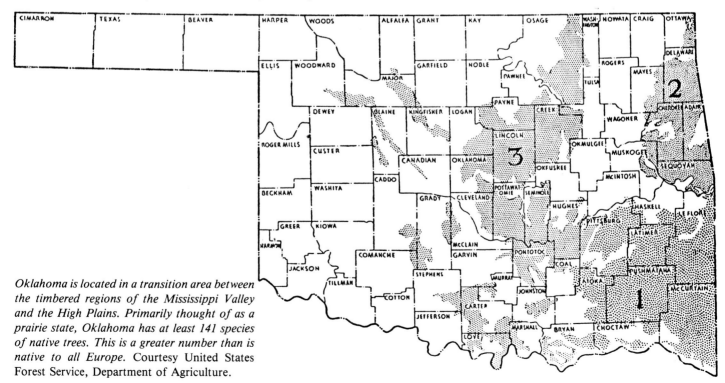

Oklahoma is located in a transition area between the timbered regions of the Mississippi Valley and the High Plains. Primarily thought of as a prairie state, Oklahoma has at least 141 species of native trees. This is a greater number than is native to all Europe. Courtesy United States Forest Service, Department of Agriculture.

These pieces of pottery illustrate the highly developed art forms excavated from the Spiro Mounds to the east of Cleveland County. In this photo W. P. Campbell is logging artifacts into the Stovall Museum record book. Courtesy Oklahoma Historical Society.

Timbers had been planted by an ancient lost race of men of the Mississippi mound builders to mark the western edge of their territory. Made up of a variety of hardwood trees, laced with a dense growth of greenbriars and grapevines, this thick woodland presented a virtually impenetrable barrier to Francisco Vasquez de Coronado when he marched north from Mexico in 1541 and crossed central Oklahoma.

Other explorers commented on the Cross Timbers as early as 1719. In 1832, during his journey through present Oklahoma, Washington Irving spoke of the wooded section this way: "I shall not easily forget the mortal toil, and the vexations of flesh and spirit, that we underwent occasionally, in our wanderings through the Cross Timbers. It was like struggling through forests of cast iron."

Sometime after 1200 A.D., hostile forces from the Plains tribes invaded the Spiro people and displaced them. When Coronado arrived, he found the Caddo, Wichita, Pawnee, and Apache Indians living on the plains. The Wichita dwelled in grass huts on the waterways and cultivated corn, beans, and tobacco. They ventured onto the prairies to hunt buffalo, as did the Caddo. The Comanches left their mountain retreats after they obtained guns from the Spanish and invaded the plains.

Three flags flew over the territory that now embraces Cleveland County. First that of Spain, then France, on the basis of Robert de la Salle's explorations along the Mississippi River in 1682. Spain regained the land in 1763 following the defeat of France in the French and Indian War then turned it back to France in 1800.

In 1803, Napoleon Bonaparte sold the land to the United States through the Louisiana Purchase. President Thomas Jeffer-

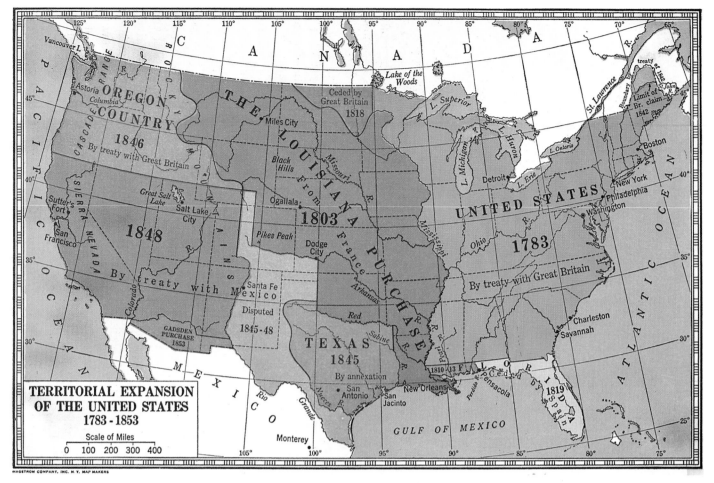

TERRITORIAL EXPANSION
OF THE UNITED STATES
1783-1853

Scale of Miles
0 100 200 300 400

HAGSTROM COMPANY, INC. N.Y. MAP MAKERS

son saw in this acquisition an opportunity to get rid of the bothersome Indians in the East, by settling them in this remote section, beyond the way of expanding white settlement. The Five Civilized Tribes — the Cherokees, Choctaws, Chickasaws, Creeks, and Seminoles — had adopted the ways of the white man in an attempt to get along with him, but the Indians still clashed constantly with the governments of the Southern states.

In 1804, Congress passed a bill giving the President authority to make a treaty with the Indians. This treaty asked them to cede their lands in the east for a like amount in the west.

The Eastern Woodlands Indians were the first to move to Indian Territory. In 1817, the Western Cherokees settled in what is now northeastern Arkansas. During the next fifteen years, the

A major accomplishment of President Thomas Jefferson was the purchase of the Louisiana Territory from France in 1803 for $15,000,000. This act nearly doubled the area of the United States. Cleveland County was included in that area comprising the Louisiana Purchase. Courtesy Bonnie Speer.

Buffalo and a variety of other game found a home on the varied terrain of Cleveland County. Courtesy Wichita Wildlife Reserve.

Washington Irving traveled through Cleveland County in the fall of 1832 with a troop of U.S. Rangers. He wrote about his adventures in A Tour of the Prairies. Courtesy International Portrait Gallery.

Col. A. P. Chouteau, a French fur trader and interpreter, established a trading post on Chouteau Creek, which he operated for three years following the peace treaty with the Plains Indians. Courtesy Shelby Fly.

COL. A. P. CHOUTEAU ~ 1786-1838
from an old print

remainder of the Five Civilized Tribes were forced by federal policy to follow suit. Hundreds of people died of hunger and exposure during the long, cold march over the infamous "Trail of Tears."

The Choctaws were the first to receive that land containing present Cleveland County. In 1833, the U.S. government assigned the Seminoles to hold joint title to the land with the Choctaws and a year later the Seminoles were given full title.

No other civilized tribe gave the goverment as much trouble as did the Seminoles. Though a small group, under the leadership of Osceola, the Seminoles started a war in the swamps of the Florida Everglades, which cost the United States ten million dollars and 1,466 lives. Eventually, over 2,000 Seminoles settled in Indian Territory, but some of that tribe are still living in the Everglades even today.

The new land of the Seminoles was bounded on the north by the North Canadian River and the Cherokee Outlet, and on the south by the Canadian River. The western boundary extended to a point near the Texas line. The Chickasaws and Choctaws occupied the land between the Canadian River and the Red River. The Creeks lived to the north of the Choctaw land.

When the Five Civilized Tribes arrived in Indian Territory, even then they found white settlers already pressing them from the east. On the west, the Plains Indians were hostile, resenting this intrusion into their traditional hunting grounds. The U.S. government established military forts in the territory to protect the eastern Indians from both the whites and hostile Indians in the area. The earliest of these forts was Fort Gibson built in 1824, followed by Old Fort Arbuckle in 1834.

The first known white man to explore future Cleveland County was Major Stephen H. Long in 1820. He had selected the site for Fort Smith three years earlier and while returning from an exploration journey to Pikes Peak, he had mistaken the Canadian River for the Red River, and followed the southern branch. On August 25, the party journeyed across the flat land north of the Canadian River where Norman now lies. Long noted in his journal that huge prairie dog towns existed in the vicinity, and elk, deer, and bear were numerous.

Washington Irving accompanied Captain Jesse Bean and a company of U.S. Rangers across the region in the fall of 1832. Irving preserved the details of this trip in his book, *A Tour of the Prairies*.

On August 1, the men camped on a creek in what is now the eastern section of urban Norman. A herd of buffalo rushed upon their camp, approaching within 200 yards before the men could turn the herd with their guns. (In March 1893, J. C. Clarke, who had homesteaded that section, cut down a tree on his property and found a bullet deeply embedded in the wood, which was presumed to have come from this buffalo hunt.)

Two days after the potentially disastrous buffalo hunt, Washington Irving and his party moved downstream to a small spring which later became known as "Norman's Camp."

Other military explorations of the region followed this. Peace among the Plains Indians became important to westward settlement.

In 1835, a three-man peace commission met with over 6,000 western and eastern Indians on a treaty site located between the headwaters of Little River and the Canadian, approximately four and a half miles northeast of present Lexington. Ft. Holmes, a small unoccupied military post, had been started there the year before. The treaty signed at "Camp Holmes" promised U.S. citizens safe passage through the western country and hunting rights to the eastern Indians on the plains.

Shortly after signing of the treaty, Col. A. P. Chouteau, member of a French fur trading family and Osage interpreter with the peace party, established a trading post on Chouteau Creek near the treaty site, which he operated for three years.

Other famous explorers who visited the area included Josiah Gregg in 1839 and Captain Nathan Boone, youngest son of Daniel Boone, who made the trip in 1843 with a group of U. S. Dragoons.

Following the 1848 California gold discovery, soldiers laid out a wagon road from Fort Smith to Santa Fe. Called the California Road, the trail followed the divide between the Washita and Canadian rivers across western Indian Territory. Many travelers took this road; others kept to the north bank of the Canadian River, crossing near the site of future Norman.

Jesse Chisholm established a trading post near Choteau's old site in 1854. The area, a rich and bountiful land, seemed delightfully removed from the rest of the world. All that was soon to change though.

Most of the Five Civilized Tribes owned slaves and wanted to remain neutral during the Civil War, but the Union soldiers

Jesse Chisholm established a trading post near Chouteau's old site in 1854. A mixed-blood Cherokee, he opposed the break with the United States during the Civil War. Courtesy Oklahoma Historical Society.

The Creeks and Seminoles held joint title to central Oklahoma from 1836-1856. Courtesy Bonnie Speer.

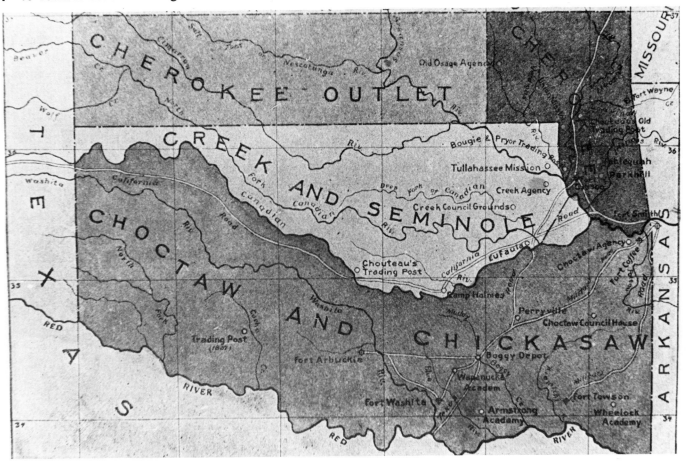

After the Civil War, Texas cattle moved north-ward through Cleveland County, headed for shipping points in Kansas. Here, a crew takes a noon break on the Chisholm Trail. Courtesy Western History Collections, University of Oklahoma.

Elias C. Boudinot, a Cherokee citizen, stated in 1879 that the Unassigned Lands in Indian Territory were public domain, setting off a tempest among land hungry white settlers. Courtesy Oklahoma Historical Society.

withdrew from the military forts in Indian Territory, thus removing their protection. Confederate troops moved into the area from Texas. Feeling abandoned by the United States, the Cherokees, Choctaws, Creeks, Chickasaws, and Seminoles signed treaties with the Confederacy.

After the war, the United States declared all previous treaties with the Indians invalid because the Indians had revolted against the government. Officials demanded the Five Civilized Tribes cede part of their lands in Indian Territory for the settlement of other tribes, predominately those in Kansas. The Seminoles gave up all their lands in exchange for 200,000 acres between the two Canadian Rivers in present Seminole County, which had been previously ceded by the Creeks. The other tribes made similar concessions.

When all the new tribes were settled, a large block of land consisting of present Payne, Logan, Oklahoma, Cleveland, Canadian, and Kingfisher counties remained in the middle of Indian Territory, unassigned to any tribe.

The cattle industry was flourishing in Texas and in the Chickasaw Nation to the south and west of the Unassigned Lands. Since there were no railroads in Indian Territory, numerous cattle trails were established from Texas to the cattle markets in Kansas. The Arbuckle Trail traversed what is today Cleveland County, passed through Norman, crossed Alameda Street just east of 12th Street N.E., then traveled northwestward to join the main Chisholm Trail near present day Kingfisher.

No one had a right to use the Unassigned Lands, but the ranchers were in no hurry to trail their cattle through the area and often grazed the entire district. Many people in Kansas who wanted free farms resented the use of the land by the cattlemen.

In 1879, a newspaper article signed by Elias C. Boudinot, a Cherokee citizen, appeared in the *Chicago Times*. The article stated the Unassigned Lands were public domain and therefore open to homesteading. The article was widely reprinted and created a furor along the frontier among land-hungry settlers.

David L. Payne, a former Kansas state legislator and a captain with General Custer's Nineteenth Cavalry during his Washita campaign, organized the Boomer movement and led band after band of would-be settlers into the forbidden land during the next six years.

Although the Boomers were arrested time and again by the soldiers sent to guard the Unassigned Lands, they were never convicted and believed right was on their side. At one time in 1883 more than five hundred of the intruders made their way into Lincoln County. There they pitched tents, and began to till the soil before being driven out. Others went into the restricted territory in smaller groups or singly.

When Payne died suddenly in November 1884, his most trusted lieutenant, William L. Couch, took over leadership of the Boomers and the invasions continued. The Boomers contended the cattlemen were intruders also. Finally the Boomers took their fight to Washington to try to persuade Congress to open the Unassigned Lands in Indian Territory to settlement and to create the Territory of Oklahoma.

In anticipation of the opening of these lands, the United States government gave the railroads permission to build two lines across Indian Territory from north to south and east to west. The Missouri, Kansas and Texas Railroad extended its line from Vinita to Denison, Texas, beginning in 1871. The Atlantic Pacific crossed the border from the east to junction with the MKT the same year. There were no extensions for ten years, but again in anticipation of opening the area to white settlement, the United States Land Office contracted in 1871 with Theodore H. Barrett to survey a broad area west of the Indian Meridian.

Working for Barrett was a young Kentuckian named Abner E. Norman, a graduate of Forest Home Academy near Louisville. Norman began as a chainman but soon was placed in charge of one of the survey units. On November 13, 1872, one of his crews established the corner of what is now Classen Boulevard and East Lindsey Street in Norman. They camped at a spring located three-eighths mile south of there. Peeling the bark from a large elm, one of the men burned the words "Norman's Camp" into the trunk of the tree.

In 1885, the Atchinson, Topeka and Santa Fe Railroad received permission to build its line from Arkansas City, Kansas,

Capt. David L. Payne headed the Boomer movement to open the Unassigned Lands to settlement, leading band after band of would be settlers into the land, only to be evicted by soldiers. Courtesy Edna Couch.

The Boomers suffered many hardships, and lived in squalid camps while they waited for the opening of the Unassigned Lands. Courtesy Western History Collections, University of Oklahoma.

William Couch took over as leader of the Boomers following the untimely death of David Payne. Courtesy Edna Couch.

south to Galveston, Texas. Railroad officials selected station grounds and watering sites along the way. They gave the name of Norman to a thirteen and a half acre site located a mile and a half north of the spring at Norman's Camp.

The line reached Norman Station on April 15 and continued to Purcell, the division point. There it connected with another line being built northward. The last spike was driven on April 26. The first passenger train moved past Norman Station northbound on June 13, 1887.

The stage was now set for the opening of the Unassigned Lands. As the fight continued in Washington, the railroads sided with the homesteaders, for without the settlers the railroads would have no business. The cattlemen sided with the Indians.

Finally, in 1889, after four years of bitter lobbying, Congress passed the Springer Bill, authorizing the President to open the Oklahoma district immediately for settlement, according to homestead laws. On March 23, President Benjamin Harrison issued a proclamation setting the date of the opening for April 22.

Handbills boosting settlement of the Unassigned Lands found their way across the country and encouraged many a Boomer to congregate on the Kansas border in hope of obtaining free land. Courtesy The Norman Transcript.

Railroad construction crews began laying track across Central Oklahoma in 1885. Courtesy Western History Collections, University of Oklahoma.

In Kansas, hats sailed into the air when men heard the news. They shouted and danced in the streets. The Boomer camps were also rife with excitement. Their hard work had finally paid off. At last they were going to have the opportunity to gain free lands. Would-be settlers began pouring into the area surrounding the Unassigned Lands to await the opening.

Following the acquisition of the Lousiania Purchase, the eastern Indians were forced by the U.S. government to remove to Indian Territory over the "Trail of Tears," experiencing much hardship and many deaths. Courtesy Oklahoma Historical Society.

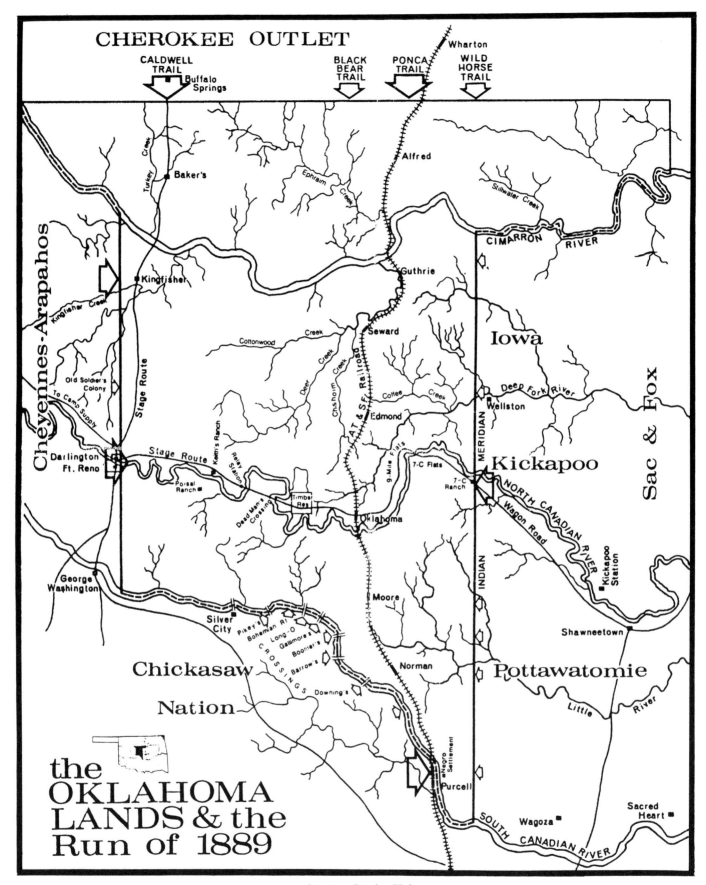

the
OKLAHOMA
LANDS & the
Run of 1889

Courtesy Stanley Hoig

CHAPTER 2

Claiming the Land

Montford T. Johnson, a Chickasaw rancher, was one of the earliest settlers in the area, grazing his herds of cattle across Cleveland County before the run. This picture is copied from an oil portrait by Ralph Shead. Courtesy Redlands Press.

The major entering point for the great land run into the Unassigned Lands from the south was at Purcell in the Chickasaw Nation, a town established two years before. Bob Love, a Chickasaw rancher, operated a slaughtering pen near Purcell Station to furnish the railroad crews with fresh beef while they were building the track.

Love, a white man, was in the Chickasaw Nation by virtue of having married a Chickasaw woman. He saw the possibility of a town being established at the division point. Taking advantage of his family's tribal rights, he selected the land next to Purcell Station on which to settle. Though all land in the Chickasaw Nation was held in common, under tribal law Love could not only retain full rights to the use of this land for his lifetime, but also pass these rights on to his heirs.

Love proposed to Edward B. Johnson, another Chickasaw rancher, that they go into the townsite business. Johnson's father, Montford T. Johnson, had previously settled north of Purcell, and Edward B. Johnson and Joe Lindsay of Silver City, near Tuttle, had established a store near the future crossing of the Canadian River railroad bridge, north of Purcell Station.

The new town of Purcell grew steadily. By 1887, it was known as the "Queen City of the Plains," and boasted a population of two hundred. Its trade area extended across the Chickasaw Nation to the north and west, and reached into the lands of the Pottawatomie and Sac and Fox tribes to the east.

During the three weeks before the land run, more than 2,000 people poured into Purcell. Travelers filled the hotels and camped along the banks of the river. Quick-buck artists and fakirs

Purcell was the major entering point for those entering Cleveland County during the run. Hundreds of hopeful settlers camped along the Canadian River while awaiting the run. Courtesy Oklahoma Historical Society.

Bob Love, another Chickasaw rancher, was the founder of Purcell in 1887. Courtesy McClain County Historical Society.

Edward B. Johnson (shown here with his family) was a co-founder of Purcell and later became a prominent citizen of Norman. Courtesy John Womack.

crowded the dusty streets, selling their wares. Gambling flourished everywhere. Merchandise skyrocketed in price, and fast horses sold at a premium.

Any man or single woman over age twenty-one was permitted to make the run. Each homesteader could claim 160 acres and was given five years to prove up on the land. The first one to plant his or her stake on the claim would be declared the legal owner. Anyone who had been in the Unassigned Lands thirty days prior to the opening was declared ineligible to make the race. But the ranks of the guarding soldiers were thin, and they could not find all the "sooners," a term that did not come into use until late in 1889.

Only four townsites had been designated in the Unassigned Lands: Guthrie, Oklahoma City, Kingfisher, and Norman. Norman had come into existence on July 4, 1887, when telegraph operator W. E. Thomas had been assigned to this location on the Santa Fe Railroad, fifteen miles north of Purcell, where he lived and worked in a boxcar on the siding. He posted the name of Norman on the side of the boxcar, taking the name from the elm tree at Norman's Camp.

Shortly thereafter, railroad workers built a section house on the west side of the tracks just north of present Duffy Street to shelter maintenance personnel. Among those stationed here was Jefferson Lehmanowsky "Lem" Hefley.

Hefley had been born in Illinois, and following the Civil War, he worked in an Arkansas City, Kansas, gravel pit. There, someone suggested he might get a job working for the railroad in Indian Territory. Subsequently, Lem and his two oldest sons traveled to Norman Station and were hired. The Hefleys set up a tent near the section house where they cooked their own meals.

Soon, Hefley became section foreman. The maintenance superintendent asked if Hefley would bring the rest of his family to Norman Station and board the railroad workers at the section house. Hefley agreed. The remainder of his family arrived in September 1888, to become Cleveland County's first official family.

It proved to be a lonely existence for the Hefley family at Norman Station, but that was soon to end. On March 23, 1889, news came to them that President Benjamin Harrison had proclaimed the Unassigned Lands would be opened to settlement by a giant horse race at noon on April 22. The Hefleys began laying in supplies to feed the horde of homesteaders they knew would soon swarm across the land.

This was a busy time for railroad personnel also. Charles M. Chamberlain, Chief of the Santa Fe Civil Engineers in Topeka, spent the three weeks preceeding the run, laying out the four designated townsites in the Unassigned Lands. In keeping with the wishes of the railroad, he placed all street crossings at right angles to the railroad.

In Norman, company surveyors named the streets, some after prominent employees of the railroad, such as Peters, Linn, Webster, Gray, and Findlay. Other streets bore Indian words including Muskogee and Tonhawa.

On April 17, five days before the run, the new station agent at Norman Station, Andrew Kingkade, along with his wife and four-year-old son Martin, moved into a small house next to the

Hefleys, to become Cleveland County's second resident family.

Those at Norman Station talked of nothing but the run. Lem Hefley made trip after trip to Arkansas City on the train to obtain supplies. Mrs. Hefley and her four daughters spent the last few days baking dozens of golden loaves of bread to feed the hungry settlers.

All this activity at Norman had not gone unnoticed by those waiting at Purcell. Many of the homesteaders intended to claim town lots at Norman. Among them was Delbert Larsh, a tall, handsome man with a large mustache. Larsh was the Santa Fe station agent at Purcell. Following announcement of the opening of the Unassigned Lands, he saw possibilities in the new town to be built at the Norman station. He suggested to Thomas R. Waggoner, chief clerk and cashier for the Santa Fe, that they establish a townsite company to take over the 360 acres there.

The two men invited several others to meet with them at the Santa Fe depot to discuss the matter. Among these men were Charles T. Gorton, Pryor V. Adkins, John Helvie, Tyler Blake, George Blake, and Ed P. Ingle.

Charles T. Gorton, a newly-wed from Harper, Kansas, had arrived in Purcell shortly before to make the run with his wife, Viola, and father-in-law Seth M. Moore. Pryor V. Adkins had been a rancher in the Chickasaw nation since 1886 and knew the area well. John Helvie was a Santa Fe locomotive engineer, whereas Ed P. Ingle published the *Purcell Register*. Tyler Blake

The "Lem" Hefley family was Cleveland County's first family, living at "Norman Station" before the run. This photo was taken in 1890. From left to right, back row: Jess, 24; Henry, 20; John 16; Harold, 22. Second row: Nora, 14; "Lem"; Mrs. Hefley; Orna, 18. First row: Belle, 11; Nellie, 9. Courtesy The Norman Transcript and Nellie Hefley.

Delbert L. Larsh, Santa Fe station agent at Purcell, organized the Norman Townsite Company and became a leading businessman in Norman. Courtesy John Womack.

Three weeks before the run, the population of Purcell rose tenfold, from 200 to 2,000 people. Gamblers were everywhere as shown in this street scene. Courtesy Oklahoma Historical Society.

and his son George were druggists and had known Larsh in Larned, Kansas.

Larsh asked White Bead attorney Albert Rennie to draw up a townsite agreement for the new company. The document would have no legal bearing, but would establish an ethical guide for those coming into the town on the day of the run and afterwards.

Rennie also drew up a plat for the new town, with the streets running in cardinal directions. He would have joined them in the townsite company but was planning a similar venture for another town to be established seven miles south of Norman Station.

Shortly before the run, Santa Fe officials issued orders prohibiting all railroad employees from participating in the run. Subsequently, Larsh quit his job in order to carry out his plan of establishing the Norman townsite, but Helvie refused to do so.

The government ordered Chickasaw rancher Montford T. Johnson to remove his cattle from the Third County, as Cleveland County was designated at that time. The last of these cattle were driven across the Canadian River on the morning of the run. The crowd was so thick lining the riverbank that the cowboys had to ask the people to move back.

In Purcell, excitement mounted to a fever pitch as noon approached. As far as one could see, eager homesteaders lined the river. During the night, a heavy thunderstorm had struck the area, but this morning had dawned fair and clear. Prairie flowers blossomed in the bright, spring grass. The homesteaders watched the muddy waters of the Canadian River with an anxious eye, fearing a sudden rise in the infamous stream. Some of the settlers beg-

ged the soldiers guarding the line to allow them to cross the river before this happened, thus preventing them from making the run. But Lt. Samuel E. Adair, Co. L, 5th Cavalry, told them no. His orders stated that none were to cross the boundary line into the Promised Land until twelve noon sharp, and he intended to obey orders.

Many of the settlers waiting at Purcell planned to enter the Unassigned Lands on special trains. The first section of the train from Gainesville, Texas, steamed on past the Purcell station, eliciting a howl of rage from those waiting to board. The train stopped just north of the town to wait until 11:40 before approaching the Canadian River bridge, which was being guarded by a soldier.

In the railroad yard, workmen made up two more special trains of twelve coaches and two engines each. Within five minutes, men filled each train to capacity, and others clung to the top, the sides and the cowcatcher. The members of the Norman Townsite Company were among those aboard the first train. Through Helvie's connections, he and Ingle rode in the cab, while Waggoner, Larsh, Gorton, and George Blake managed to find space in one of the cars. Tyler Blake jumped onto the cowcatcher of the locomotive.

Then the trains began to move. They puffed slowly around Red Hill to join the earlier train waiting to cross the turbulent Canadian River. The other settlers on horses, in wagons and buggies, stood poised on the riverbank waiting for "Harrison's horse race." Those who did not intend to make the race climbed Red Hill at the north edge of town to watch the activity.

When the bugles sounded at noon on April 29, 1889, signaling the start of the run, the homesteaders surged forward in "Harrison's horse race," as depicted in this oil painting by Robert Lindeaux in 1934, now in the Phillips Collections. Courtesy The Norman Transcript and Western History Collections, University of Oklahoma.

Charles T. Gorton made the run and claimed the quarter section where the University of Oklahoma is now located. Courtesy John Womack.

The tension became almost unbearable as noon approached. Suddenly the bugles that signaled the start of the race sounded and the homesteaders were off, splashing through the muddy water, wary of quicksand. The trains moved out, traveling at a slow rate of speed so they would not take advantage of the other homesteaders.

Those on Red Hill watched the drama unfolding below them. Shortly, someone noted a white flag being erected by a Sooner on a claim a half-mile north of future Lexington. He noted that was "Dr. Johnson's claim," and that the good doctor was riding toward it "for all he's worth." All supposed Dr. Johnson would lose the claim, but he rode straight for the choice piece of property, which he had located prior to the run, and "managed to take over" from the Sooner.

Many had similarly located their land in advance of the run though technically this was in violation of the law, which clearly stated that "until such lands are opened no persons shall be permitted to enter and occupy the same." But the homesteaders took a liberal view of this statement in that as long as they did not physically occupy the land before the land run, there was nothing illegal about entering and selecting a claim in advance.

As the race continued, homesteaders spread out over the land in a frenzy of excitement. Others dashed in all along the eastern and western boundaries of the Third County. Everywhere the Sooners popped up out of the brush to speed before them.

At Norman Station as time for the race drew near, the Hefleys and the Kingkades took time out from their work to watch the anticipated excitement. They expected to see the riders coming toward them from Purcell, but they heard a shout behind them and turned to see riders approaching from the west. Nellie Hefley, who was fifteen years old at the time, recalled the event in later years:

> "All of our family were out in the yard. The section house was on the west side of the tracks, so we were lined up along the fence, looking southeast. . . . We heard them coming up in back of us and

This is the only known picture of the run into Cleveland County from Purcell, the major entering point from the south. Here soldiers escort a wagon across the tricky quicksands and the special train can be seen in the background. Courtesy The Norman Transcript and Western History Collections, University of Oklahoma.

This section house, where the Hefley family lived, was built in 1887 on the west side of the railroad tracks just north of present Duffy Street. Courtesy John Womack.

turned to see them. The horses and carriages came first, and then the wagons and men on foot. They came from every direction. We didn't know where they were coming from. I heard my parents say later that these were the sooners, camping out on the streams. They had been there three or four days and no one knew it.

"They went by us. And there was lots of noise, more noise and excitement than you can imagine. . . . I saw the train come in, with twenty-two cars on it. It was spectacular. The engine just barely pulled it. Men were all over it, on top, hanging out the windows and doors and on the steps, holding to anything they could. Anyone could get on the train, so long as he could hold onto it. We had talked about nothing else around the section house for days except the expected arrival of the train.

"This train made such an impression on me as a child, just running so slowly, puff, puff, puff. . . . Men would drop off at intervals and start running out into the country. They knew a townsite would be started and a lot got off to get a claim in the townsite."

Among the first ones to step off the train at Norman Station were the members of the Norman Townsite Company. Delbert Larsh carried with him the plat and townsite agreement for Norman, which Attorney Albert Rennie had drawn up. Much to Larsh's surprise, he found a number of white tents already erected on the townsite. Quickly, he found a representative of the railroad and learned these tents belonged to the Santa Fe surveyors. These men had staked Main Street and several other blocks along the railroad tracks to protect the railroad sidings and buildings from being claimed by agriculture homesteaders.

Larsh showed the representative his townsite agreement and plat for the new town. The representative informed him a previous plat had already been drawn up for Norman and most of the surveying was done. Therefore, Larsh agreed to accept Santa Fe's plat, and he put away his own.

The Santa Fe representative, Frank E. Clark, caught the train and rode to Guthrie, where he filed as trustee for the townsite at 3 p.m. that afternoon. The railroad surveyors folded their tents and went away, leaving the Norman Townsite Company in possession of the land at Norman Station.

Each member of the townsite company filed on two city lots that day, plus a 160-acre homestead adjoining the townsite. Pryor V. Adkins drove his stake down at 101 East Main, the site now occupied by Sooner Theatre. Larsh chose two lots at the southeast corner of East Main Street and Santa Fe Avenue. Tyler Blake took business lots near East Main Street and Peters Avenue and residence lots where the Cleveland County Courthouse now stands. George Blake chose residence lots.

Helvie and Ingle took possession of adjoining homesteads north of Robinson Street, while Larsh and Waggoner filed on quarter sections south of the townsite. Adkins claimed the quarter section at McGee Drive, south of Lindsey Street. Charles T. Gorton drove his stake down on the quarter section where the University of Oklahoma now stands. While Gorton stood guard over the land, Seth M. Moore, his father-in-law, caught the special train to Guthrie to file on their claim.

All in all, the settling of the Norman townsite was done in a fairly orderly manner. In part, this was due to the lack of interest in the area from the Boomer movement. Boomer leaders had concentrated their efforts mainly at Oklahoma Station, eighteen miles north of Norman Station, and at Guthrie, the expected capital of the new territory.

Though government officials had planned only four townsites in the Unassigned Lands on the day of the run other small towns sprang up. Most of these were along the railroad tracks. Among those in the Third County were Moore, located seven miles north of Norman; Noble, seven miles south of Norman; and Lexington, which developed across the Canadian River from Purcell.

The land surrounding these townsites was rapidly claimed. The most desirable quarter sections were those located close to the townsites. Sometimes more than one claimant drove his stake down on a choice piece of land. As a result, much litigation was to

Pryor V. Adkins, a Chickasaw rancher, drove his stake down at 101 East Main Street in Norman on the day of the run, the site now occupied by Sooner Theatre. Shown in this picture, taken on an early fishing trip are from left to right: John Adkins, Green Taylor, C. D. Adkins, Pryor Adkins, and Lewis F. Adkins. Courtesy Betty Adkins Melton.

Tents went up quickly on the day of the run on the various townsites in the Unassigned Lands. Location of this scene is unidentified. Courtesy The Norman Transcript.

north of Norman; Noble, seven miles south of Norman; and Lexington, which developed across the Canadian River from Purcell.

The land surrounding these townsites was rapidly claimed. The most desirable quarter sections were those located close to the townsites. Sometimes more than one claimant drove his stake down on a choice piece of land. As a result, much litigation was to follow in the wake of the run.

Such was the case of James Bishop, an older man who filed on the quarter section containing the spring at Norman's Camp. Two other men claimed the same site. One soon withdrew from the contest, but the other determined to fight it out in court. After four years Bishop was finally named the winner. Thereafter, the spring and small stream feeding into it were known as Bishop's Spring and Bishop's Creek, respectively.

Sometimes "Winchester law" prevailed when more than one person chose the same land. The legal age for staking a claim was 21, but the story is told of one eighteen-year-old Sooner, who successfully held three claims with his gun, near what is now Indian Hill Road and Highway 74, until the rest of his family could arrive.

R. M. Graham of the Chickasaw Nation, who along with his two sons, one daughter and a hired hand, laid claim to an entire section of land a mile north of Noble. Graham built a home on his quarter section. When Graham's youngest daughter turned twenty-one-years-old that August, the hired hand, by pre-arranged agreement, relinquished his claim to her.

The law required each homesteader must live on his claim six months out of the year. That fall Graham built a house at the point where the four family claims joined, so that each of his children had a bedroom on his own land to meet the residence requirements of the law.

Businesses sprang up at once in the new towns to meet the needs of the settlers. In Norman, A. D. Acers, manager for the Carey Lombard Lumber Company of Wichita, Kansas, sold lumber from a boxcar on a Santa Fe siding; Charles Gorton hauled a small building into town the day of the run from which to sell supplies. Others set up businesses in tents.

As time went on, other small communities such as Stella, Slaughterville, Willowview, Franklin, Etowah, and Denver developed within the Third County.

Norman, though, was to reign as the main trading center from its advantageous position beside the railroad. Soon other events were to make the town even more important to the county.

Wiggin's map of Cleveland County shows all claims filed upon during the run and by whom. Courtesy John Womack.

CHAPTER 3

The Struggle For Survival

The day after the run, the Third County found itself with a diverse population. Businessman and farmer stood shoulder to shoulder as did the wealthy and poor, black and white, Northerner and Southerner, young and old, the educated and uneducated.

The majority of those making the run had come from the surrounding states, with the largest number coming from Kansas; next largest from Texas; then from Missouri and from other drought ridden states in the Midwest. Many came in ethnic groups.

Some were speculators hoping to obtain a choice agriculture claim near a town or a desirable town lot—land which they could sell shortly in a relinquishment, thereby making a profit. Others saw this as an opportunity to create a new community from the ground up, and they wanted to be a part of it.

Still others saw the run as their last hope in obtaining a home for themselves. Signs painted on the sides of their covered wagons often expressed their emotions. A newspaper reporter noted one sign which stated, "Plenty of damn fools like us." Another homesteader expressed his sentiments this way: "Chints bugged in Illinoy, siclooned in New brasky, white caped in Missoury, prohibited in Kansas. Oklahomay or Bust."

All of the people were taking a gamble. The government

Norman looking south, June 29, 1889. Courtesy Mrs. Harold Belknap and The Norman Transcript.

had bet them five years of their lives in exchange for a barren piece of ground in an isolated section of the country. There were no roads, no stores where they could easily purchase needed supplies, no doctors for the sick, or schools for their children. There were no means for the rural settlers to make a living except off the land and that would take time. For most of the settlers the big question was whether they could survive long enough to prove up on their land and make it a paying proposition.

Added to this was the fact the national government, in its haste to open the land to settlement, had failed to provide any kind of local government for the territory. There were no guidelines for the newly established towns on which to operate. Nothing had been said about cemetery lands. There was no place in the county where people could tend to legal business.

The lack of law and order in the Unassigned Lands brought hordes of outlaws and crooks into the territory. Only a handful of U.S. deputy marshals and soldiers were available to help preserve law and order.

Nevertheless, most of the new settlers looked forward with vision. All were chasing a dream. The J. M. Chastain family was exemplary of these settlers. The Chastains had left Alabama and were living in Midland, Texas, when they heard about the opening of the Unassigned Lands. Mr. Chastain decided to make the run because, as his son Earl said later, "We were long on family and short on money, and my father wanted moving room for all nine of us children, eleven counting himself and Mother."

Many rural settlers lived in their wagons that first summer and cooked over an open fire while they tried to get a crop into the ground. Courtesy Western History Collections, University of Oklahoma.

Often the homesteaders had nothing to build their homes out of but the soil itself. Some built dugouts; others erected sod houses like this one. Courtesy Pioneer Multi-County Library and The Norman Transcript.

Earl, though only sixteen years old, made the run across the Canadian River with his father at Adkins Crossing. They staked a claim at Norman's Camp, but found James Bishop had already beaten them to it. They rode on east and found a man with a staked claim who was willing to trade his rights for four horses.

William Polk had teamed up with a friend in Texas to make the run. They pooled their resources so they would not be burdened with too many personal possessions. Each of them owned a mule. They left their covered wagon at the soldiers' camp on Adkins Hill and made the run on their mules.

"I rode that old gray mule as fast as he would go, my arms flapping, for about ten miles before I found the land I wanted," Polk recalled later.

"I staked my claim at the four corners of the quarter section and rode round and round the borders. A man thought he could bluff me and chase me off, but I was the biggest and most threatening. He gave up to go on to find other land."

The majority of homesteaders arrived on their claim with nothing more than a horse and a gun. Speed was the essence of the day, and only the fleetest riders could be assured of gaining a piece of land. They could not be encumbered with heavy wagons, women and children, and household goods.

Once the homesteader had succeeded in staking his claim, he had to hold it against claim jumpers. One of the surest ways of doing this was to erect some kind of temporary shelter on the land. For example, many put up a tent.

As soon as it was possible, the new resident of the Third County had to travel to one of the two designated land offices, Kingfisher or Guthrie, to file on his claim. This required a $20 filing fee. If, however, someone contested his claim, he could expect a long litigation period.

The crowds at the land offices were so large that sometimes the homesteader had to stay a week before his turn to file came. People camped for miles around, but the crowd was good natured for the most part and passed the time telling jokes, singing, and talking among themselves. They stood in line to get a filing

Breaking new ground was laborious work as shown here in this 1916 photo of a six-mule hitchup on the Tim Fishburn farm on Jim Blue Creek. Lester Blankenship is driving with Tom Irvin, left, and Tim Fishburn holding the plow. Courtesy Pioneer Multi-County Library, The Norman Transcript, and L. R. Fishburn.

number; then they had to wait for it to be called. Women were given filing privileges ahead of the men.

After the ordeal of filing their claim was over, the homesteaders began plowing the land. They were given a limit of six months to erect a house and to plant at least five acres. As soon as it was feasible, the homesteaders sent for their families.

Among these homesteaders, records show that sixteen of them were single women who made the run and were successful in obtaining a homesite in the Third County. Laura Troy, 23, who was a native Iowan, was one such woman. Previous to the run, she had worked as a housekeeper in a large home near Tuttle in the Chickasaw Nation. She made the run in a covered wagon and staked a claim nine miles west of Moore. Her father failed to obtain a claim, so she gave him eighty acres of her land.

Many of the rural settlers lived in their wagons that summer and cooked over an open fire while they tried to get a crop sowed. This in itself proved difficult. The eastern half of the county was covered by the dense forest of the Cross Timbers. Cutting the trees down and hauling the stumps out required back-breaking labor.

However, those who settled in the western half of the county were not much better off. There, thick grasses covered the prairie, often waist high. Over-sized plows and several teams were required to break up the thick sod with tough root zones. A number of the settlers, such as William O'Haver, brought oxen to handle the heavy duty chore.

Often, all of this work required help. Those who could afford it hired someone, but most of the settlers depended upon each other for assistance, neighbor lending neighbor a hand.

That summer most of the planting was restricted to small garden patches to provide food for the family that winter. The summer was hot and dry. That fall was to become known as "the year of the turnips" because turnips were about the only thing that grew, providing food for both cattle and human beings.

Some of the families brought enough provisions to last a year, including flour, lard, cured pork, dried beans, home canned vegetables, and dried fruits. Those who were fairly well off, drove herds of cattle, horses, and mules before their wagons, and brought flocks of caged chickens with them.

Others, down to their last cent, were forced to live off the land. Fortunately rabbits were plentiful in the county, wild turkeys strutted through the brush, prairie chickens and quail were numerous, and deer bounded through the thickets along the rivers. An occasional bear could be seen roving through the woods.

The women, with the help of the children, collected wild plums, opposum grapes, crab apples, blackberries, mulberries, and other wild fruits and berries and turned them into delicious jams, jellies, and pies. When their gardens matured, the women preserved the food, spending long hot days canning the vegetables, or storing them in root cellars for the winter.

The men, once the first seeds were in the ground, turned to the task of providing shelter. Those in the Cross Timbers, where timber was plentiful, built log cabins. They cut poles, twelve to fourteen feet long, notched them and laid them on top of one another. They chinked the cracks between the logs with clay.

Those settlers on the prairies found it more difficult to obtain building material. Little was available to them but the tough prairie sod. Some made dugouts, literally digging into the earth, and roofing the excavation over with long poles and brush which they covered with sod. Others cut the sod into thick blocks which they stacked on top of each other like bricks, building up their walls and leaving space for windows and doors. Again they covered the roofs with long poles and more layers of sod. Or, if they had a little money, perhaps they invested in real glass for their windows and wood shingles for the roof.

The sod houses and dugouts were susceptible to insects of all kinds and occasionally a snake. The roofs leaked. The floors were earthen and soon became hard packed.

The women strived to make the houses as comfortable as possible. They covered the walls of the dugouts and sod houses with cheese cloth, burlap, or other lightweight cloth to keep the insects and dirt from falling in their beds and in their food.

Those who lived in the Cross Timbers found abundant trees from which to build their homes. Courtesy The Norman Transcript.

The settlers were starved for fruit and planted large orchards such as this one belonging to Mr. and Mrs. Armstead M. Reeds, in northwestern Cleveland County. Courtesy The Norman Transcript.

Sometimes they managed a piece of cloth with which to cover their windows as curtains. More than one enterprising woman sewed burlap bags together and laid them upon her earthen floor as a makeshift rug.

Cupboards were often nothing more than packing cases fastened to the wall. The furniture in many of these first homes might be homemade, crude tables with sawed logs for chairs. Beds consisted of a frame attached to the wall and strung with rope to support a thick feather tick covered with homemade quilts.

At first, water for these new homesteads was carried from the creeks and rivers. After the first crops were in and a home of some kind was provided for, the men dug wells. Often, good water could be found at thirty to forty feet. Others found only "gyp" water, too laden with minerals to be drinkable.

That summer of 1889 was hot and dry, and everyone had a difficult time. The Charles Moses family of Lexington thought seriously about returning to Illinois and would have, but they did not have the money. Many others who could afford to return home did so, unable to cope with the raw, new land.

There was much sickness that summer and few doctors in the territory. Dr. R. E. Innis was the first to arrive in Norman, followed shortly by Dr. R. D. Lowther, who had been practicing in Noble. Dr. Chesney lived in the Denver community. Later, Dr. Capshaw moved to Norman.

The doctors rode horses in all kinds of weather to aid the sick. They dispensed medicines, which consisted principally of calomel, quinine, paregoric, bismuth, castor oil, chloroform, morphine, codeine, and eventually ether (which had been recently discovered). Most of them performed operations in the patient's home or in the doctor's office.

Many settlers survived that first year by leaving their homes temporarily to work elsewhere. The government permitted them to be absent from their homestead six months out of the year. Others survived by hiring out locally to more prosperous farmers and ranchers.

Contrary to popular belief, not all the land in the Third County was filed upon immediately. Ed P. Ingle, publisher of the *Purcell Register*, who rode the train to Norman the day of the run, said later that he did not stake his quarter section north of Robinson Street until 4:30 p.m. the day of the run.

In January 1890, a map distributed by T. J. J. Wiggins, a Norman real estate man, showed that only 1,300 of the 1,500 homesteads in Cleveland County had been filed on as of December 31, 1889. A few of these farms lay adjacent to the Canadian River, with a good portion in the riverbed. Most were in the northeast section near the Shawnee-Pottawatomie reservation, which had little tillable land.

The drought continued through 1890. Many of the homesteaders could not overcome the obstacles that faced them no matter how hard they worked. The number of crops in production that year was limited. Farmers with bottom lands fared best. Row crops on upland fields and late gardens were hard hit. Urgent requests for relief went out to Governor Steele. He formed a territorial relief board that provided $44,800 for basic foods for the destitute. The commodities were dispensed through the county agents. The able-bodied could receive rations of flour, meal, beans, and salt. In addition, the sick and infirm were allowed coffee, tea, sugar, rice, oatmeal, and crackers. *The Norman Transcript* argued for a program of work relief instead of handouts, except for the disabled.

Many of the families were proud, and did not wish to accept charity. Out of desperation, some accepted assistance only under cover of darkness. Though scanty, these rations helped many subsist through that second winter.

The Santa Fe Railroad helped the settlers also. The company shipped in 25,000 bushels of seed wheat, making it available to those who wanted to plant the 1891 crop. One carload came to Norman. Farmers signed promissary notes, purchasing the wheat

There was much sickness in Cleveland County that first year. Dr. and Mrs. Madison T. J. Capshaw settled in the Denver community and later moved to Norman. Dr. Capshaw rode a horse when visiting his patients in the country and pedaled a bicycle around town. Courtesy John Womack.

By 1891 most of the farmers had plowed enough land to plant cotton and wheat, the two most profitable crops. This unidentified haying crew was photographed near Moore. Courtesy Moore Public Library.

at 90 cents a bushel. Reportedly, more than 95 percent of the loans were paid off the following summer.

The railroad also announced that beginning January 31, 1891, it would limit its purchase of crossties to the settlers for a three month period. Specifications were announced. The settlers received thirty cents each for white oak crossties delivered to the right of way in lots of fifty or more and twenty cents each for those of burr oak. Culls, which were used in sidings and freight yards, brought half price. The remainder sold as firewood.

Hard times forced most of the homesteaders to become self-sufficient. They raised their own vegetables and meat, and kept perishables in springs or cellars. The Armstead Reeds family developed an unusual method of early refrigeration when they built a sandstone cellar with deep recesses on either side of the entryway.

Artie Reeds recalled, "Mother used to keep these filled with water, and kept milk, butter, and eggs down there."

The homesteaders traded any surpluses they had in town for shoes and other staple items such as flour, which they could not produce at home.

By 1891, most of the farmers had plowed enough land to plant cotton and wheat, the two most profitable crops. Norman gained early fame as a market place. W. R. Jennison began erecting a cotton gin just south of the Planters Hotel, late in May 1890, the first in Oklahoma. The Jones and Berry cotton yard, on the present day courthouse square, quickly followed as did the Norman Cotton Gin and Cotton Seed Oil Mill; agitation began for a flour mill.

Though hard times were to persist until 1897, thanks to the drought, low prices, and economic recession, by 1891 things began to look up. The farmers in Cleveland County harvested a tremendous wheat crop that summer, and vegetables were plentiful. Agricultural lands rose in value to seven dollars an acre.

Even so, nature was to take another swipe at the hardworking homesteaders. On April 23, 1893, not one but two tornados

In May 1890, the Jennison Brothers announced the construction of the first cotton gin in Norman, which was built in the 100 block of West Eufaula. Samuel A. Ambrister later purchased the Norman Cotton Gin and Cotton Seed Oil Mill Company. Photo taken circa 1909. Courtesy The Norman Transcript.

raked the area. Early in the afternoon, a small twister moved in from the south and struck east of Norman, killing one person and injuring several others. All doctors responded to the emergency.

About 5 p.m., the clouds began to look ominous again. A tornado dipped down near the Canadian River west of Norman. The funnel crossed the river and swept across the Ten Mile Flat in a path two miles wide, leveling houses and barns. Twenty-two people were killed, including eight members of the John O'Conner family, at their farm home near present 48th Avenue Northwest and Franklin Road, and six in the D. F. Banks family. More than one hundred people were injured.

Many miracle stories were told about the storm. The William Polk family were all in the cellar, but the cellar was so new the door wasn't even on. Nothing was saved of their home except a clock that had been fastened to the wall. The clock, found a quarter of a mile from the house, began running as soon as it was picked up. The storm lifted a horse out of a lot and set it down across the fence. Chickens were stripped bare of feathers but lived, and the family found a straw driven through a fence post.

A man who lived across the road from the Polks had no cellar and jumped into a well he was digging. At the Banks' home five people were saved when they crawled against an embankment.

Food, clothing, bedding, furniture, and family heirlooms were blown away. The rain that followed the storm destroyed what was left.

Help from outside the area came at once. As soon as the people in Norman heard the news, they arrived in droves to assist the survivors. The Red Cross moved in, turning a two-story house on the west side of Norman into an emergency hospital. Children wandered aimlessly around the yard, their heads, legs, and arms bandaged. A relief committee collected $2,000 for the storm vic-

Norman quickly gained fame as a market place. The Jones and Berry cotton yard stood on the site of the present Cleveland County Courthouse. In the fall of 1890, at least 2,000 bales of cotton were ginned in Norman and sent to St. Louis. Courtesy Pioneer Multi-County Library and The Norman Transcript.

Norman continued to be a booming market place for cotton. Farmers from all parts of the country came into town with their cotton on November 24, 1901, the day this picture was taken at the intersection of Main Street and Peters Avenue. Courtesy The Norman Transcript.

tims. Total damage in the storm was estimated at over $100,000.

Most of the farmers rebuilt their homes, and planted their crops again. Though down, they were not out, showing their hardy pioneer spirit.

The economy continued to grow. Farmers marketed 1,000 bales of cotton at Norman during the first two weeks of October 1893. Great piles of corn, hay, and rows of cotton bales, stood stacked along the Santa Fe right of way, awaiting shipment.

In November 1895, rumors of a gold strike in Cleveland County spread quickly. Located on the Whittier homestead, seven miles northeast of Norman, an assay of the ore reported rich findings. A gold rush ensued, and numerous gold claims were staked in the area. Further prospecting in the vicinity reported even richer finds "at points two to three miles distant." In May 1896, plans were made to bring ore crushing machinery into Cleveland County to develop the gold fields. Such was subsequently done, but the ore never proved rich enough to be a paying proposition. Coincidently, the gold fields were restricted to the same area where Cleveland County's famous rose rocks are found.

In 1897, when rainfall became more plentiful, farmers marketed more than 4,000 bales of cotton in Norman. This figure increased to 9,000 bales in 1902. The banks bulged with money, and stores did a tremendous business. Elevators and cotton gins were overworked. Most of the farmers built new houses after their first good crop.

Today's generation in Cleveland County owes a great deal to the perseverance of these intrepid men and women who settled the land following the run. Surviving untold hardships, they provided the financial base for the growth of all the towns and numerous crossroad villages in the county during those first

critical years. By the time statehood rolled around in 1907, Cleveland County was well on its way to becoming a prosperous farming community, justly earning its title, "Garden Spot of Oklahoma."

The Farmers Financier Creamery meant big business to early Moore. Farmers brought their cream here, then wagons hauled it to Oklahoma City. Courtesy Moore Public Library.

The Oklahoma City Mill and Elevator Company built this feed mill in Moore, providing the farmers another outlet for their crops. Courtesy Moore Public Library.

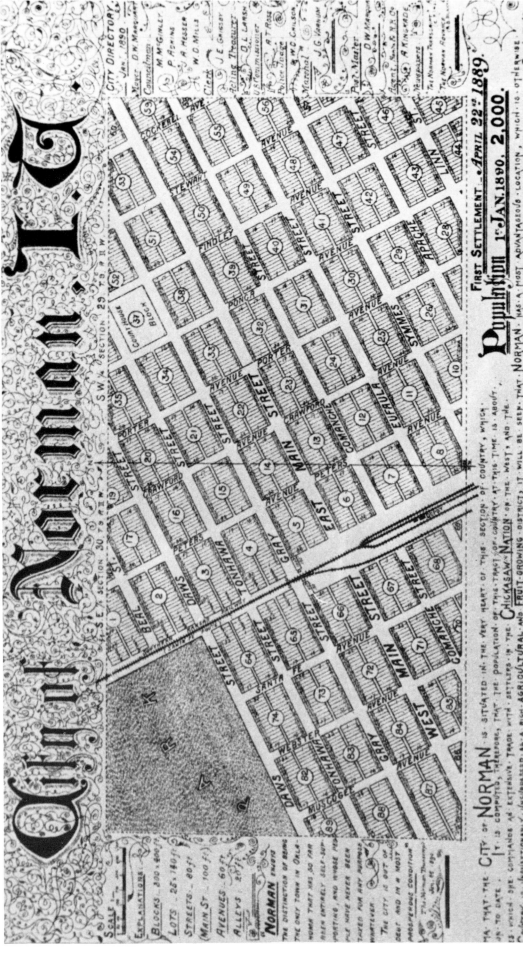

Realtor T. J. J. Wiggins' 1889 map of Norman. Courtesy of John Womack Collection.

CHAPTER 4

Norman, A Territorial Town

Pryor V. Adkins typified the quality of the first settlers in Norman. An older man and a former commissioned officer in the Confederate Army, he soon became a leading figure.

Adkins was well familiar with the area long before the run. A native of Tennessee, following "the war between the States," he had brought his wife and six sons to settle in the wilderness near Eufaula on the Canadian River. Here, they operated a ferry for several years.

In 1885, following the marriage of Adkins' son Columbus (better known as C. D.) to Sarah Jane McKinney, a member of the Choctaw tribe, Pryor Adkins and his sons, C. D., James, Frank, John, Hughell, and Art came to the Norman area in search of a better place to live.

Here they found an unsettled wilderness, "it was beautiful indeed," with acres of wild flowers, vast forests and pastureland for miles and miles, where wild animals roamed. This was the home they sought.

They camped that first night on the flat piece of ground that was soon to become Norman. The next day they crossed the Canadian River, then about 800 feet wide, and made their way to the scenic hill rising out of the misty blue April morning. Here, they built a log house on what was to become known as Adkins

Though Main Street was still a grassy track, in June 1887, construction was proceeding quickly. The building on the left was the first frame building erected in Norman, by Pryor V. Adkins. The site is now occupied by the Sooner Theatre. Courtesy The Norman Transcript and Mrs. Harold Belknap.

This building is reported to be the first store in Norman, hauled there on the day of the run by Charles T. Gorton, from which he dispensed a small supply of merchandise. Courtesy John Womack.

Charles Chamberlain, townsite location engineer for the Santa Fe Railroad, laid out the townsite for Norman. Courtesy John Womack.

Hill, and because of C. D.'s tribal rights, were allowed to lease as much Indian land as they could fence. At one time this amounted to thousands of acres on which they ran an estimated 20,000 head of cattle.

When the Santa Fe Railroad began its survey in the area, the surveyors visited the Adkins and a warm friendship developed between them. Before the surveyors left, Abner Norman, the young Kentuckian in charge of the survey crew, reportedly presented the survey chains, with which the railroad had been routed, to C. D.

The last three years before the run, Pryor Adkins and his sons had cut and baled hay on the Norman townsite. When the time came for settlement, Adkins knew exactly where to go to stake the best claims.

He built the first permanent frame building in Norman on his business lot, completing the Planters Hotel in early May. He operated a corn mill below Adkins Hill and established a saw mill there which supplied lumber for many of Norman's first buildings.

Norman was lucky in that, unlike other towns in the territory, settlement of the townsite was conducted in a fairly orderly manner, thanks to the railroad surveyors that Charles Chamberlain had sent in before the run and to the efforts of the Norman Townsite Company.

This contrasted sharply with what happened at Oklahoma Station, eighteen miles north, where the government had taken no part in the development of a town plat. Subsequently, two townsite companies, the Seminole Townsite and Development Company and the Oklahoma Town Company fought it out to have their plats accepted by the new citizens. Settlement was haphazard and there were many legal conflicts. Finally, a committee of fourteen, which had been elected the day following the run to establish streets, alleys, and blocks, effected a compromise between the townsite companies, heard arguments, and settled ownership disputes.

On the day of the run in Norman, Lem Hefley succumbed

to the frenzy of excitement around him when the special train steamed into Norman Station, and laid claim to the quarter-section of land on which the railroad section house was located. The rest of the day his family was kept busy feeding the hungry town lot claimants and disappointed land seekers who showed up on their doorstep. Mrs. Hefley and her daughters baked biscuits, which they sold six for a dollar with hot coffee. When they ran out of food, Lem sent two of his sons to Purcell on a handcar to purchase more supplies. Nellie Hefley recalled later that she had never seen so many quarters in her life.

Hefley rented a frame structure on Main Street and put up two tents behind it, where he operated a hotel until he could finish building the Hotel Norman on his claim, a short distance east of the railroad tracks on the south side of Symmes Street.

Hefley's claim was contested though, and he lost it in 1894 because he had not begun the run outside the boundary line of the Unassigned Lands. Ordered to vacate the land, he moved the Hotel Norman to another location.

Andrew Kingkade did not attempt to stake a claim the day of the run. However, he bought a claim several months later with his mother. He soon became a prominent citizen of Norman.

The exact population of Norman at the end of that first day is in dispute. One report said ten to twenty-five persons staked lots there that day. Another placed the figure at five hundred new residents. Twenty-four years after the run, Delbert Larsh estimated the number at one hundred and twenty-five people.

Nevertheless, a tent city sprang up at once. New businesses burst into being. Charles T. Gorton is credited with establishing the first business building in Norman. He hauled a box-like structure across the river the day of the run and placed it on his business lot on Main Street. Here he sold a small supply of staple foods and merchandise.

Delbert Larsh completed the first residence building in the

Abner E. Norman, a young Kentuckian heading one of the Santa Fe Railroad surveying crews in 1872, loaned his name to "Norman's Camp," which was later borrowed to designate the townsite of Norman. Courtesy John Womack.

Teams of oxen were a common sight on the streets of Norman following the run in Cleveland County. Possessing considerable strength and endurance, these animals were favored over horses or mules for clearing the new ground. Courtesy The Norman Transcript.

Andrew Kingkade, Norman's first Santa Fe agent, arrived at Norman with his family three days before the run. He became a prominent businessman in Norman. Courtesy John Womack.

A. D. Acers, manager of the Carey Lombard Lumber Company, had faith in Norman. Courtesy John Womack.

Norman vicinity. He had a small one-room structure built in sections in Purcell then shipped to Norman on a flat-bed car the day of the run, where he put the building together on his lot at 115 East Johnson Street.

Pre-fabricated buildings such as this were popular during those first days in Norman. Called "squares," these buildings, were usually twelve by twelve feet, and built in sections at some central location such as a lumber yard, then hauled to the site and quickly nailed together. Costing about $75 each, these buildings notified claim jumpers at once that these lots were already taken.

At first few of the new townsite residents seemed to have the capital or confidence in the new town to make extensive improvements on their lots.

A letter from the Carey Lombard Lumber Company to their manager in Norman exemplified this reluctance.

Hotel Carey
Wichita, Kansas
May 4, 1889

Mr. A. D. Acers, Manager
Carey Lombard Lumber Company
Norman, Indian Territory

You will not build any expensive place. Four yards can not live in your town and we may have to move and do not want a big loss in the building. You will put up rough structures, easily taken down — just enough to keep goods dry. Don't want a lumber shed or office.

We will probably abandon Moore, and there is another town starting below you that will have lumber. Do you think it is advisable to stay at Norman? Answer by wire.

Yours truly,

W. P. Carey

Mr. Acres must have answered in the affirmative for the Carey Lombard Lumber Company was to become the longest operating business in Norman, serving the community until 1986.

By the end of April 1889, a few crude buildings had been erected on East Main Street. M. McGinley opened the first general merchandise store on a permanent basis. Larsh and Waggoner built a furniture store on Larsh's lots. The first drug store, the Pioneer Drug Store, owned by Mayfield and Bellamy, opened in a tent, then moved to permanent quarters. George and Tyler Blake opened a drugstore in mid-summer, the third in Norman, on the site of the present City National Bank. In the early fall, the Nolan Brothers, "Tony," James and John, who had made the run, opened a general merchandise store. A short time later they added a slaughterhouse.

Choice residential lots were still available in Norman, not

far from the business section, through July 1889. Most of these were irregular patches, or near drainage areas.

Lots in the eastern part of the townsite were still open as late as October 1891, thanks to a controversial agricultural homestead claim which produced much litigation.

While living at the Hotel Norman, R. Q. Blakeney, owner of the *Norman Advance* with his brother Benjamin, a Norman attorney, had noticed no businesses had been located on the east eighty acres of the townsite. Contending this left the land subject to homesteading, he filed on the land, stirring up a major protest among the Norman settlers. Over one hundred families took up residence lots in the contested area.

Lard, vinegar and molasses came in barrels during those early days and crackers sold for 25 cents a peck. This unidentified grocery store was located in Norman. Courtesy The Norman Transcript.

Cleveland County's first grand jury was called in September 1891 to investigate irregularities in office. The only identified members in this photo are Tom Luttrell, top row, fourth from left; Ed M. Goodrich, fifth from left; _____ Boston, second from left, and bottom row, Charles Cox, center, and Martin Endicott, right. Courtesy The Norman Transcript and Mrs. E. W. Delay.

Jack Kahoe, an early contractor, built most of Norman's early masonary structures. Courtesy John Womack.

Many of Norman's early buildings were financed by the Commercial Bank, Norman's first bank, which opened on August 8, 1889. It moved into permanent quarters at the northwest corner of East Main Street and Peters Avenue in December of that year. Courtesy John Womack.

When the townsite trustees visited Norman in late 1890 to secure a patent on the townsite, they found they could not do so because of Blakeney's claim. Numerous hearings followed. Eventually Blakeney was overruled. Soon after, the townsite trustee board was formed and secured a patent for the townsite and began issuing deeds to the lot claimants. Blakeney made so many enemies during this time that soon after he and his brother sold their newspaper.

Despite such setbacks, Norman began to develop, slowly but steadily. During those first days, the town obtained its water from the springs and river. Malcom Fulkerson had a going business for a time, hauling water from the spring at Norman's Camp, which he sold for five cents a barrel. Shortly, the town dug a well at the center of the intersection of Peters Avenue and Main Street. Equipped with a rope, a pulley, and two oaken buckets, the well provided free water for everyone. A second well was located on Santa Fe property.

Ice was a luxury that summer. A crowd gathered at the depot to purchase the precious commodity each time a freight car arrived with a shipment of beer packed in ice.

The settlers were starved for fruit and bought oranges from the newsboys on the trains. They planted large orchards on their town lots and claims, mail ordering their stock from Stark Brothers Nursery.

Mud and dust were commonplace in the new town. No money was available to drag the streets or to purchase equipment.

That fall, Pryor V. Adkins manufactured street grading equipment at his ranch south of the river, and helped drag the streets, winning the thanks of everyone.

Births and marriages went on as usual. Almost every issue of the *Norman Transcript* carried items about young men going home to return with a new bride. Norman's first burials were made on ten acres of school land at the southwest corner of what is now Berry Road and West Main. Most of these were later removed to the I.O.O.F. cemetery after it was established in 1891, though some headstones were still seen in the first burial site as late as 1934.

Of primary importance to the settlers in Norman that first summer was the lack of law and order. When Congress opened the Unassigned Lands to settlement, it failed to make any provisions for such. Two deputy marshals, headquartered in Norman, attempted to keep the peace throughout the county but were hard pressed to do so. The land opening had attracted all kinds of people, the good with the bad. The bad were unwelcome among those attempting to establish a new life here.

Pryor V. Adkins called a mass meeting in Norman on May 4, 1889, to elect a provisional municipal government. The election was held from the back of a lumber wagon in the small park just north of the depot. Elected to office were: Thomas R. Waggoner, mayor; George Blake, clerk and recorder; Pryor Adkins, E. C. Hall, Andrew Kingkade, and Delbert Larsh, councilmen; and Fred Sevier, city marshal.

Charles H. Bessent, Norman banker and businessman was a leader during territorial growth period. Courtesy John Womack.

Levi Briggs came to Norman in 1891 from Yell County Arkansas. He built many of the buildings in the 200 and 300 blocks of East Main Street. He was the great-grandfather of actor James Garner. Courtesy John Womack.

In the first order of business, the group adopted the townsite plat that Larsh had accepted from the Santa Fe representative on April 22.

Blake kept a record of lot claims and transfers for which he pocketed a filing fee of 75 cents each. Considerable protest arose over this.

On July 15, the trusteees passed Ordinance #2 which required the city clerk to hand the filing fees over to the Board of Trustees, thus providing Norman's first operating revenue.

The intent of the registration was to prevent lot jumping. A major incident had occurred on July 4, during Norman's first big holiday celebration. A man and his wife had illegally erected a "square" on a lot on the south side of East Main Street. Mayor Waggoner ordered the city marshal to remove the building. The marshal deputized twenty men to help him, and they picked up the building and set it in the street. A crowd immediately surrounded them but the soldiers, who were still stationed in town at the Planters Hotel, maintained the peace.

A short time later, the lot jumper swore out a warrant against the mayor, town marshal, and several others. They were arraigned by the newly appointed U.S. Commissioner Albert Rennie. But Rennie was uncertain of his duties and dismissed the case.

Those first eight months in city government could be described as nothing but chaotic. There were many arguments and a frequent turnover in officials.

In August a hundred delegates met at Guthrie and petitioned Congress for an organized government. There were now twenty-seven towns established in the Oklahoma district, with a total population of about fifty thousand law abiding citizens.

No Man's Land

Congress created the Territory of Oklahoma on May 2, 1890. This included all of Western Oklahoma, the Unassigned lands, and the Panhandle.

Daniel W. Marquart was appointed the first postmaster at the Norman post office which was established on May 27, l889. Courtesy John Womack.

These citizens could not will their property, legally marry, or provide for the poor, sick, and insane. There was no provision for burial grounds, or taxation for any purpose.

On May 2, 1890, Congress passed the Organic Act creating the Territory of Oklahoma. Included in the new territory was all of present Western Oklahoma, along with the six numbered counties in the Unassigned Lands, and No-Man's Land in the Panhandle.

The Act provided for a legislative, judicial and executive department in the new territorial government, with Guthrie being designated as the Capital.

President Harrison nominated George Steele of Indiana as the first territorial governor, and he was ratified by Congress. On August 5, 1890, in the first territorial election, voters of the Third County adopted the name of Cleveland for their county in honor of President Grover Cleveland, and elected two senators, R. J. Nesbitt from Lexington, and Mort L. Bixler from Norman, to serve them in the new legislature, along with representatives W. C. Adair and Thomas R. Waggoner from Norman, and James M. Stovall of Lexington.

Norman had been previously selected as a county seat by Congress. Early bills had named Oklahoma City, Reno, Guthrie, Edmond, and Kingfisher as county seats. Norman businessmen felt slighted and began the fight to have their town named as a county seat, too. Their cause won support in Washington, D. C., and William Couch notified Mayor Marquart in February that Norman, too, had been designated as a county seat.

Controversy between those businessmen on the east side of the railroad tracks and those on the west side began as soon as the county government was established. Court was held in Wiesehann Hall on the east side of town, the only building large enough for the purpose. Other county offices were scattered about town, most of them on the east side.

During the summer of 1893, the businessmen from that part of town built a two-story county office building on East Gray

Edwards Park, Norman, Okla.

Street, which they turned over to the county commissioners on October 7 for $1. In a residential area, the building proved inconvenient to the businessmen on both sides of the railroad tracks. Opposition developed, and a petition was circulated requesting that the county commissioners condemn the building, but nothing was done.

Then on February 11, 1904, the courthouse mysteriously burned and many county records were lost, but no one seemed to regret the building's loss. Under the leadership of Delbert Larsh, the two factions got together and bought the lots where the present courthouse stands.

Norman had been incorporated as a village in July 1890 under the Nebraska Laws. It incorporated again as a town on May 13, 1891, under the new Oklahoma Territory Municipal Corporations Act, and adopted a five member board system of government, which soon increased to six members, with each ward electing one member to the board.

The population of the town now stood at 1,218. With law and order taken care of in the area, the citizens of Norman turned to improving the quality of life in their town.

Several enterprising men had opened brick plants in the area, and by the end of 1889 the town had begun to take on a permanent look as brick buildings began to spring up on Main Street.

A number of these buildings were financed by the Commercial Bank, Norman's first bank, which opened for business on August 8, 1889, in temporary quarters, then moved to its permanent location on the northwest corner of East Main Street and Peters Avenue a week before Christmas. A year later, the parent

The small plot of ground, just north of the Norman depot, remained a mudhole until Lewis J. Edwards, upper right, got the Santa Fe Railroad to fill it in. Edwards then planted and tended the area until it became a small but attractive park. Dedicated to Edwards in 1913, today, Edwards Park is maintained by the Norman Park Board, garden clubs, and Rose Society. The second Cleveland County courthouse can be seen in the background. Courtesy The Norman Transcript.

Eastside School was built on East Gray Street in 1894 at a cost of $12,375. The structure was also known as Norman's first high school, which occupied the upper story. The school was renamed Jefferson School in 1909. This building was condemned in 1916. Rock salvaged from it was used in the present house at 502 East Gray Street. Courtesy The Norman Transcript.

Westside School was also built in 1894, on the site of present Washington School. This photo was taken in 1896. From left to right, back row: Oscar Cruce, Sam Wilkins, C. W. White, teacher, Hardy Story, Lucker Miller, Lee Williams, Kate Williams, Clara McCoy, Cassie Warren, Janie Howery, Pearl Ingle, Alice Reynolds, Lulie Hughes. Middle row: Martin Kingkade, Auro Butts, Nannie Hughes, Lena Corn, Irene Elledge. Front row: Unidentified, Alice Boyd, Myrtle Hartley, Blanche Morgan, Jeanette Jeddems, Jessie Ringo, Margaret Applewhite, Mary Hughes, Grover Fulkerson. Courtesy The Norman Transcript.

The first brick building in Norman was built by Pryor V. Adkins on his lot at 101 East Main. Completed in May 1890, the Planters Hotel contained fourteen rooms and no bath. Courtesy The Norman Transcript.

The first exclusive housing district along North Peters was called "Silk Stocking Row." This unidentified front parlor, shown in 1901, was typical of the times. Courtesy The Norman Transcript.

Norman's first school was built by subscription. It opened on November 2, 1889. Courtesy The Norman Transcript and Western History Collections, University of Oklahoma.

Norman's first schoolteacher, Mattie Dollarhide, came to Oklahoma with her husband just after the run, and the couple homesteaded 160 acres one and a half miles north of Norman. Courtesy John Womack.

bank in Newton, Kansas, ran into financial difficulties and the Commercial Bank was closed. Two weeks later, it was reopened as the Citizens Bank.

No schools existed in the town that first spring or summer because many of the settlers did not bring their families until later.

On November 2, 1889, a subscription school opened in the newly completed Methodist Episcopal Church. Taught by Mattie Dollarhide, who had made the run with her husband, the school had a total of 68 pupils enrolled before the end of the term.

The first public school building, a one-room structure, was built early in 1890, just north of the present Norman Public Library. The students soon outgrew this building. In 1894, Jefferson School, which soon became known as Eastside School, was built on East Gray Street. Later that same year, Westside School was built at the present site of Washington School.

By June 1893, Norman streets were much improved. In response to public outcry, wooden sidewalks had been built, extending from the Santa Fe Railroad tracks to Crawford Avenue. Now walks were completed as far north as Hughbert Street along Peters Avenue, and the walk from downtown to the university on University Boulevard was finished.

Until now, Norman's alleys had been virtual dumping grounds for garbage. In June, the city council appointed a "town scavenger" whose duties included cleaning the streets of debris and the toilets of offal. The job was an undesirable one, but necessary. Much of the waste was dumped in an area adjacent to South Pickard Avenue near Boyd Street. Those on the south side of town complained about the stench, and rats proved a problem everywhere.

By now, Norman's population stood at 2,000 people and water became a pressing issue. In 1893, the town dug a new well west of the city limits in a pasture better known today as Lions Park. A small building housed the engine, pump, and boiler room.

The standpipe consisted of a sheet iron cylinder 100 feet high in the 700 block of East Main. Water was pumped across town through a 15-inch pipe. Once full, the standpipe could serve the city the rest of the day. Each house had a hydrant on the back porch and a stock trough stood at Peters Avenue and East Main Street. Water cost each household one dollar a month.

But as Norman continued to develop, its need for a better water system grew. On January 9, 1894, a waterworks bond issue was placed before the citizens. It carried and the town dug two more wells in the 400 block of South Flood Avenue. Soon Norman was the envy of all other towns in the Oklahoma Territory, with water service in its downtown district.

In 1895, city officials approved installation of eight gasoline street lights on Main Street. These sufficed until electricity came to the town on May 8, 1903, after six years of agitation by *The Norman Transcript* editor, Ed P. Ingle. The Norman Milling and Grain Company had an electrical system that turned a large grinding machine during the daytime. After dark, the company agreed to connect its electrical system to a 440 kilowatt generator to provide power for the city. The electricity was turned off at 10:30 p.m.

The Women's Coterie Club opened the first circulating library in June 1895 over the Bell Store in the Hullum Block. The library contained over 250 volumes and subscriber fees were set at $1 a year. By the end of the century the library had over 600 books, which were later transferred to the Carnegie Library at the University of Oklahoma.

The first exclusive residential district became known as "Silk Stocking Row," because so many of the prosperous

Church going was an important part of early Norman history. The Methodist Church South gained distinction as being the first church in Norman. It was built at the southeast corner of Crawford Avenue and Tonhawa Street in July 1889. This building, second from left, top row, replaced the first in August 1896. Other major denominations quickly followed. Top left, the Baptist Church; bottom row, Roman Catholic Church and the Presbyterian Church. Courtesy The Norman Transcript.

The Farmers National Bank of Norman was the forerunner of present City National Bank on the northwest corner of Main Street and Peters Avenue in Norman. The Fred Reed Drug Store is to the left of the bank. Mr. Reed's wife was the daughter of Tyler Blake, a member of the Norman Townsite Company. Courtesy The Norman Transcript.

The Colemon Harness Shop featured a variety of leather goods much of which was manufactured in Norman. Courtesy Pioneer Multi-County Library, The Norman Transcript, and Western History Collections, University of Oklahoma.

The Buckhead Saloon, located next door to the Mayfield Drug Store on Main Street, was only one of a number of saloons in Norman where thirsty men could slake their thirst. Seen in this 1901 photo from left to right, are Scott Prince, Ike Elledge, owner Theo Jensen and two other unidentified men. Courtesy The Norman Transcript.

The J. D. Maquire Hardware store was built at 113 West Main Street in 1889, Norman's first hardware store. Courtesy John Womack.

The Norman Milling and Grain Company brought even more business to Norman. This photo was taken in 1895. Courtesy of The Norman Transcript.

Sunday School outings such as this one were popular among early residents. Courtesy Pioneer Multi-County Library and the Norman Transcript.

members of the town lived here. The district was located on North Peters in the vicinity of the present day Cleveland County Historical House.

Although the population of Norman was small by some standards, the town always had an active social life. Nearly everyone went to church, even the gamblers and saloon keepers. At first, meetings were held in homes and store buildings. The Methodist Episcopal Church South built the first church in the territory at the southeast corner of Crawford Avenue and Tonahawa Street in Norman in July 1889. This was quickly followed by other churches in the area.

Sunday School outings were popular, and the congrega-

tions held ice cream socials to raise money for their churches.

The settlers worked hard and took their holidays seriously. The first one occurred on Fourth of July 1889. Over 1,500 people thronged into the new town to join in the celebration. The festivities featured a stomp dance by Big Jim's band of Absentee Shawnee Indians, who lived ten miles east of Norman.

Local talent provided music for community dances. The Norman Cornet Band, which was organized on January 29, 1890, claimed the distinction of being the first band in the territory. It played at numerous celebrations.

The Seawell Opera House brought culture to Norman and Cleveland County. Completed near the end of 1890 at 109 East Main Street, the Opera House was the only three-story building in town. It presented local productions as well as traveling shows. In 1892, John Faning purchased the Opera House, rearranged it and furnished it in splendor. The town gained distinction as the "Athens of Oklahoma" because of its cultural and educational facilities.

Picnics were popular during the early days. This Old Settlers Picnic, was held on July 19, 1900, at Franklin. Families present included Tom Vincent, Teen Cook, Joe Stowe, Mrs. R. C. Berry and son Ray, Addie Berry with daughters, Alpha and Avo, Frank Meyers, and R. L. Reisinger. Courtesy Pioneer Multi-County Library.

This section of the Norman business district on Main Street, shown in 1901, burned in a disasterous fire in September 1923. Courtesy The Norman Transcript.

The Norman Cornet Band, which was organized on January 29, 1890, was the first band in the territory. It serenaded F. J. McGinley on his wedding night. From left to right: Unidentified, Dutch Fred, Oscar Wimberly, Kid Mills, Tony Nolan, Mead Hoover, George Blake, Unidentified, Fred Reed, Mert Hoover, _____ Tracy. Courtesy John Womack.

The Woodman Circle Drill Team provided entertainment in this public demonstration in 1907. Courtesy The Norman Transcript and Mrs. Bess Johnson.

Even so, life in the new territory could still be a lonesome thing. The custom of ordering mail order brides was not unusual. In 1892, an enterprising group of Norman citizens banded together to supply the local demand. They called themselves the Widowers Mutual Protective Association. Their bylaws and constitution appeared in the February 27, 1892, issue of *The Norman Transcript*.

The intent of the group, so they said, was to "encourage matrimonial alliance" with all widowers and widows of Norman. Anyone joining the association and not adhering to its code could be fined one dollar. The Association agreed to furnish the entertainment for the wedding feast, in addition to a covered wagon, stove, and provisions for at least twenty days after the wedding so the couple could take a trip to the "Pott country," or to any part of the country of equal distance.

However, most people felt their matrimonial plans could do without the assistance of the Association, and the Association

fell apart after James Bishop, one of their leaders, got married.

As time passed, economic growth in Norman came slowly, advancing only as the surrounding farmers cleared their land and began producing good crops. In 1890, the U. S. government opened a new land office in Oklahoma City in preparation for additional land openings. The first of these was the Pottawatomie-Shawnee lands on September 22, 1891. Located on Cleveland County's eastern boundary, ten miles east of Norman, the opening added a strip of land, six miles in width, to the county. Many people outfitted for the run in Norman, after registering at the new Oklahoma City land office. Numerous disappointed land seekers returned to Norman and settled here, helping the economy grow. By the turn of the century, Norman was the most prosperous town in Cleveland County.

Cleveland County celebrated its first Fourth of July with a ceremonial dance by Big Jim's band of Absentee Shawnee Indians. Over 1500 people attended the celebration. John G. Lindsay, second from left, became mayor of Norman in 1905 in a landslide victory over Dr. Capshaw. Courtesy The Norman Transcript.

By 1895, brick buildings were beginning to replace many of the wooden ones on Norman's Main Street. Looking east from the railroad tracks, the Adkins brick building is on the left, and the Carey Lombard Lumber Company, right center. This group of wooden buildings, on right, was swept away in the fire of 1902. Courtesy of John Womack.

The first bridge across the Canadian River was this suspension bridge west of Noble, designed and built by Charles Edwin Garee. This photo was taken on opening day in August 1898. Courtesy The Norman Transcript and Mrs. Clyde Black.

The Grand Central Hotel at Gray Street and Peters Avenue in Norman was built in 1890 and accommodated many travelers. This site was later occupied by the Phillips Motor Company. Photo taken in 1929. Courtesy The Norman Transcript and E. W. Smalley.

CHAPTER 5

Transportation and Communication

Cleveland County has always had a good transportation system. Even before there were any towns in the Unassigned Lands the railroad existed. By the time of the opening, the Santa Fe had a daily schedule of eight trains a day running north and south through the area, connecting with the Gulf Coast and into Kansas.

The trains hauled freight as well as passengers. Before the run, the railroad was deluged by heavy freight traffic, with 487 freight cars of farm implements, merchandise and prefabricated houses piling up on sidings, waiting for shipment. The pressure increased after the run as the population of the county grew.

In Norman, the small depot erected beside the railroad tracks in 1887 soon become inadequate. In late summer 1890, in response to pressure from local businessmen, Santa Fe built a new

The automobile was rapidly replacing horse drawn wagons during the early 1900s as seen in this photo taken on Norman's Main Street after 1913 when Main Street was paved. Courtesy Pioneer Multi-County Library and The Norman Transcript.

This depot was built in 1910. The building to the right is the express building while in the background can be seen the second Cleveland County Courthouse which was completed in 1906. Courtesy The Norman Transcript.

*Ed P. Ingle, editor of the **Purcell Register** and a member of the Norman Townsite Company, printed the first issue of **The Norman Transcript** in July 1889. Courtesy John Womack.*

depot on the west side of the tracks at Eufaula Street, and added cattle shipping pens a month later.

The first settlers found few, if any, established trails in Cleveland County when they arrived. The land was verdant, and the grass hip high in certain areas.

The government had made no provisions for roads in the new territory. After settlement, trails led every which way across the land, following the path of least resistance. These first roads crossed private lands and were no more than paths in the grass, which deepened into ruts. As early as mid-summer of 1889, people were complaining that some settlers living south and east of Norman were fencing in their claims without leaving public roads as they should.

"This causes trouble for one who fences without regard to public highways. They are a necessity and should be kept open and in good repair," stated the editor of *The Norman Transcript*.

It was not until the Federal government established the postal roads in 1890 that there was much improvement in rural roads. In 1916, Federal funds became available to the counties for road building purposes. After World War I, road building took off in a big way with the state highway system.

One of the biggest obstacles facing the first citizens of Cleveland County and those in the adjacent Chickasaw Nation who wanted to trade here, was lack of bridges and ferries over the rivers, in particular over the Canadian River.

The Canadian River was a treacherous stream with much quicksand, and it was subject to rampaging floods, especially in

The Canadian River was aptly described by pioneer geologist Dr. Charles E. Gould as being a thousand miles long, a mile wide and three feet deep. Bearing treacherous quicksands it could flood with sudden walls of water six-feet high during the spring thaw. In this aerial view, taken during the 1970s, the main channel is seen to the right with the Norman bridge in the background. Topsoil and water conservation practices upstream since the 1930s have tamed the river's violent nature. Courtesy The Norman Transcript.

B. B. Blakeney, Norman attorney, was copublisher of **The Norman Transcript**, Norman's first newspaper, along with his brother, Robert Q. Blakeney. The paper began publication on July 11, 1889. Courtesy John Womack.

the spring when the snow melt came down from the Rocky Mountains. The stream had its headwaters high in the mountains in New Mexico, above Raton. Properly the name of the river is the Canadian River, not the South Canadian. The North Canadian River is simply a branch of the Canadian River.

Dr. Charles E. Gould, pioneer Oklahoma geologist, who was head of the department of geology at the University of Oklahoma and director of the Oklahoma Geological Survey for many years, described the Canadian as being a thousand miles long, a mile wide and three feet deep. All this could change suddenly, however, in the spring when huge walls of water two to six feet high cascaded down the wide sandy riverbed, sweeping all before them, tearing out trees by their roots, and destroying all that got in their way.

Shortly after settlement, the small son of Mr. and Mrs. George Grissom lost his life in the turbulent flood waters near Adkins Crossing. Farmers from miles around searched for him but no trace of the body was ever found. The Grissoms lived in the Chickasaw Nation and had to travel seventy miles to reach Norman when they could not cross the river.

Norman had one of the busiest freight stations in the country. This photo was taken in the AT&SF freight office about 1915. From left to right: John Jerome Baker, _____ Mooney, and _____ Jepson. Courtesy Bob Nolan.

During that first year of settlement in Cleveland County, the merchants of the new towns became concerned because they were losing business from the farmers and ranchers across the river as there was no safe, convenient passage across the Canadian River. They knew that if they wanted their towns to grow that they must do something about the situation.

The first bridge across the Canadian River in this area was constructed at Noble by the South Canadian Bridge Co., organized by F.A. and C. E. Garee and M. and N. C. Rigg.

The bridge was a suspension-type with a center span of 264 feet in length and two 400-foot approaches on each side of the river. Dedicated in August 1898 and operated as a toll bridge, it served for five years. Then a sudden rise in the river cut around the west end of the structure. A group of Noble businessmen bought the bridge but their efforts to force the river back under the bridge failed. They gave up and built another bridge one-fourth mile south of the first one, using materials from the first bridge. The company completed the bridge but it was swept away in the great flood of 1904, along with the remnants of the old suspension bridge.

The first bridge to span the river at Lexington-Purcell was completed in the fall of 1899. It lasted until the flood of 1904. Seven years passed before an Oklahoma City industrialist conceived the idea of a toll bridge across the river here. The bridge opened in December 1911. The toll fee was twenty-five cents for a two-horse vehicle or a car to cross the bridge, fifteen cents for a one-horse buggy, ten cents for a horseback rider, and five cents for someone on foot. This bridge operated as a toll bridge until 1935, and continued to serve as a free bridge until the present bridge was constructed in 1938.

Norman's first bridge across the Canadian was not built until 1913 near Adkins Crossing at the end of 24th Avenue Southwest. To insure this as a free bridge, the city voted $20,000 in bonds and obtained another $20,000 by subscription for construction of the bridge.

Frequent floods and channel changing forced the city to take another look at financing. When part of the bridge was washed out in 1920, the city turned the structure over to a bridge company, which charged a toll to finance repairs.

Ferries over the Canadian River brought trade from the Chickasaw Nation into Cleveland County. This unidentified ferry boat operated near Norman. Courtesy Western History Collections, University of Oklahoma.

On January 1, 1894, Rock and Hudson initiated a hack line from Norman to Tecumseh. The service also carried mail. The stage left Norman at 8:00 a.m. and arrived in Tecumseh at 1:00 p.m. The line kept the reverse schedule on return. The line operated for several years but ownership changed frequently. Courtesy The Norman Transcript.

Another flood in 1923 took out another section of the bridge. Workers constructed dirt ramps so that the bridge could continue in use.

Bruce Drake recalled the treachery of the Canadian River during one of the periodic times when the bridge was out. Crossing the river in his auto enroute to a golf tournament, he hit the water too fast, and his car stalled and began to sink. He opened the car door and by the time he got out the car had sunk to the window level, although he was standing in water only knee-deep. He watched the vehicle sink until only the antenna stuck out.

Two young men stopped and asked him if the water was deep. Drake warned them of the quicksand, but they decided to cross the river anyway. "Then give my car a shove while you're down there," Drake told them. They quickly changed their minds and decided to drive back through Oklahoma City rather than chance the Norman crossing.

The State Highway Department took over the Norman toll bridge in 1927. Sections of the bridge were washed out in May 1937, and twice in 1953, but the repaired structure continued to serve until replaced in 1955. The latest structure was built in 1987.

To serve the needs of the first settlers, several ferries also operated in the area. In those days, there was a greater level of water in the rivers and streams, before the farmers began damming them up and diverting the water.

In 1905, Norman merchants, feeling the pinch as Chickasaw Nation farmers and ranchers were lured into the thriving community of Tuttle across the Canadian, convinced Diedrich

"Dick" Borjes to establish a ferryboat at Downing Crossing, near the present end of West Robinson Street. A master craftsman from Germany, Borjes took on R. A. Butterfield as a partner. They began operating on May 23 with twenty wagons crossing that day. On May 31, a cable broke on the ferry, injuring Harold Redmond, a five-year-old boy, when the scaffolding supporting the cable above the waterline fell. Operations did not resume until mid-July. The ferryboat continued in use until 1907.

E. M. Yates operated a ferryboat at Adkins Crossing for a while. C. E. Garee attempted a similar venture at Noble but this proved shortlived.

A hack line furnished transportation and mail service between Norman and Tecumseh for several years. On January 1, 1894, the line was owned by Rock and Hudson. In operation less than a week, the driver of the open carriage and his passenger, a Tecumseh lawyer named Alcott, were both injured when a kingpin broke on the carriage and they were thrown out. Returning to Norman, they had their injuries tended and tried the trip again the next day.

On May 1, R. C. Self took over the line, offering service to all hotels each morning on a regular schedule, seven days a week, leaving Norman at 7 a.m. and arriving in Tecumseh at 1 p.m. The same schedule was in effect in reverse on the return trip, providing direct connection with the Santa Fe railroad.

By 1920, a network of roads crisscrossed Cleveland County. Often muddy and ill-kept, these roads were a source of much criticism by the residents.

With the advent of the automobile and the release of federal funds for highway construction to the counties, the roads began to improve with grading and graveling. Highway 77, built

Edwin W. Smalley, shown here at a stock show in Fort Worth, Texas, jumped in a ditch for self-protection when he saw his first automobile. Courtesy The Norman Transcript and E. W. Smalley.

This was the first horseless carriage seen in Cleveland County, though this picture was not taken locally. It was a promotional vehicle owned by Montgomery Ward & Company. Courtesy John Womack.

The I. M. Jackson Understaking Firm operated this horse-drawn hearse in Norman in 1909. the driver is Roy Cook. Courtesy The Norman Transcript and Western History Collection, University of Oklahoma.

Claude Pickard, left, and Roy Berry, right, operated the Norman Motor Company on North Peters Avenue. There were few cars in town and no service stations. People bought gasoline by the barrel. Courtesy The Norman Transcript and Mrs. Bess Johnson.

Business quickly motorized with the advent of the automobile in Norman. In the mid-1920s the Norman Milling and Grain Company ran an ice plant with nine trucks for deliver. Drivers from left to right are Major Oder, George Naill, Ed Skaggs, Don Lenby, Cliff Reach, Charles Stowe, _____ Larsh, and Arthur Stowe. Standing on the loading platform are Harold Larsh and Gus Miller. Courtesy The Norman Transcript and Mrs. George Naill.

The Adkins family show off a variety of automobiles in this 1916 photo taken at the Adkins home on Adkins Hill, south of the Canadian River. The house later burned and the family rebuilt on the same site. From left to right: Hughell Adkins, John Adkins, W. A. Adkins, Oliver Adkins, C. D. Adkins with wife Sarah Jane Adkins and children Betty and James in car, A. W. Boshers, Stella Adkins Boshers (in car), Pryor Adkins, L. F. Adkins, Sr., and Frank Starzer. Courtesy Betty Adkins Melton.

during the late 1920s, soon became known as the "football road" due to the amount of traffic driving into Norman for the University of Oklahoma football games. "Deadman's Underpass," on the south edge of Moore where the highway made an S-Curve under the railroad tracks, became the scene of many fatal accidents. Cars sped around the curve and collided head-on at the narrow underpass.

Sight of their first automobile proved a startling experience for some people. Edwin Smalley recounted one example of this. "My brothers and I were walking on old Highway No. 77 when we heard a terrible racket. We looked toward the noise and saw the horseless carriage. We ran and jumped over a fence to make sure we were safe and out of the way of that car."

In those early days, there were no filling stations in the towns. Like other car owners, the Edgar Cralle family, who owned a "Kritt," bought their gasoline by the barrel. They loved to go riding with the car's top down, but when gas went from eight cents a gallon to ten cents, Cralle advised his family they would have to stop pleasure driving and use the car only for necessities.

Another form of transportation was added to Cleveland County during the first decade of the twentieth century. The Oklahoma Railway Company had begun in Oklahoma City in 1905. With its own power plant at Belle Isle, the Oklahoma Railway Company extended its Capitol Hill line into Moore in 1910. In 1913, the interurban reached Norman. The line opened officially on November 15 with three special cars carrying 139 Oklahoma City businessmen. A big celebration was held at the Norman terminal. The shortest of the company's three interurban lines reaching to Norman, Guthrie, and El Reno, the Norman route soon proved to be the busiest with students bound to and from the university. Cars ran every half-hour from the main station located on West Main beside the Santa Fe Railroad tracks. For a time, *The Norman Transcript* had economical access to United Press news, utilizing the interurban. The news agency was then headquartered in the Black Hotel in downtown Oklahoma City. Every day except

The interurban streetcar line reached Norman in the fall of 1913, bringing a new form of transportation to Cleveland County. This building, as seen in 1928, was built in 1917. It is now occupied by the Interurban Eating House. Courtesy The Norman Transcript and Western History Collections, University of Oklahoma.

During World War II passengers could buy a ticket to Oklahoma City on the interurban, round-trip, for seventy-seven cents. Courtesy The Norman Transcript.

Sunday, a copyboy picked up a handful of dispatches at the hotel and handed them over to the motorman on the departing interurban. A staff member from *The Norman Transcript* then picked up the copy in Norman. This method proved cheaper than transmitting the news by telegraph or teleprinter circuits.

In 1942, two naval bases were built at Norman, greatly increasing the traffic on the Norman line. Everything went fine until June 17, 1944, when a tragedy occurred. Most of the Norman line was protected by block signals, but a section in the middle was not. On that fateful day, 150 passengers had boarded the four sections of No. 258, which left Norman at 8:10 p.m. The first section of the train stopped at Berry station, six and a half miles south of the Oklahoma City terminal to await a southbound car scheduled to take the siding at that point.

Suddenly sailors, riding at the back of the first car, saw the second section of the train bearing down upon them. They shouted in warning. The second car telescoped into the first, derailing both cars. Three passengers were killed as well as the engineer of the second car, and thirty-five people were injured.

During the war years, the fare on the interurban to Oklahoma City from Norman cost forty-four cents, or one could purchase a round trip ticket for seventy-seven cents.

The war ended in August 1945 and abruptly the naval bases in Norman closed. Industries in Oklahoma City laid off workers and revenues on the Norman line fell.

In the fall of 1945, operators of the Oklahoma Transportation Company, a major Oklahoma City intercity bus line, bought the failing Oklahoma Railway Company, and reorganized it. The new company petitioned the corporation commission to abandon the three interurban lines and all of the remaining Oklahoma City streetcars.

A great uproar arose in Norman. The Moore and Norman Chambers of Commerce protested, as did the officers of the American Legion. Dr. George Cross, president of the University of Oklahoma, added his voice to that of the others, stating that hundreds of students commuted to the university from Oklahoma City, and with the war over, hundreds of others would soon be doing so. Norman could not house all the returning veterans who would be going to school on the G.I. bill. Events soon proved him right, for that fall the interurban had to schedule two and three-section trains to handle all of the commuting students.

But the end of the interurban was in sight. By April 1947, the last of the Oklahoma City streetcar lines had been replaced by buses. In September 1947, the Oklahoma Transportation Company, scheduled thirty-nine round-trip buses to Norman, duplicating the rail system. Business on the interurban fell off. At the same time, visions of new freeways came into being. The Norman Chamber of Commerce decided it wanted a street on the interurban right of way where the line ran through the town. The Oklahoma Transportation Company petitioned the corporation commission a second time for abandonment. This time there was no opposition and the petition was granted.

The last car to run between Oklahoma City and Norman did so on the night of September 26, 1947. The car left Oklahoma City at 9:05 p.m. As the interurban lumbered through the night, passengers sang "Auld Lang Syne" with a note of sadness. As the car approached the Norman station, operator E. L. Hodge gave a farewell "toot-toot" of the whistle. The car gave a memorable

The last interurban car to run between Oklahoma City and Norman left Oklahoma City at 9:05 p.m., September 24, 1947. Aboard for the final ride were left to right: Emil R. Kraettli, who had ridden on the first interurban to Norman in 1926; J. L. Lindsey; operator E. L. Hodge; and Dr. Edward Evertt Dale, OU Professor. Courtesy Pioneer Multi-County Library and The Norman Transcript.

lunge and ground to a halt. Today, the old interurban station is occupied by the Interurban Restaurant.

Following World War II, the government turned its naval facilites in Norman over to the University of Oklahoma. Westheimer Field reopened. Commercial air service began here in September 1951, and ran until April 20, 1953, when a CAA ruling suspended the airline.

Today, Westheimer Field is the world's largest university-operated airport. FAA traffic figures list 100,000 takeoffs and landings here each year, making it one of the 150 busiest airfields in the nation.

A feeling of sadness touched Cleveland County on October 1, 1979, when the last Amtrak train on the Chicago-Houston Lone Star route ran through the area. The county had been privileged to daily passenger service since before the run. The Santa Fe Railroad donated the depot at Norman, which was built in 1909, to the City of Norman. Plans got underway to establish a public multi-use building.

While the transportation system in Cleveland County was developing so was the communication system. Telegraph service came in with the railroad in July 1887. In the first issue of *The Norman Transcript*, after the run, Editor Ed Engle predicted, "A telephone system connecting our thriving little town with our enterprising neighbors, both north and south, is one of the possibilities of the near future."

The first line in Cleveland County ran from Abernathy's Drug Store in Lexington to the Santa Fe depot and one of the hotels in Purcell in late 1893. This one-wire line grew into the Lexington-Purcell Telephone Company. By 1900, this company had fifteen miles of line in Lexington.

In September 1898, The Missouri-Kansas Telephone Co. extended long distance phone service from Oklahoma City, through Moore, to Norman, and on to Noble in 1900. Two years later, the line reached Etowah, Colo, Maquire, Hico, and Franklin. By 1904, the system included Stella in the northeast part of the county.

The Norman Telephone Exchange began providing local service in January 1901. Owned by J. D. Phillips and C. G. Munsell, it started with seventy-two phones and doubled its number of subscribers in one year. The switchboard was located

Max Westheimer Field began operation in Norman in 1942. It was turned over to the Navy Department during World War II. Today, it is the world's busiest university-operated airport, with over 100,000 takeoffs and landings a year. Courtesy Bonnie Speer.

Daisy Armstrong Clement operated the first telephone switchboard in Norman. Owned by the Norman Telephone Exchange and located upstairs in the McGinley-Berry building in the 200 block of East Main Street, the switchboard has sixty positions. Courtesy Besse A. Clement.

J. J. Burke, editor of **The Norman Transcript,** *relaxes in foreground in the back shop in 1912. Other early day staffers included Van Endicott, Russell Smith, Jeff Griffin, J. D. Womack, and Fred Andrews.* Courtesy The Norman Transcript and Van Endicott.

upstairs in the McGinley-Berry building in the 200 block of East Main Street.

Daisy Armstrong Clement, who had moved to Norman in 1898 to live with her sister and brother-in-law, Edwin H. Kendall, became the first telephone operator for the company. The Pioneer Telephone Company bought out the Norman company in September 1916.

Newspapers were equally important in early Cleveland County. The first settlers into the area possibly carried with them a copy of *The Purcell Register,* which Editor Ed. P. Ingle began publishing in 1887. A member of the Norman Townsite Committee, the first thing Ingle did on the day of the run was to locate a town lot in Norman where he could publish *The Norman Transcript.* The first two issues of that paper were published in July 1889, and then it was not issued again until late that fall, reportedly due to ill health. The newspaper has been published continuously since then.

The first newspaper published in Norman though was *The Norman Advance,* published by brothers Robert Q. Blakeney and B. B. Blakeney, on July 11, 1889, beating *The Norman Transcript* by two days. The Blakeney's ownership lasted only six months. Following Robert's growing unpopularity among the residents of Norman, after his attempts to homestead the east eighty acres of the Norman townsite, the brothers sold the newspaper in February 1890 to a pair of Kansas brothers. Mort Bixler, who had been associated with two Oklahoma City papers, bought *The Advance* in 1891.

A half-dozen other short-lived newspapers were printed in Norman during the 1890s. While the Norman newspapers were getting started, so were others in Cleveland County. Lexington claimed a total of five newspapers after the run. An organ of the Democrat party, *You Alls Doins,* founded by O. M. Stevens in 1899, was the most popular publication. Eight newspapers were founded at Noble during those early years, but only the *Noble News* survived. In Moore, Tom Kennedy established *The Moore Monitor* in 1891.

Early editors painted glowing pictures of their towns and claimed them to be the best places in which to live in Oklahoma. Boasted the editor of *The Norman Transcript* in the first issue: "Norman is a natural location for a town as everyone agrees, after viewing it and the beautiful surrounding country with its many prosperous settlers."

During those days, the newspapers were sharply divided along political lines. The vitrolic editors often carried on running feuds which got them into trouble. Such was the case in 1894 when Mort Bixler, editor of *The Norman Transcript,* ran a story accusing the new postmaster, T. J. Johnson, of placing copies of *The Oklahoma Call* in patron post office boxes, thus insuring every family in the county of receiving a copy. Johnson denied the accusation. One day he met Bixler outside the post office and gave him a trouncing.

Radio communications came into Cleveland Country in September 1922 when WNAD, the oldest university-operated sta-

WNAD was the oldest university-operated station in the nation. It went on the air in 1922 on the University of Oklahoma campus, and is now known as WWLS, a private company. Here, OU President George Cross presents former football coach Bennie Owen an on-the-air award for his many years of service to OU. Courtesy Western History Collections, University of Oklahoma.

tion in the nation, went on the air. It was the second broadcasting station in Oklahoma. WKY had begun transmitting a month earlier in Oklahoma City.

WNAD began in the home of Maurice L. Prescott, a university engineering student, who obtained a frequency and set up an experimental transmitter in his home on Eufaula Street. In September 1923, a group under the name of the Oklahoma Radio Engineering Company, decided to help Prescott gather broadcasting apparatus, and the station was soon put into operation with 50 watts of power, using Prescott's parlor as a studio.

In the beginning, programming on WNAD consisted mainly of playing records and play-by-play descriptions of athletic events. The following year, the station was installed as part of the electrical engineering lab, and work began on the construction of a 100-watt station. WNAD was housed in the tower of the Memorial Union Building after the tower's construction in 1936.

Early stars at WNAD included John Dunn, director, Homer Heck, Walter Emery, and Fisher Muldrow. Walter Cronkite, who went on to network fame, broadcast here during the summer of 1937.

The call letters of WNAD were changed in 1980 to WWLS. Today, the original voice of Soonerland can be heard all through Oklahoma at 0640 on the AM frequency.

KOMA was born on Christmas Eve, 1922, in Oklahoma City, under the call letters of KFJF, with 15 watts of power. The studio operated on the fourth floor of the Kerr Building for a number of years, before moving to the twenty-fourth floor of the Biltmore Hotel in 1932.

William "Bill" Morgan operated radio station KNOR in Norman from 1948 to 1972. Morgan also served three terms as mayor of Norman: 1965-1969, 1975-1979, and 1979-1983. Courtesy June Morgan.

On January 8, 1929, KFJF began its long affiliation with the Columbia Broadcasting System, relying on CBS for most of its programming during the 1930s and 1940s with the exception of local news.

In 1932, the call letters of the station were changed to KOMA when the owner, Dudley Shaw, retired and took the original call letters with him.

During the 1950s, television was forcing radio into a period of change. The old radio shows were quickly fading into the past. Changing with the times, KOMA ended its affiliation with CBS in 1958 and became a true "rock" station.

In 1961, the KOMA studios and transmitter were permanently combined at one site on West Fourth Street in Moore. Today, the station operates with 50,000 watts power at 1520 on the AM dial.

KNOR went on the air in 1948 at its present location on East Alameda Street in Norman. William "Bill" Morgan had come to the University of Oklahoma in 1947 from Nebraska to teach radio speech. He soon became program director of WNAD. When he learned radio station KTOK in Oklahoma City had been reassigned to a frequency of 1000 on the AM dial, he and a silent partner, Tol Dickenson, applied for the vacated frequency of 1400 and got it. Construction began on the East Alameda building at once.

Bill Morgan and his wife June ran the station with the assistance of OU students until 1972. Well-known Oklahoma sports announcer Bob Barry got his start with KNOR. Today, the station operates with 1,000 watts power.

KIMY came to the county in 1985 as a sister FM station of KOMA. In 1987, it changed its call letters to KRXO.

With its early advances in transportation and communication, Cleveland County was pushed to the fore in the development of Oklahoma. Today, it still maintains a steady growth rate because of these characteristics.

Lexington was a regular bus stop on the McIntire Transportation Line which connected it with other towns across Oklahoma. This photo was taken in 1915. Courtesy McClain County Historical Society.

Village stores and community blacksmith shops often served as meeting places for area residents. With the advent of the automobile, the necessity of these small trading centers faded away. **Courtesy Western History Collections, University of Oklahoma.**

70

CHAPTER 6

Other Towns Of Cleveland County

Community ties have always been important in Cleveland County. Any site that had one or more stores, a post office, and a school building, which usually doubled as a church, readily received a name and served the basic needs of the community. Cleveland County had many settlements of this type in the beginning. The village store and post office served as a meeting place for the area residents, and social and religious functions at the schoolhouse further strengthened these ties.

As time passed, with the invention of the automobile and the development of better roads, many of these small trading centers faded away. People drove to the larger towns to purchase their necessities or to sell their farm products. Rural free delivery blanketed the county before statehood, eliminating fifteen country post offices. During the next two decades, schools consolidated, often doing away with the last social tie.

Today, many of these small communities that burst into being following the run are remembered in name only but they played a large role in the development of Cleveland County. A few such as Etowah, Franklin, Slaughterville, and Stella, have hung on, a reminder of the days that were. Moore, Norman, Noble, and Lexington have grown into the largest towns, and each is unique in its development.

As soon as they could, the rural communities built crude schoolhouses for the education of their children. These schools also served as a meeting place for religious activities and other social gatherings. This is Red Hill School, a half-dugout building located three miles north of Little Axe in 1893. The teacher is Mrs. Vic English. C. D. Ross is standing next to her. The others are unidentified. Courtesy of The Norman Transcript and C. D. Ross.

MOORE

Moore, Cleveland County's northernmost town, slumbered along as a peaceful little place for more than eighty years, then suddenly boomed into a large city during the 1970s.

Located twelve miles south of Oklahoma City and eight miles north of Norman on Interstate 35, Moore can trace its roots back to 1887 when the Santa Fe Railroad built into the area. Railroad officials planned a watering stop on the Santa Fe right of way, every nine miles. They designated Moore—or Verbeck as it was first called—as the thirteenth stop south of the Kansas border.

Reportedly, Chief Engineer Charles Chamberlain named the site Verbeck after his hometown in Barton County, Kansas. However, the story goes that Al Moore, a railroad employee who lived in a boxcar at the watering stop, had trouble receiving his mail. Therefore, he painted his name on a board and nailed it to the side of the boxcar. Soon the place became better known as Moore rather than Verbeck. Postal authorities officially accepted the name of Moore for the village in May 1889.

The original townsite of Moore extended only a few blocks on both sides of the railroad tracks between present Northeast Third Street and Southeast Fourth Street. Only half of the allowable land was claimed for the townsite on the day of the run leading historians to believe that there was no organized group behind the town's founding. At first most of the businesses were located on the east side of the railroad tracks but these soon moved to the west side.

The town dug two water wells to serve the needs of the community. One well was located at the intersection of Main Street and Broadway, and the other at Southeast Third Street and Broadway.

One of the primary concerns for the new town following the run was the need for a schoolhouse. The community constructed a one-room wooden building for that purpose on South Howard Avenue, just south of the present First Baptist Church.

A second small building followed, then in 1899, the town built its third schoolhouse, a two-story building with one room upstairs and two down. All grades one through ten were taught here until 1920. Those students desiring to graduate from high school had to transfer to either Oklahoma City or Norman.

1893 . . . Looking west from the railroad tracks. The buildings on the north side of Main Street, were destroyed by fire in 1910, and the merchants rebuilt on the south side of the street. Courtesy Moore Public Library.

In 1920, Moore consolidated with five other school districts and built Moore High School in the 200 block of North Broadway. Fire destroyed this building in 1927, and a second high school was not completed until 1929.

In 1987, Moore High School had the distinction of having the largest high school student body in Oklahoma, 2,020 in only two grades, 11th and 12th. That all ended in August 1988 when the school divided and Westmoore High School opened at SW 12th Street and South Western.

Today, the boundaries of Moore Consolidated School District C-2 encompasses a 177 square mile area, primarily in northern Cleveland County, and extending into southern Oklahoma County.

Higher education came to Moore in 1977 with annexation of Hillsdale Free Will Baptist College in the southern part of the city, when the forty-one acre campus was de-annexed by Norman.

From the beginning, religion played an important part in Moore. The First Baptist Church was founded on July 5, 1890. The Moore Methodist Church South alternated every other Sunday with the First Baptist Church in holding services in the one-room schoolhouse.

The Baptists constructed a new building at 201 Howard Avenue in 1899. The Methodists erected their first building in 1901. When the church was nearing completion, someone set fire

The original townsite of Moore covered only a few blocks on each side of the railroad tracks. The citizens dug two wells to furnish water for the town. One of these wells can be seen in the center of the street. Courtesy Pioneer-Multi County Library.

A few brick buildings were beginning to appear on Main Street in Moore, lending an air of permanency when this photo was taken in 1908. Courtesy Pioneer Multi-County Library.

The Albert J. Smith store furnished a variety of merchandise and groceries for early residents of Moore. Courtesy Moore Public Library.

Moore served as a trade center for a wide area in the northern part of Cleveland County. Here, ladies gather around the display of an enterprising merchant. Courtesy Moore Public Library.

to it and a bucket brigade, two blocks long, saved the building. It remained another sixty-one years to serve the community.

In 1893, the citizens of Moore decided to incorporate as a town. But first they had to conduct a census. The story is told that when the two census workers were about to complete their count, totaling ninety-nine residents, a jackass belonging to grocer Bud Cottrell began braying down the street. "Let's count him in to

make it an even one hundred," proposed William C. Jury. So they did and Moore's first census officially tallied one hundred.

During those early years, the town survived as a trading center for the farmers in northern Cleveland County. Among the businesses catering to their needs were Albert J. Smith's livery stable and grocery store, Bud Cottrell's grocery, Sam G. and

This is Moore's third school building. Students attended here from the first grade through the first two years of high school. To graduate they had to transfer to either Norman or Oklahoma City. Courtesy Moore Public Library.

The first brick building in Moore was used for a variety of functions as shown by the various signs. From left to right, Mildred Sims, her father P. R. Sims, and Henry Applegate. Courtesy Moore Public Library.

This Methodist Church was one of the earliest churches in Moore. Its members shared a schoolhouse with the Baptists until each denomination could finance its own building. Courtesy Moore Public Library.

C. Dyer's drug store, the First National Bank of Moore, Ruedy Lumber Co., H. P. Dreessen's Hardware, and Henry Applegate's Iowa Hotel.

The Oklahoma City Mill & Elevator Company built a 5,000-bushel elevator on the west side of the railroad tracks at Southeast First Street in 1898. Two years later, the Norman Milling & Grain Company constructed a second elevator near Main Street. Both of these elevators did a brisk business buying corn and wheat, thus bringing new trade into the community from the Chickasaw country.

Most of the businesses in Moore that were located on the north side of Main Street were destroyed by fire in 1910. Undaunted, the merchants rebuilt on the south side of the street.

Those days, Main Street turned into a quagmire following a rain. In 1918, a gravel pit opened in the area and the town obtained several wagonloads of gravel from it, which it spread on Main Street, improving it greatly. About four years later, the State of Oklahoma built Highway 77 through Moore, thus providing easier access to Oklahoma City and Norman.

During the first twenty-seven years of its existence, Moore had little fire protection. The Moore Volunteer Fire Department was organized on July 18, 1916. Four months later, it proudly purchased its first piece of fire fighting equipment, a Badger chemical fire engine.

A town marshal maintained the peace in Moore during the early 1900s, assisted later by a town watchman. The town did not hire a full-time policeman until 1955. Today, the Moore Police Department numbers about forty-five officers who patrol twenty-two and a half square miles.

In the beginning, Moore was governed by a three-man town board, later in a four-man board, and then a five-man board. In 1962, the city incorporated, and changed its form of government to that of a city manager. The charter provided for seven city councilmen, one of whom the members selected as mayor. This continued until 1971 when a change in the City Code specified that the mayor be elected by popular vote.

Electricity came to Moore in 1918. Gas lines were not laid until 1930, and a sewer system was developed in 1933.

In 1958, library services were established in Moore when it affiliated with the Pioneer Multi-County Library system, which included Cleveland, McClain, and Garvin counties. A bookmobile served the community until 1965 when the town passed a $200,000 bond issue to construct a new library. The building opened on April 29, 1967, with a total of 6,000 volumes. Today, the Moore Public Library lists nearly 45,000 books in its holdings.

Dr. C. C. Nail delivered the first baby in Moore: Dick Kitchen, in 1890. During the early 1900s, Dr. R. D. Lowther of Norman obtained one of the first cars in the area and visited many patients in Moore. The Moore Municipal Hospital opened its facility on May 25, 1971, establishing a new order in medical care in the town.

Moore slumbered along as a quiet little country town until the early 1960s when a building boom erupted in the town. The area's proximity to Oklahoma City and Norman was the principle factor in this. Moore called itself the "Minute City," for it was located fifteen minutes from Tinker Air Force Base; seventeen minutes from Western Electric; and thirteen minutes from the Federal Aviation Aeronautics center at Will Rogers Airport, all principle employers. Then on March 31, 1977, General Motors Corporation announced plans for a new car manufacturing plant on I-240, west of Tinker Air Force Base. The plant, when it opened, employed 5,000 people. Many of these workers sought housing in nearby Moore, and the town began to boom. Its population soared from 942 people in 1950 to 33,000 in 1977, one of the fastest growing cities in the nation. Today, Moore is Cleveland County's second largest city with approximately 43,000 citizens.

Mildred Sims Moore collected, organized, and stored the first library books at the American Legion Hall, which became Moore's first public library. Later, this collection was moved to this little white building, which was formerly a barbershop. Courtesy Moore Public Library.

NOBLE

Noble, the county's third largest town, could be termed the town that was never meant to be. When the Santa Fe Railroad built its tracks through future Cleveland County, it designated Walker, a site two miles below the present location of Noble, as a future townsite.

However, Albert Rennie, a White Bead attorney, had other ideas. When he first came to Indian Territory from Canada in 1883, he worked as a cowboy for his brother, James Rennie, in the Chickasaw Nation. Albert Rennie rode over the high ridge east of the Canadian River many times, and he thought the spot would be ideal for the location of a town. Before the run, he drew up a townsite plat and convinced the railroad authorities to choose his location for a town instead of theirs. He named the town Noble in honor of Secretary of Interior John Noble, who helped open the land to settlement.

On the day of the run, Rennie possessed the 160-acre townsite along with several other businessmen. The group had great plans for Noble, anticipating it would become the future county seat. But they defeated their own purpose by keeping such tight control on the townsite and maintaining the price of lots so high that many prospective businessmen moved on to Norman.

Before the opening, the area was part of a vast cattle range, the center of which was the Montford B. Johnson ranch across the Canadian River. The earliest known settler was Charley Campbell, who farmed the rich bottom lands near the river.

After the opening, Noble thrived as a business center with a general merchandise store, two cotton gins, and a grain elevator.

Business increased in 1898 when C. E. Garee built a new suspension toll bridge over the Canadian River. On opening day, August 13, several hundred people gathered on the Chickasaw side to celebrate the occasion, and everyone crossed over the bridge free of charge.

During Noble's first year, W. J. Reid, 18, the depot agent, received word that the Comanches were on the warpath. He advised all men to have their firearms in readiness. When he gave the word, they were to get the women and children to the depot. Later, news came that U. S. soldiers had corralled the Indians and the citizens sighed in relief.

Noble's first school was a subscription school, which

Albert Rennie, a White Bead Hill attorney, drew up the townsite plat for Noble and possessed the site on the day of the run. Courtesy John Womack.

Construction was proceeding rapidly on Main Street in Lexington when this picture was taken on May 21, 1889. Courtesy McClain County Historical Society.

opened in 1890 and lasted only a few months. Miss Mary Anne Klinglesmith taught the first class and Miss Carr Wilson the second one.

In 1891, members of the town established the Noble Academy, taught by Professor E. D. McCredy, and constructed a one-room building on the future site of the Noble grade school. Unable to obtain clear title to the land, the group moved the school building to the northeast side of town and added two classrooms. The school progressed rapidly, boarding as many as 150 students from the Indian Territory and Texas. But the town could not accommodate so many new people and some students had to live in half-dugouts. The school closed in 1895, forced out by its high tuition and lower costs at the state university in Norman.

Noble built a one-room public school in 1897, which was expanded in 1899, but operating funds proved scarce. One year, board members had only enough money to provide for a six month term. For a while, it looked as if the public school would have to close for good but the citizens were prevailed upon to make monthly payments into the school fund and the school kept going.

Noble's first high school was built in 1911. The school system received a big boost in attendance in 1948 when the state legislature eliminated the majority of rural schools in the area.

The Noble School District suddenly encompassed 143 square miles, extending as far as Little Axe and creating tremendous transportation and space problems. The present high school was built in 1970.

The Noble Methodist Church organized on April 22, 1890,

The Noble Academy was established in 1891 and drew students from the Twin Territories and Texas. The school closed in 1895, forced out by the lower tutition at the state university in Norman. This picture was taken during the school's last year. Courtesy Western History Collections, University of Oklahoma.

Charles Edwin Garee was one of Noble's earliest businessmen. He built the first bridge over the Canadian River in 1898 and established the Noble Nursery in 1899. He is shown here with his wife Elva in the fall of 1897. Courtesy Mrs. Harry Dean.

The Santa Fe Railroad completed this depot at Noble in August 1889. The last passenger train stopped here in 1944 and the depot was moved away. This photograph was taken in 1897. Courtesy Western History Collections, University of Oklahoma.

with eight members. In August that same year, the First Baptist Church also organized with eight members, followed by the Church of Christ and Presbyterian Church.

Noble had little fire protection during its first years. On February 22, 1905, fire destroyed half of the business buildings on one side of the street. A year later, the opposite side of the street burned. Eventually, the town organized a volunteer fire department. A city marshal and night watchman kept peace within the town during those early days.

Sidewalks were among the town's first improvements, followed by the installation of a telephone system. Central office was located in the back room of the Noble bank. Water mains were laid in 1912, then electricity came to town, and after that came paved streets and natural gas.

Noble Nursery was among the earliest businesses in Noble, providing day work for many people. Francis Albert Garee came to Noble in 1895 with his parents. He had a great love for nature and in the fall of 1899, he planted a few grape cuttings and some peach seeds. From these, he gradually developed a variety of fruit trees which he grafted onto the seedlings. Later, he added other trees and shrubs. He shipped his stock all over Oklahoma, and outside the state, too. Noble Nursery existed until 1970 when it was sold to Brockhaus Nursery which is still in operation.

The Noble First Methodist Church was organized on April 22, 1890, with eight members. This picture was taken in 1900. Courtesy Western History Collections, University of Oklahoma.

Noble built a one-room schoolhouse in 1897. These high school students were photographed in 1898. Courtesy Western History Collections, University of Oklahoma.

Gus Leslie of Noble helped keep the peace as a Cleveland County deputy sheriff. With him in this picture is his wife Louisa. Courtesy Gus Leslie.

Ike Graham's Hardware Store was located on Main Street in Noble. The woman in the picture is "Okie" Graham. Courtesy Gus Leslie.

For a time, a distillery operated a mile and a half northwest of Noble. The facility closed with the coming of statehood and prohibition. The remnants of the old still and bonded warehouse remained for a long time as a landmark.

Other early businesses included Bob Stogner's barbershop, Flitner Hardware, Stufflebean's Store, Smith Hardware Store, and W. J. Scott's brickyard. For a time, a saloon operated on the east side of Main Street, but was voted out in 1899. A later saloon, which opened in one of the new rock buildings on Main Street, failed for lack of business.

For a few years, Noble served as a major shipping point for cattle from both sides of the Canadian River. Then the suspension bridge washed out in 1904. About the same time the communities of Blanchard and Washington began to develop, and there was no longer any need for the farmers and ranchers in the Chickasaw Nation to cross the river to trade in Noble.

The last passenger train stopped in Noble in 1944. The depot, which had been built at the time of the run, was moved away.

The town went quietly about its business until the mid-1970s when it experienced a building boom. Today, the population of Noble stands at approximately 5,000 people.

The town's largest employer is Award Design Medals Inc. which produces hydrastone and bonded porcelain figurines. Established in 1973, the company maintains a workforce of 230 people, plus another 150 cottage workers who paint the figurines.

Noble's first hotel was located just south of the present city hall. Dr. and Mable Ward lived here, and in 1915, Dr. Ward, a drug addict, murdered his wife. Courtesy Western History Collections, University of Oklahoma.

Noble School was located on Fourth Street between Chestnut Avenue and Cherry Avenue. The school was built in 1910. All twelve grades attended here. Courtesy Gus Leslie.

The First State Bank, shown on the left below, was located on the west side of Main Street in Noble. On the right is the Farmers State Bank. Courtesy Gus Leslie.

This photo of the first and second grades was taken in September 1912 at the west entrance of Noble School. The teacher is Miss Nell Payne. From left to right, top row: Mary Hendry, Leona Stogner, _____ Hover, Ruth Vance, Wilneth Nemecek, George Russell, _____ Avants, Jim Carmon, Cora Manley, Roy Kurkendoll.
Second row: Lola May Lumper, Ethel Mefford, Nora Petty, Elizabeth Garee, _____ , Lola Wagner, Margie Grissom, Lottie Mae Mills, Ruth Bryant, Wilma Sandel, Bernice Stufflebean.
Third row: Ocelor Ward, R. F. Ellinger, Jr., _____ Luper, Ruby Manley, John Hobaugh, Vema Craddock, Gracie Dilbeck, Darwin Childs, James Roberts, Clara Mae Riggs, _____ Bryant.
Fourth row: Buck Grissom, Sam Oliver, _____ McFerron, Jack Childs, Alvin Mefford, Herbert Black, Charles Morris.
Kneeling at front: Worth Roberts and Jimmy Brown. Courtesy Elizabeth Garee Bullard.

LEXINGTON

Lexington had a unique beginning. Born on the day of the run, April 22, 1889, the village soon became known as "Fun City," and the "Booze Capital of Southern Oklahoma Territory."

Territorial law at that time prohibited the introduction of liquor into Indian Territory. But when Oklahoma Territory was established, it was no longer officially a part of Indian Territory. Though liquor dealers—principally druggists—were supposed to be licensed by federal officials, the lack of organized government in the Oklahoma Territory invited infractions of this law.

Within a month after the run, twenty-one saloons had sprung up in Lexington stretching all the way from the Canadian River to what became known later as the "bank corner." With these saloons, came all sorts of other vices including gambling and prostitution. A number of robberies and murders occurred in the area despite the U.S. soldiers and deputy marshals stationed there to maintain law and order.

Many of the saloons were located in the Canadian River, on a sand bar near the east bank. Congress had established the boundary line between Indian Territory and Oklahoma Territory as the center of the river. The saloon nearest "dry" Indian Territory logically had first chance at obtaining the most business.

Among the most famous of these saloons in Sand Bar Town was the Sand Bar Saloon built by Charley and Sam Lassaur. At first, the small building stood on wooden piles driven deep into the sand. After several small rises in the river, the owners placed the saloon on a flat-bottomed boat and waterproofed the bottom half of the building. The saloon soon became better known as the "ark." A catwalk stretched from the saloon and over the narrow river channel, placing the saloon within easy reach of the busy Santa Fe depot, inviting all to come over.

Another well-known floating saloon was the "City of Purcell" launched by Fred Perry in October 1890. Periodic rises in the river gave Perry more trouble than the local lawmen, washing the stern-wheeler down river and beaching it in "dry" country.

Busy hacks plied the trade between Lexington and Purcell, braving the treacherous quicksands in the river. All went well until February 1891 when a big rise washed away most of the saloons on the sand bar, "just one house and the 'ark' left," reported the *Purcell Register*. The saloons quickly rebuilt only to be washed away again in September 1892.

Following the Organic act of May 1890, all liquor licenses were issued by local government. At first the town trustees of Lexington set the saloon fee at $200 a year, but soon reduced this to $25 when some of the saloons closed because the owners thought the license too high.

In a further attempt to control the wanton activities within their jurisdiction, the city council passed an ordinance, on July 27, 1891, prohibiting gambling within the village limits and for two miles outside it.

On March 11, 1897, the Fourth Oklahoma Legislature outlawed all saloons within two miles of an incorporated town. This spelled an end to the sand bar saloons, though those within the town continued to operate.

Lexington also boasted the largest distillery in Oklahoma Territory. The Weitzenhoffer-Turk distillery had a capacity of 70 gallons of liquor a day. The first barrel, tapped December 4, 1901, was reported to be "as clear as pure well water" with "a flavor that would make a judge on an article in that line say that it could not be beaten."

But all of the liquor industry vanished with statehood on November 16, 1907, when Oklahoma came into the union as a dry state. On that final day before prohibition took over, drunks could be seen everywhere as the remaining thirteen Lexington saloon keepers gave their stock away as a goodbye gesture.

In spite of having inherited so many empty buildings by the demise of the liquor business, Lexington prospered during the next few years as the trade center of southern Cleveland County.

B. L. Higbee, Sr., shown here with his family, served as a deputy sheriff for the south end of Cleveland County. He was first appointed in 1907 by Sheriff Ike Sales. Courtesy Pioneer Multi-County Library and The Norman Transcript.

Lexington soon became known as the "Booze Capital of Southern Oklahoma Territory." Many of its saloons were located on a sand bar in the Canadian River, in "wet" territory adjacent to the "dry" Chickasaw Nation. Courtesy The Norman Transcript and Ray W. Isom.

Lexington soon became a trading center in the southern part of Cleveland County for cotton farmers. Courtesy Pioneer Multi-County Library.

The G. Ille grocery store in Lexington stocked a variety of merchandise. On the left in this photo, which was taken in 1909, is Mr. Ille, and right, his son, Adolpf Ille. Courtesy McClain County Historical Society.

Prior to the run, a group of Purcell businessmen including Amos Green, Morgan Abernathy, Bill Hocker, Frank Beeler, George Beeler, and Percy R. Smith, had seen the possibility of establishing a town across the Canadian River from Purcell. Amos Green, a lawyer, drew up a townsite plat. As all the men on the townsite committee were from Kentucky (except the Beeler brothers, residents of Purcell, originally from Kansas), it seemed only natural to name the new town Lexington. On the day of the run, Green selected George Beeler, who had opened Purcell's first bank four days before the run, to make the race on his trusted

pony to claim the townsite. Beeler was successful in his effort but never claimed the 100 town lots as a reward.

A few tents went up in the business district on the day of the run. Two weeks later there was only one frame building in town: One-Armed Ed's Saloon. Other businesses were far outnumbered those first months, but gradually more merchants began to build. The first census, taken on June 4, 1890, reported a population of 183 people.

By 1894, Lexington listed six grocery and dry goods stores, among twenty-four essential businesses, and had grown to a population of 350 people. A fire destroyed most of the stores on Main Street that year.

The town bounced back, and in 1900, *You All's Doin's* reported: "Lexington now has a population of about 1,500. It has two telephone exchanges—one bank and one loan company—electric lights—and the only broom factory this side of Olathe, Kansas . . . two shoe shops—four millinery stores—five blacksmith shops—four wagon yards—three livery barns—two lodging houses—three hotels . . . four lawyers and six doctors."

The Purcell Bridge and Transfer Company completed a toll bridge over the Canadian River in September 1899, providing Lexington with a direct connection to the railroad. However, the bridge washed out in the big rise of 1904 and those in Lexington were back to fording the dangerous river to reach Purcell. There was much rejoicing in Lexington when the bridge was replaced in 1911. But this feeling was shortlived. In this new era of better roads and automobiles, shoppers in Lexington began to travel over the bridge to Purcell and Lexington stopped growing.

A Chickasaw-by-marriage, George Rylie Beeler, established Purcell's first bank, owned a 2,000 acre ranch south of Chickasha and in the Run of 1889, raced across the Canadian river on "Brownie," his favorite horse, establishing the Town of Lexington. Courtesy Julia Beeler Smith.

Lexington's first public school as shown in 1899. Courtesy McClain County Historical Society.

A big issue in the statehood election in 1907 was prohibition. Demonstrations such as this Women's Christian Temperance Union parade helped swing support toward making Oklahoma a dry state and put an end to Lexington's thriving saloon business as it did elsewhere. Courtesy The Norman Transcript and Western History Collections, University of Oklahoma.

Grandma Bettes lived in the Franklin community. The women of the new settlements worked hard to make their homes comfortable. They collected wild fruits and nuts, and preserved their gardens so that the families could have food during the winter. Courtesy The Norman Transcript and J. H. Muldowney.

Today Lexington, Cleveland County's fourth largest town, numbers approximately 1,800 people. The Lexington Pre-release Center, a sub-unit of the Oklahoma State Penitentiary, is the town's largest employer.

OTHER COMMUNITIES

Denver exemplified the numerous crossroads villages which sprang up in Cleveland County during settlement days. Finding time on his hands during the fall when his field work was done, M. C. Runyan set up a saw mill, a sorghum mill, and a small general store at the crossroads near the farm he had homesteaded. Located on Dave Blue Creek, Runyan named the village after his oldest son, Denver Runyan.

The first post office at Denver was established on May 24, 1892, with Dr. Samuel O. Chesney as postmaster. By the turn of the century, Denver had two general stores, two cotton gins, a sawmill, an elementary school, an I.O.O.F. Lodge, a Baptist Church, a drug store, a hardware store, a cemetery, and several residences.

Much excitement reigned in the village in the early 1900s when it was rumored that the Frisco railroad was going to build into Denver and nearby Franklin, but nothing happened. In 1965, Denver was inundated by Lake Thunderbird.

Another typical crossroads village, Franklin was established May 10, 1892, and the village was named after the first postmaster, Franklin Blackburn.

Etowah was located on the main road to Tecumseh from Lexington and Purcell. Its post office was established on August 8, 1894, and it was the last inland post office to be discontinued when rural free delivery was extended across Cleveland County.

History rings with the names of other crossroad communities, such as Stella, Hico, and Slaughterville.

Most of the crossroad communities in Cleveland County began to lose their importance after rural free delivery was

extended into the areas from the larger towns during the spring of 1906. Within the next decade, schools consolidated and agriculture production reached its peak. There was a drop in population and in economic prosperity in the rural communities during the Depression years when many farmers moved away. In addition, better transportation eliminated the need for rural stores and cotton gins. By World War I, most of these small crossroad communities had all but disappeared.

Wolves were a major problem in the countryside, sometimes killing livestock. This group is displaying wolf cubs captured during a wolf hunt two miles north of Norman in 1913. From left to right: L. C. Lindsey, Tom Dilbeck, Clyde Pickard, Claude Pickard, Dr. Capshaw, Ralph Hardie, Mr. Hughes, and M. C. Runyan. Courtesy Pioneer Multi-County Library and The Norman Transcript.

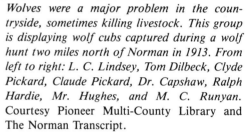

Wild game was plentiful in Cleveland County during those early years. Here, E. H. Stubbeman and rancher Joe Phillips display the quail they shot. Farmers often sold the quail to produce companies for fifty-five cents a dozen for shipment to swank restaurants in Chicago. Courtesy Pioneer Multi-County Library and The Norman Transcript.

A number of university coeds were housed in this building at the northwest corner of Main Street and Webster Avenue. Constructed in 1892, it was originally known as the Arline Hotel. Later, it became the First Christian Church. The structure was torn down in 1936. Courtesy The Norman Transcript and Western History Collections, University of Oklahoma.

John Merkle built this farmhouse in 1895 on the section line road which was to become the 2000 block on West Main Street in Norman. The building soon became a landmark. The house was moved to Noble in 1979 by the Merkle family for restoration. Today, this site is occupied by The Carriage Plaza. From left to right: Bea Stevens, Ruth Thelma Stevens, Bessie Merkle O'Halloran, and Priscilla Merkle. Courtesy Elizabeth Merkle.

CHAPTER 7

A University Town

Norman's future as a university town was first hinted at in May 1890 when a group of citizens met at the Methodist Church to discuss the matter. Congress had made no provisions for schools and left each district to formulate its own education plans. First thoughts turned to local schools, then to higher education.

The first Oklahoma Territorial Legislature met in Guthrie on August 27, 1890. Its primary purpose was to locate the territorial institutions. These included the capitol, a university, a mechanical and agriculture school, and a normal school.

The territorial capitol was the most coveted prize, and the wrangling began at once. Those in Guthrie had always considered the capitol theirs and were determined to have it. Oklahoma City was equally determined. Strong combinations formed in the legislature to secure the capitol for each favored town. When the combinations fell apart, the politicians accused each other of disloyalty and graft. Some resorted to threats of violence.

Cleveland County had sent five members to the legislature, two Councilmen (Senators), R. J. Nesbit and Mort L. Bixler, and

The first classes at the University of Oklahoma were held upstairs in this rock building at 202 West Main Street. Built by Pryor V. Adkins, the building was incorporated into Landsaw Furniture Store about 1948. Courtesy The Norman Transcript.

Of the fifty-seven students to enroll in the University of Oklahoma that first year, none qualified for freshman standing. Seen here in 1892 are from left to right, top row: Oliver Richardson, Odessa Wallace, Carrie Rockefeller, Elbert Longwell, Lem Dorrance, Lizzie Pool, James Wadley, Perry Alexander, John T. Hefley, Etta Allen, Maude Gossett, W. N. Rice (faculty), and Ray Stoops.

Second Row: F. S. E. Amos (faculty), John Barbour, Marvin Miller, Agnes Pool, Ona Barrow, George T. Leavy, Alice Johns, Marion Donehue, Harry Brown, Leah Warren, Attie Roberts, Miss French, Ollie Hunt, Will Depue, Hattie Jacobs, Otis Houghton, Pearl Trimble, Winnie Edwards, and Roscoe Helvie.

Third row: Edwin DeBarr (faculty), Joe Merkle, Jennie Jarboe, Jesse Hefley, Etta Warren, Ethel Wadley, Clara Wallace, Marshall Tucker, Wallace Jacobs, Willie Allen, Jennie Barbour, Mrs. Minnie Ritter, Ed Barbour, Maud Compton, J. F. Taylor, Helen Marr, Rose Compton, J. N. Coulter, and David R. Boyd (faculty and president).

Fourth row: L. R. Bond, Beulah Wood, Alma Dickard, Herman Mueller, Mrs. Lucy Dill, Hillie Braden, Kathryn Barbour, and Mamie Martin. Courtesy Pioneer Multi-County Library.

three Representatives, W. C. Adair, James M. Stovall, and Thomas R. Waggoner.

Nesbit was a farmer near the Canadian River, a man reportedly of good judgment and common sense. Bixler was bright and educated, the editor of *The Norman Advance* and former assistant editor of the *Oklahoma City Daily Times.*

W. C. Adair, a former school teacher, was said to be a weak, vacillating man, and a smart alec. It was rumored he was the first to betray the Oklahoma City combination. He left the territory soon after this first legislative session. Col. James M. Stovall had fought in the Civil War and was a big, generous man, as honest as his word. Thomas P. Waggoner, 29, had served as the first provisional mayor of Norman, and was a shrewd and scheming businessman.

All of the Cleveland County legislators believed that securing the territorial university would bring a better and wealthier class of people to Norman. Bixler helped organize the Oklahoma City combination, but it was Waggoner who was credited with throwing Cleveland County's votes to Oklahoma City in return for locating the university at Norman.

As a result, the legislators designated Norman to receive the territorial university, Stillwater the Agriculture and Mechanical College, Edmond a normal school, and Oklahoma City the capitol. All of these choices were written into one bill. Waggoner saw the danger in this and presented a resolution that each item should be considered separately. His foresight paid off, for the institutional bills all passed but the capitol bill did not.

The territorial legislature stipulated that the residents of Cleveland County must provide a forty-acre site within a half-mile of Norman for the university, and $10,000 cash for a construction fund.

Times were hard, and few people had any excess cash. There was no taxable property in the new territory except for personal property because all of the land still belonged to the government. It would take the settlers up to five years to prove up on their claims and to officially gain title. Nevertheless, the citizens of Cleveland County were able to raise the $2,000 needed to purchase the required land.

A legislative site selection committee approved a forty-acre tract bounded by present Boyd Street and Brooks Street, and Elm Avenue and Asp Avenue. The land had been claimed on the day of the run by Charley Gorton. Since then he had signed the quarter section over to his father-in-law S. M. "Dad" Moore, reportedly in an attempt to forestall foreclosure because of some shaky business dealings in the livestock industry. Moore signed the property over to the state on July 8, 1891, in exchange for $2,000. Delbert Larsh, Thomas P. Waggoner, and W. T. Wallace each donated a strip of land forming a broad road, which connected the university to the town. This became known as University Boulevard.

It was much harder for the citizens to obtain the $10,000 for the construction fund. Undaunted after a massive advertising campaign, the Norman Board of Trade undertook to float a bond issue which was presented to the voters of Cleveland county, and it passed on May 18, 1891.

The next problem became how to get rid of the bonds. By law they were required to sell at par, with no more than five percent interest. Interest rates at the time were about ten percent, and the rate of return proved to be so low, that the county commissioners could obtain no more than seventy-two percent par value.

The commissioners hired an agent to sell the bonds, which were purchased by an Oklahoma City bank for $7,200. The balance of the required sum was raised by subscription, with the president of the Atchinson, Topeka & Santa Fe, pledging $1,800 and Carey Lombard Lumber Company $1,000. On December 14, five days before the deadline, Cleveland County delivered $10,000 in cash to the territorial treasurer. Governor Steele appointed a Board of Regents and construction of the university got underway in April 1892.

The search for a university president, also began. After several months, the selection committee chose Dr. David Ross Boyd, Superintendent of Schools at Arkansas City, Kansas. Boyd hesitated. He had been offered a position as superintendent of schools in Wichita at $3,000 a year. But a friend advised him to take the university job at $2,400, stating that a state university had

Marion Donehue was the first student to enroll in the University of Oklahoma, according to local tradition. Donehue later served as tutor to the Adkins children. Courtesy Cleveland County Historical Society.

The University of Oklahoma's first building was a grand structure with three floors, a basement, and a winding staircase which had "bannisters of the most elegant design." Completed in 1893, this building burned in 1903, destroying more than 8,000 books, as well as many geological and botanical collections. Courtesy John Womack and Western History Collections, University of Oklahoma.

S. M. "Dad" Moore signed over the property, on which the University of Oklahoma is now located, to the state on July 8, 1891. Moore had gained title to the quarter-section of land from his son-in-law Charley Gorton, who had filed on it the day of the run. Courtesy John Womack.

Dr. David Ross Boyd was appointed as the first president of the University of Oklahoma in 1891 at a salary of $2,400 a year. He served until 1907 when he was dismissed because of politics. Courtesy John Womack.

never been known to fail. So Boyd accepted the job. He stated that school would begin in September.

Within a week from his appointment, Boyd had selected his faculty. He named William N. Rice, from the faculty at Southwest College in Winfield, Kansas, as professor of ancient languages and literature; Edwin C. DeBarr, professor at Albion College, professor of chemistry and physics; French S. E. Amos, who had been teaching at Lampasas, Texas, instructor of English, history, and civics. Dr. Boyd designated himself as professor of mental and moral science.

Boyd arrived in Norman on August 6. Years later he recalled that hot afternoon. "I looked off to the southwest where our university was to be located. There was not a tree or shrub in sight on the hard-pan desert," he said. "Not a sign of activity, just the monotonous stillness of the prairie grass.

"To the southwest led a trail; it couldn't possibly be called a road. I was to learn that this trail led out to Adkins Ford which was near the present bridge across the South Canadian. It was the trail followed by the thirsty cowboys who came into Norman on Saturday nights. They couldn't get liquor in the Chickasaw Nation across the river, so they made plentiful use of Norman's fifteen saloons . . . Behind me was a crude little town of 1,500 people and before me a stretch of prairie on which my helpers and I were to build an institution of culture. Discouraged? Not a bit. The sight was a challenge." He went to his room at the Agnes Hotel and washed up for dinner.

The rest of his faculty arrived soon thereafter. Because it was hot, they held their first planning session outdoors, and the first order of business was to cut a watermelon.

Construction on the new university building had barely begun. Boyd rented temporary classroom space for $20 a month, upstairs in what was known as the "Rock Building," which had been built by Pryor Adkins at 202 West Main.

William Rice commented on the structure later. "In comparison with the magnificent plants of older and wealthier states, it seemed a gross exaggeration to call that stone building and its modest contents a university. Only three rooms without ornament, barely comfortable, cheaply furnished with tables for teachers' desks and chairs for the students; no libraries, laboratories, traditions."

The university opened on September 15, 1891. Fifty-seven students presented themselves for admission. Of these, none qualified for college work but were placed in the preparatory school. There were few high schools in the territory those first two years and those in existence had not had time to graduate any students.

Dr. Boyd personally enrolled each student so that he could get acquainted with each and determine where he or she should be placed. Some of the students were young, and some were as old as forty-five, and the student body was equally divided between men and women. The majority of the students lived in Norman with their parents or other relatives and the rest stayed in "boarding clubs" for two dollars a week. The men wore high-topped riding boots and denim trousers, while the women dressed in gingham gowns and braided their hair. The students did their studying by

Edwin DeBarr, member of the first faculty, came to the University of Oklahoma from Michigan, as professor of chemistry and pharmacy. Courtesy John Womack.

William N. Rice taught at Southwest Kansas College before being hired to teach ancient languages and literature on the first faculty at the University of Oklahoma. He served as superintendent of Lexington Public Schools from 1904 to 1918. Courtesy John Womack.

French S. E. Amos, the only Democrat on the first faculty at the University of Oklahoma, previously taught at Centenary College in Lampasas, Texas. He taught English, history and civics at Oklahoma University. Courtesy John Womack.

candlelight or kerosene lamps. All were poor and acutely conscious of their position.

In addition to registering students and teaching classes, Dr. Boyd hitched his horse, Jock, to his rubber-tired buggy and scoured the countryside from the Red River to Kansas searching for new students.

This was not an easy task. Few of the parents saw any need for higher education those days, and the boys and girls were needed at home to help get the homestead started.

In addition, the university had to compete with private schools in the area. High Gate College, sponsored by the Methodist Episcopal Church South, had erected a building on the east side of Norman. The Norman Business School was located nearby, and seven miles south, the Noble Academy was making a strong bid for students. Guthrie had several private institutions, and Oklahoma City and Kingfisher each had a college.

Boyd also ran into difficulty with the "back home" spirit of the settlers. They kept close ties with their former hometowns, and when they thought about sending their children off to school, they sent them back home to stay with relatives. In addition, they did not trust the fledgling school with its lack of facilities.

Boyd continued his recruitment of students, making speeches wherever he could, until he became one of the best known men in Oklahoma Territory. The main thrust of the university was free tuition for those from within the territory. If a family could not afford to send their child to school, Boyd promised to find the student work when he arrived. His efforts paid off. By the end of the first semester, the university had 119 students enrolled.

The university spent two years in the Rock Building. Construction on the first university building was slow, and the contractor, Charlie Holcraft, had run out of funds before the first story was finished. He continued working on faith until the territorial

Reverend A. J. Worley took over as president of High Gate College in January 1893. He found the enrollment discouragingly low, and its proposed building still unfinished. Nevertheless, he set about seeing that the facility was completed, and at his own expense, erected a girls' dormitory building nearby. Courtesy John Womack.

The registry office at the University of Oklahoma in 1900. From left to right, William Kendall, George Bucklin, and S. R. Hadsell. Later a Rhodes scholar, Kendall served as superintendent of Lexington Public schools in 1902. Courtesy Multi-County Library and The Norman Transcript.

For bicycles only, this was the 500 block of University Boulevard, looking south. Dr. David Ross Boyd's first home can be seen in the background, located at 526 University Boulevard. Courtesy The Norman Transcript.

legislature could allocate new funds. At last, the building was completed, and the students moved into it at the beginning of the third school year, on September 6, 1893.

The building was a grand structure, three floors and a basement, with winding staircases which had "bannisters of the most elegant designs," and a domed top. The twenty-two rooms were well-lighted and ventilated.

"The first building," Rice reminisced later. "Do you realize what it meant to us? Can you understand the promise which this mound of brick and mortar, upreared on the flat red sand and clay, gave us? I'm afraid you cannot. You, with your splendid campus of today, your steam-heated buildings, your clipped borders and flower beds, your steel-framed gymnasiums, will never be able to appreciate the fact that such a building meant to us comfortable quarters, classrooms which could hold our already increasing enrollment, a library which was a rarity in the territory, and always, always the opportunity for learning and more learning."

That year the university had 142 students enrolled, including its first college student, Nahum E. Butcher. The school added a music department and the Department of Pharmacy in 1893. The town laid a wooden sidewalk along University Boulevard to the school.

That same year Dr. Boyd began another important project. He said he could not imagine a campus without trees. He undertook a tree planting program. Local residents ridiculed his efforts, saying it was impossible to grow trees in the hard-pan. They had tried it and knew. Boyd scoffed at this, knowing they had dug up saplings along the river and planted them in shallow holes. When the summer drought came, the trees died.

Boyd bought the entire stock of a bankrupt Arkansas City, Kansas, nursery out of his own pocket. He planted these trees all

over the campus, tending them with water purchased for five cents a barrel. When these trees were gone, he bought a variety of seeds from a man in Wisconsin, and planted five acres in rows behind the present administration building. When the seedlings came up, he distributed them to the citizens of Norman. If the trees lived, they were free; if they died, the people would have to pay for them. Not many trees died that summer. Soon the campus and town began to flourish with greenery, transforming the area from a barren prairie to an oasis.

As the university grew, High Gate College found itself in trouble. It could not compete with free tuition. By December 1895, all of Highgate's teachers and students were gone.

The University of Oklahoma graduated its first two students in June 1898, Carleton Ross Hume and Roy Philston Stoops, each with a B.A. Hume went on to become the first student to receive a master's degree from Oklahoma University.

In 1903, the university constructed a frame building immediately south of the present student union building to be used as a gymnasium. Work began on a new University Hall.

Disaster struck the university on the night of January 6, 1903, when fire destroyed the first building, now known as Science Hall. The blaze started in the basement. No one ever knew the cause. A night watchman gave the alarm, and a bucket brigade attempted to fight the fire, but when the flames broke through the first floor, all knew everything was lost. Heroic efforts were made to save what they could. George Bucklin and Walker Field climbed through a window and saved most of the valuable records, in-

The University of Oklahoma String Band is shown here in 1898. Mrs. Grace King Maquire, chorus director, is in the middle of the second row, wearing a hat and coat. Hired as an instructor at the University of Oklahoma when she was sixteen years old, Miss King's first instinct was to flee back to Kansas when she saw the barrenness of the land. Courtesy The Norman Transcript.

Built by Dr. David Ross Boyd in 1905, the "White House" at the corner of Boyd Street and University Boulevard served as the home for the University of Oklahoma presidents for more than fifty years. The State of Oklahoma bought the house from Boyd in 1914. Dr. Stratton Brooks remodeled the building extensively inside and out during his administration. Courtesy The Norman Transcript and Western History Collections, University of Oklahoma.

cluding students' credits and grades. Finally about midnight, the dome on top of the building turned over with a groan and crashed into the basement. The onlookers watched in silence as the flames consumed the rest of the structure. For a decade this building had been the university. Now it was gone.

Classes resumed the next day in the Rock Building and in the Christian Church, as well as in the gymnasium and other buildings on campus. Construction on a new administration building got underway shortly after. It was completed in 1904 along with the Carnegie Library.

Unfortunately, the second administration building was to suffer the same fate as the first one. Oklahoma became a state on November 16, 1907. In honor of this event, President Boyd decided to give the roof of the administration building a new coat

The University of Oklahoma as it appeared in 1906 with University Boulevard and Boyd Street in the foreground. From left to right: Gymnasium, Carnegie Library, University Hall and Science Hall. Courtesy The Norman Transcript and Western History Collections, University of Oklahoma.

of tar. On a cold day in December, at the beginning of Christmas vacation, workmen were heating the tar in the dome of the building, when the tar boiled over onto the stove. The flames spread rapidly. Again those at the scene of the fire attempted to save what they could, but much was lost.

For the third time, the Rock Building was called into use. Other classes were crowded into Science Hall, the Carnegie Library, and other buildings on campus.

Perhaps an even greater disaster lurked in the wings. With the coming of statehood, the citizens of Oklahoma elected their first Democrat governor. One of the first things Governor Charles N. Haskell did was to fire six of the Republican teachers at the university, including Dr. Boyd. With these went seven other

University of Oklahoma suffered its second big fire on December 8, 1907, when University Hall burned. The fire began when workmen were re-tarring the roof and the tar boiled over onto a hot stove. Courtesy Western History Collections, University of Oklahoma.

Dr. David Ross Boyd began a tree planting program on the Univeristy of Oklahoma campus and in Norman which was to change the face of the barren prairie. In the early 1920s, the new administration building can be seen in the center and in the upper right are the remains of the tree nursery planted by Dr. Boyd. Courtesy The Norman Transcript and Slim Wiley.

Methodist High Gate College was located at the east end of Main Street in Norman in 1893. This school for young women competed with the new territorial college on the south side of town for students. Courtesy John Womack.

The Oklahoma Sanitarium Company selected the site of the former High Gate College as the new Oklahoma State Asylum. Today, this is the location of Central State Hospital. Courtesy John Womack.

teachers who quit. Haskell's action did irreparable damage to the school. It would take a good decade to recover from this act as the Board of Regents tried to take over administration of the school and appointed inept teachers. Later, Haskell admitted that his firing of Dr. Boyd and the other Republican teachers was one of the greatest mistakes of his career.

Angry, Dr. Boyd wrote numerous letters to other universities seeking positions for his displaced staff. Many went on to greater careers. Vernon Parrington, professor of literature, for instance, went to the University of Washington and in 1927 received the Pulitzer Prize for his *Main Currents of American Thoughts*. Dr. Boyd went to New York as head of educational work for the Presbyterian Board of Missions. In 1912, he became president of the University of Mexico.

Enrollment at the University of Oklahoma remained stagnate during the presidency of A. Grant Evans as people lost faith in the institution. It was not until the coming of President Stratton Brooks in 1912 that things began to turn around.

As the university grew, so grew Norman. The citizens gave the school their wholehearted support and soon began to reap the economic benefits thereof.

In addition, the town received a second political plum which was to provide further economic security. During the first year of territorial government, the officials had looked around for a facility to care for the mentally ill. Eventually they contracted with a place in Illinois at a cost of twenty-five dollars per person, per month. This soon proved too costly. Also, the distance from Oklahoma Territory hindered relatives from visiting the patients.

In 1891, Governor William Renfro determined the territory should have its own facility to care for the insane. There was fierce competition among the towns for the hospital. For a time, it looked as if Perry would be the winner of the facility, but Norman finally triumphed.

The Oklahoma Sanitarium Company selected the site of the former High Gate College for Young Women for the new asylum. The first patients arrived from Illinois in especially designed railroad cars with barred windows and doors.

A year later, *The Norman Transcript* decribed the facility

as "an institution that ranks with the best and largest asylums in the Southwest." However, when Dr. David W. Griffin was hired as an assistant at the hospital in October 1899, he was horrified to find little attempt was being made to cure the patients. Many were restrained to prevent them from injuring themselves or others. Some were placed in isolated cells and were often forgotten by relatives.

Dr. Griffin immediately instituted more humane treatment and attempted to cure the patients. He was soon named superintendent of the hospital, a position he was to retain for fifty years. In 1950, the facility was renamed Central State Griffin Memorial Hospital in his honor.

By the time of statehood, Norman was looking quite progressive. Its streets had been graded and drained. Electricity and running water had come to the town. Citizens could subscribe to one of three newspapers. The farmers could sell their cotton to the Jennison brothers, or their wheat to the Norman Milling and Grain Company. They could deposit their money in one of four banks or buy their groceries at any of a half-dozen grocery stores, where they could purchase crackers for twenty-five cents a peck, and lard, molasses, and vinegar by the barrel.

The men frequented Stubbeman's harness and leather shop and had their hair trimmed at Ira Wheeler's or Bob Risinger's barbershop for ten cents. The women could buy calico for five cents a yard at Sam McCall's dry goods store, or purchase a soft drink at one of the three drugstores. Perhaps the families met at Charles Irving Shears' jitney lunch, which stood where the Norman Paint and Paper Company is now located. Here they could buy a sandwich for five cents, or a drink or pastry for the same amount. Ham and eggs cost twenty cents, while a roast beef, pork, or ham lunch could be had for fifteen cents.

Dr. David W. Griffin, shown here with his wife, served as superintendent of the Oklahoma State Hospital in Norman for fifty years. The facility was renamed Central State Griffin Memorial Hospital in 1950 in his honor. Courtesy Vera Griffin Willard.

Norman's Main Street was a mudhole following a rainstorm. Contractors paved the downtown business district in the fall of 1911. Courtesy The Norman Transcript and Don Frensley.

The Barbour Drug Store in Norman was a favorite place to meet friends during the early 1900s. Courtesy Jeanette Barbour.

Men patronized Ira Wheeler's barbershop, an elaborate structure with a marbled and mirrored interior. Each man had his own shaving mug. Located next door to Barbour Drug Store, the barbershop stood at 104 East Main. Courtesy The Norman Transcript and J. H. Muldowney.

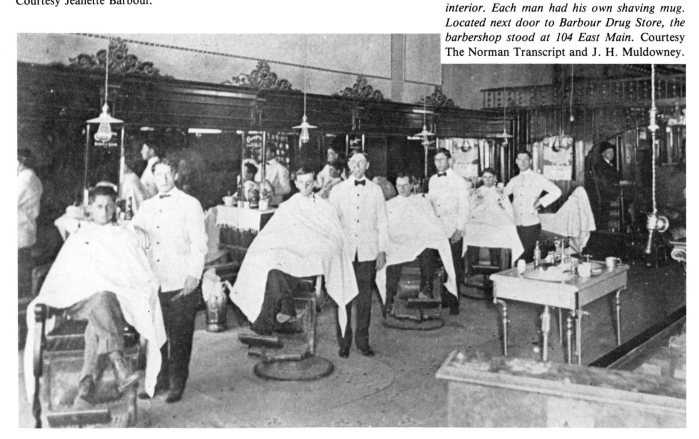

The biggest fire in Norman's history occurred on Main Street, July 7, 1902. The first started in Holland's restaurant in the wall next to Pedro Ramos' Chili Joint. The blaze destroyed all the buildings on the south side of the street, west, from the Carey Lombard Lumber Company to the Santa Fe Railroad, and badly damaged buildings and merchandise on the north side of the street. Many considered the fire a blessing as those buildings that burned were some of the first built in Norman. Most were mere shacks. Courtesy The Norman Transcript and Western History Collections, University of Oklahoma.

In 1908, the city sold bonds for an extension of the water works and a sewer system.

Vaudeville was popular during the early 1900s. The cultural center in Norman was the newly refurbished Franing Opera House. John Franing had bought the Seawell Opera House and redecorated it. The building comfortably seated 850 people. At the dedication program on November 17, 1902, Franing brought in the Gordon-Shay Grand Opera Company to present *Il Trovatore*. The *Norman Transcript* editor confessed that the majority of those attending the performance were not fully up on grand opera, but the program was most enjoyable with "first class" singing.

In 1908, a new type of entertainment came to town when three picture shows were installed in Norman. Mary Pickford, star of the silent films, became everyone's sweetheart.

The need for a new railroad passenger depot became a pressing point in 1909. Santa Fe completed the work in December, laid brick sidewalks around its yards, and began construction of an express building south of the new depot.

In October 1910, citizens in Norman were told to build sidewalks before their homes and to see that their houses were numbered. Free delivery of mail would begin as soon as this could be accomplished.

Norman's Main Street was scarcely passable following a rainstorm, or when snow melted. In the fall of 1911, a bond issue was voted and the downtown business district was paved. After Fred Tarman became editor of *The Norman Transcript*, he urged a major paving program. West Main Street, University Boulevard, and North Peters Avenue were the first three assessment districts to be formed.

About this time the Klu Klux Klan appeared in Norman. Following prohibition when statehood came in, a syndicate of bootleggers with Chicago connections attempted to operate in

Following prohibition, a syndicate of bootleggers moved into Cleveland County. On August 24, 1917, Deputy Sheriff Grover Fulkerson, right, was killed while guarding the Canadian River bridge against these "Night Riders." To the left is his brother, Boise Fulkerson, former fire chief of Norman, and center, father Malcom Fulkerson, former Norman city council member. Courtesy The Reverend Canon F. Grover Fulkerson.

Cleveland County. The "Night Riders" so intimidated local lawmen that in some communities hired killers and other criminals were going about unchecked. On August 24, 1917, Deputy Sheriff Grover Fulkerson was shot and killed while guarding the Canadian River bridge. Vigilante groups formed. In Norman, the Klu Klux Klan was given credit for helping drive out the organized crime that had begun to plague the area. Some claimed Edwin DeBarr, University of Oklahoma professor, headed the Klan. DeBarr was to die in 1950 following an altercation in his yard with the husband of his granddaughter.

By 1917, the future looked promising for Norman and the rest of Cleveland County. But war clouds and those of economic depression loomed on the horizon.

The Regime Club, one of the oldest clubs in Norman, organized in March 1908. Its motto was "The world is advancing - advance with it." Bimonthly speakers touched on current events, world affairs, travel and literature. This picture was taken February 1, 1912, at the home of Mrs. H. G. Lindsay, 508 North Peters Avenue. From left to right, back row: Mrs. H. G. Lindsay, Mrs. Tom Smith, Mrs. John Franing, Mrs. Bob Berry, Mrs. John Taylor, Mrs. John Hardy, Mrs. Lowther, Mrs. Will Hayes, Mrs. W. S. Moore, Mrs. D. W. Griffin, Mrs. Pritchett, Mrs. Felgar, Mrs. S. P. Renner, Mrs. Campbell, Dr. Lucille Dora. Front row: Mrs. Judge Anderson, Mrs. Evans, Mrs. Bobo, Mrs. Pucker, Mrs. Grant Evans, Mrs. J. D. McGuire, Agnes Wantland, and Mrs. Cheadle. *Courtesy Pioneer Multi-County Library and The Norman Transcript.*

The Norman Milling and Grain Company provided electricity for Norman in 1903, allowing the town to use its generator for three hours after dark. Shown in the office are, from left to right: Miss Hyla Ford, stenographer; W. J. Higgins, McClain County farmer; Frank Carder, clerk; John H. Anderhub, truckdriver; _____ Murphy, electric supply salesman; Guy R. A. Spottswood, assistant manager and bookkeeper. This building, which was completed in 1903 at 100 West Main Street, is now occupied by Denco Cafe. Courtesy The Norman Transcript.

Women purchased their hats in millinery shops such as this in Norman. Courtesy Cleveland County Historical Society and Historic House.

Cleveland County benefited from numerous WPA construction projects during the 1930s including the National Guard Armory at Jones Avenue and Santa Fe Street in Norman. Home of Co. D 179th Infantry and Co. C 120th Engineers, the building featured a spacious drill hall capable of seating 2,000 people. The dome of the Cleveland County Courthouse can be seen behind the armory. Courtesy The Norman Transcript.

By 1924, Norman had a thriving business district, the streets were paved, and Main Street had a "white way" of electric lights downtown. Courtesy The Norman Transcript and Mrs. J. L. Rodgers.

CHAPTER 8

War Clouds and the Depression

Before the entrance of the United States into World War I, most Cleveland County residents believed its geographic location would limit American participation to naval and financial aid. But the Allies desperately needed fighting men. On April 6, 1917, America entered the "war to end all wars."

In a spirit of high idealism, young men in Cleveland County, as elsewhere, flocked to the recruiting stations, determined to fight for the survival of democracy, and for peace on earth.

As the full impact of the war hit, the University of Oklahoma became involved. Students who enlisted were promised a full year's college credit. Hundreds of young men enlisted in the Student Army Training Corps and drilled daily on campus before the sorority houses.

In May 1917, Congress approved the Selective Service Act. Cleveland County registered 1,540 young men. In the first draft, 154 of them expected to be taken.

As the full impact of WWI hit, hundreds of young men enlisted in the Student Army Training Corps and drilled daily on the University of Oklahoma campus. Courtesy Pioneer Multi-County Library The Norman Transcript.

OPENING OF
THE W.S.S BANK
NORMAN OKLA.

Patriotic citizens erected a War Savings Bank in the center of Main Street in Norman. Everyone was encouraged to buy savings bonds and savings stamps to help fight the Kaiser. Courtesy The Norman Transcript and Mrs. J. L. Rodgers.

On September 20, 1917, thousands gathered at the Norman depot to bid goodbye to the troop train with a parade and patriotic speeches. As the soldier special pulled in, townsfolk shared 150 slices of watermelons with those on the train. The citizens wished good luck upon the fifteen from Cleveland County who went off to war that day. Soon, no one was left on the University of Oklahoma campus but women, old faculty men, and very young men.

Fletcher Pledger, from Norman, became the first Cleveland County soldier to give his life in the war when the troop transport ship *Tuscania,* enroute to France, was torpedoed off the coast of Scotland on February 14, 1918. Pledger's body was returned home in September 1920. He was buried in the I.O.O.F. Cemetery with military honors. The American Legion Post changed its name to the Pledger Post, thus beginning its custom of adding to its name that of the first dead in each American war.

During World War I, educators abolished German as a course of study at Norman High School. The school became one of the few in the state which adopted military drill as part of its curriculum. One hundred and thirty-five young men drilled daily under the supervision of N. H. Edwards, city superintendent of schools. City fathers organized a company of home guards.

Meat markets in Cleveland County closed once a week to enforce meatless days to help conserve food for the soldiers, and citizens were urged to plant victory gardens. Women and girls knitted socks for the soldiers and joined Red Cross chapters to roll bandages.

Patriotic citizens erected a War Savings Bank in the center of Main Street in Norman. Everyone was encouraged to buy savings bonds and savings stamps to help fight the Kaiser.

The Armistice was signed at 2:15 a.m., Oklahoma time, on November 11, 1919. The news spread quickly and hundreds of jubilant people formed an impromtu parade through downtown Norman, tooting their automobile horns and shouting at the top of their voices in relief at the cessation of hostilities. Schools were dismissed that day in celebration.

With the end of the war, those in Cleveland County expected a return to normalcy. But this was not to be. Many consumer goods were still in short supply and prices spiraled as the nation began a wild spending spree in reaction to wartime inhibition.

A period of rapid growth in Norman followed. The population of the county seat reached 5,000 in 1919. With this came new problems in providing city services. To meet this need more efficiently, the town changed to a city manager form of government. Voters elected five commissioners, one from each ward plus one member at large. The five commissioners hired an experienced city manager to handle the affairs of the town.

In 1920, the nation suffered a recession. This hit hard in Oklahoma. The economy of the state was based on agriculture and

Patriotism was the keynote for Fourth of July parades held during WWI. This float features Uncle Sam, Miss Liberty, flags, bunting, and red, white and blue flowers. Courtesy Norman Transcript and University of Oklahoma.

Merchants eagerly displayed the American flag during WWI. This is Main Street in Norman, looking east. The War Savings Bank can be seen in the middle of the street. Courtesy The Norman Transcript.

The 1920s were known as the age of the flappers, the Charleston, coonskin coats, goldfish swallowers, flagpole sitters, and speakeasies. Ethel Smalley's dress was typical of the style of the time. Courtesy The Norman Transcript and J. H. Muldowney.

oil. Several attempts had been made to discover oil in the Unassigned Lands after the run. During WWI, geologists began exploring the region in earnest. In January 1917, much excitement developed when a well was spudded in on the E. R. Braman farm near Big Jim Crossing, and another well on the Clay Bowlan place twelve miles east of Lexington. By May, the Seven Oil Company had over 100,000 acres under lease in Cleveland County.

The war kept oil and agriculture prices high. Many farmers expanded with the promise of future profits. They went in debt for expensive equipment. The bottom fell out of the market with the end of the war, forcing the farmers into bankruptcy. The effect of these bankruptcies spread into other areas. Soup lines formed, real estate values plunged, and the ranks of the unemployed increased.

In 1921, the economy of Cleveland County showed signs of recovery. Building in Norman began to push west and south. In the spring of 1922, the city council termed all wooden buildings in the business district fire hazards, and ordered them torn down. With this, the tempo of construction in Norman increased. City National Bank erected a new building at the northwest corner of Main Street and Peters Avenue, a site which it still occupies today.

On September 3, 1924, fire swept the south side of the 200 block of East Main Street. Of undetermined origin, the blaze broke out in the R. C. Berry Department Store about midnight and spread to eight buildings between Peters Avenue and Crawford Avenue with a loss of $301,000. The Security National Bank lost everything except its vault. President C. H. Bessent announced the firm would be open for business the next day. He found a vacant building, obtained new furniture and fixtures, and carried out his promise. The bank rebuilt at the southeast corner of East Main and Peters Avenue shortly after.

The McFarlin Memorial Methodist Church was completed in Norman that same year at a cost of over $600,000, as a memorial to Robert McFarlin, who had lived in Norman for many years. The building was acclaimed the finest church east of the Rocky Mountains and west of the Mississippi River.

From the day Norman was founded until 1925, the town had no hospital such as we think of it today. However, Dr. John L. Day saw the need for a hospital after World War I, and he interested the American Legion Post in establishing a facility. On April 5, 1925, the American Legion Hospital opened at Johnson Street and North Ponca Avenue. It had fourteen beds.

The hospital ran into immediate financial trouble. In 1927, City National Bank took over operation of the facility. Later that year, Dr. W. T. Mayfield, Dr. Ben Cooley, and Mrs. Pearl Dunscomb, R.N., purchased the hospital, which they operated until 1944, when it closed due to lack of trained personnel during World War II. The city of Norman took over the institution shortly thereafter, renaming it the Norman Municipal Hospital. Today, it is known as the Norman Regional Hospital.

The Federated Women's Club of Norman had been talking about the need for a public library for some time. In earlier years, the city had been the recipient of a small Carnegie Library which was taken over by the University of Oklahoma. In 1927, the club women, headed by Mrs. A. J. Williams, Mrs. Emma Engleman, and Mrs. Myrtle Lee Autrey, collected 4,000 volumes. Mrs. Autrey donated a frame bungalow for the library at the corner of West Main Street and Webster Avenue.

Efforts to open a permanent library continued. The city allocated funds for a new building. But a state law said no town where a Carnegie Library existed could allocate funds for another library. After two years of struggle, this law was changed. A $25,000 city bond election passed by nine votes. In 1929, the Norman Public Library opened at 329 South Peters Avenue with Mrs. Engleman as librarian. This old library building is now home of the Norman Senior Citizens Center.

The "talkies" came to Norman in February 1929 with the opening of the Sooner Theatre, 101 East Main. Designed by Norman architect Harold Gimeno, grandson of a Spanish theatrical producer, the auditorium of the three-story building seated 819

Army ROTC cadets contributed their talents to the University of Oklahoma's nationally known championship polo teams beginning in 1923. The main building of the old stable complex, which housed instructors, officers, a saddleshop and an equipment room, is now occupied by the Museum of Natural History. Courtesy University of Oklahoma Sports Information Office.

Over 100 people attended the dedication of the No. 1 Bugher wildcat on May 20, 1938, on the L. B. Bugher homestead south of Noble. The famous well opened a new pool in Cleveland County and brought new business to the area. Courtesy The Norman Transcript and Mrs. J. H. Walker.

people. Its Spanish style architecture, with bright heraldic shields, custom-designed stained glass windows and light fixtures, and red and gold striped ornamental moldings helped make it one of the most beautiful cinema places in the state.

The discovery of the Oklahoma City Oil Field had roared in with a boom on December 4, 1928, with the drilling of Oklahoma City No. 1 at what is now S. E. 59th and Bryant. Oklahoma City quickly became the state's newest boomtown. The pursuit of "black gold" continued with an unabated fever in the following years, and not even the stock market crash on Wall Street in October 1929 could slow the pace of drilling. The boom spread southward into Cleveland County.

At daybreak on March 26, 1930, a tired drilling crew was leaving the Mary Sudick No. 1, located four miles north of Moore, when the well blew in. Tools and mud shot from the hole as if blown from a cannon. Frantically, the crew tried to cap the well, but the well ran wild for five days. Crude oil covered the countryside, falling as far south as Norman. The danger of fire ran high. All roads leading to the oil well were closed to the public. The news of the blowout was broadcast to the world by radio announcer Floyd Gibbons. The well was finally closed in on April 4 bringing a sigh of relief to all, and the cleanup began.

By 1931 though, the state was facing the calamity of overproduction, and the East Texas Oil Field blew in, adding to the problem. Oil prices plummeted to sixteen cents a barrel as the market became glutted. Governor William H. "Bill" Murray threatened to close the oil fields until the price came back to one dollar a barrel. On August 4, 1931, he made good his threat, and halted all oil production in the state, and Texas followed suit. Murray relented though when oil reached seventy-five cents a barrel and Texas went back into production. Murray kept close control over oil production in Oklahoma for the next two years until state legislators could enact laws controlling production.

In spite of the oil activity within the state, the Great Depression was beginning to be felt in Oklahoma. The price of wheat had dropped below one dollar a bushel on February 24, 1930. The widespread effects in the wheat belt were comparable to the crash of the stock market in the financial district the year before. Unemployment began to rise.

Large families drifted into Cleveland County looking for work. In 1931, those who stopped at the Norman police station asking for "just a place to get my family out of the cold until tomorrow morning," were sent across the street to the old Grand Central Hotel. Here, a warm fire crackled in the heating stove of the nearly deserted building, and matresses, laid on the floor, offered a place for the homeless to sleep.

Charity funds were rapidly exhausted in Norman and the Norman Chamber of Commerce conducted a citywide search for temporary employment for the jobless.

In 1933, dust storms swept the drought stricken region. On April 26, one of the worst yet lashed Cleveland County all day and all night, halting traffic, making breathing difficult, and sending chickens to roost at midday.

For two years, the dust storms continued to transform the once fertile wheatlands of the Midwest into a desert. In the spring of 1935, the storms continued in the western half of Oklahoma almost unabated. On April 14, they reached an unprecedented intensity with a wall of dust 10,000 feet high boiling over the Oklahoma horizon. When the dense, black wall hit, visibility dropped to zero. Dust drifted across the fields and around the buildings.

Even so, the Depression was not felt as severely in Norman

One of Norman's most disastrous fires occurred on September 3, 1923. The blaze broke out in the R. C. Berry department store in the 200 block on the south side of East Main Street about midnight. Eight buildings were destroyed between Peters Avenue and Crawford Avenue. Security National Bank lost everything but its vault. It reopened next day in a rented building, as promised in this sign. Visible behind the rubble is the roof of the Masonic Temple. Courtesy Security National Bank.

McFarlin Memorial Methodist Church was completed in Norman in 1924 as a memorial to Robert McFarlin by his parents Mr. and Mrs. R. M. McFarlin at a cost of $600,000. At the time, it was said to be the finest church building between the Mississippi River and the Rocky Mountains. This photo was taken in 1933. Courtesy The Norman Transcript.

Norman was a bustling city by 1930. The Sooner Theatre on the north side of the street featured Maurice Chevalier in ''The Big Pond'' on the day this photo was taken while across the street William Boyd starred at the University Theatre. Courtesy The Norman Transcript.

as it was in other Oklahoma towns because of the presence of the state university and state hospital. Although salaries had been cut at both institutions, employment remained steady. Nevertheless, some students had to trade wheat, apples, onions, canned beans, and blackberries for three meals a day and a place to sleep, but they contributed enough to the local economy to keep business moving. Perhaps the hard-pressed farmers were the luckiest of all, though they could not sell their products, they managed to eke enough out of the land to feed their families.

In November 1932, Democrat Franklin D. Roosevelt won the presidential election by a tremendous margin over Republican Herbert Hoover, with Cleveland County casting 6,056 for Roosevelt and 1,880 for Hoover. The nation eagerly awaited Roosevelt's New Deal program.

The road to recovery included the Public Works Administration (PWA), the Civilian Conservation Corps (CCC), and the Works Progress Administration (WPA) each of which helped put the public back to work through federal aid.

Cleveland County benefited from numerous WPA construction projects. The first of these was the American Legion building erected on East Main Street in Norman, in August 1933, followed by a swimming pool on the University of Oklahoma campus, and a clock tower on the Student Union Building in 1936.

The National Guard Armory at Jones and Santa Fe was also built in 1936 with WPA labor. The amphitheater in City Park in 1938 was another WPA project, as was the present Cleveland County Courthouse, which was begun in 1939. WPA workers constructed the new building in front of the old courthouse, which was then torn down.

The WPA also provided work for the arts community, bringing cultural activities to Cleveland County. The massive 116 volumes of Indian-Pioneer interviews supervised by Grant Foreman is now housed in the Western History Collections of the

University of Oklahoma, providing one of the most important collections on Oklahoma history.

Radio came into its own during the Depression years, and free movies were shown at City Park in Norman, as people sought to forget the harsh reality of their existence in the fantasy of the screen.

By 1937, war clouds were gathering again in Europe as Germany and Italy set out to extend their territories. Recognizing that they could no longer maintain a policy of isolationism as thought during the first World War, the United States began a massive campaign of foreign aid and national preparedness. The scramble for war contracts boosted the American economy out of the Depression.

In 1940, the Board of Regents at the University of Oklahoma, recognized the growing importance of aviation in the nation's affairs. They made plans for the development of a flight training center at the university. Their plans took a big step forward when Walter Neustadt, of Ardmore, announced a gift of $10,500 from the estate of Max Westheimer, his father-in-law, to the university for the purchase of an airport.

The university obtained a quarter-section of land northwest of Norman for the site. When officials learned this would not be enough land for the airport, the city of Norman voted bonds for the purchase of another 128 acres which it leased to the university for ninety-nine years for one dollar a year. In October 1941, the university constructed a dirt runway at the airport, which would accommodate light planes. This early development of Max Westheimer Field was to play an important part in the future of the university and of Norman.

The Sooner Theatre opened at 101 East Main Street in Norman in February 1929, and with it came the town's first talking pictures. The theatre, designed by Norman architect Harold Gimeno, seated 819 people. Its Spanish style architecture with bright heraldic shields, custom-designed stained glass windows and light fixtures helped make it one of the most beautiful cinema theatres in the state. The theatre closed in 1974. Today, it serves as a civic and entertainment center. Courtesy The Oklahoma Daily.

The rural areas continued to remain an economic mainstay of Cleveland County during the Depression years. This wheat threshing scene was photographed on the George Nemecek farm near Lexington in the 1930s. Courtesy The Norman Transcript and L. R. Fishburn.

By 1930, the Great Depression was beginning to be felt in Cleveland County, and Mrs. Ward trucked her produce to Oklahoma City to be sold. Courtesy The Norman Transcript.

On December 8, 1941, President Roosevelt signed the joint congressional resolution declaring a state of war with Japan. Again, hundreds of Cleveland County men rushed to enlist. Once more the university was left with the very young men, the old faculty members, and women on campus.

Early in January 1942, a coincidental circumstance happened which would bring the war right to Norman. Savoie Lottinville, Director of the University of Oklahoma Press, traveled to New York City on university business. On the train, he chanced to meet Captain K. B. Salisbury of the Bureau of Aeronautics of the Navy Department, Washington, D. C. During the course of their conversation, Lottinville told Salisbury about the university's new airport. Salisbury asked if the university would be willing to loan the field to the Navy Department for the duration of the war. Lottinville said he didn't know but he could find out.

On his arrival in New York City, he telephoned University President Joseph Brandt and obtained permission to go to Washington to discuss the matter with the government. Two weeks later, he returned with news that plans were pretty well set for the Navy to take over Max Westheimer Field for a flight training center.

After working out the final details, the Navy took immediate action and leased the airport from the university. Officials purchased additional land to total 1,500 acres. Work began shortly after on a large complex of hangers, housing, service buildings, and administrative facilities. The Navy hoped to have the Naval Flight Training Center (NFTC) in operation by July and expected to have 1,200 cadets stationed there by September 1.

The Navy determined, also, it would need facilities for a mechanics training center. Instead of using existing structures on the university campus as first planned, the Navy decided to build its own school near Norman. University personnel and Norman civic leaders convinced the Bureau of Aeronautics to build immediately south of the university, and east to Highway 77.

Subsequently, the Navy purchased 11,000 acres of land immediately south of Lindsey Street. Construction began at once on barracks, shops, a hospital and an administrative building for the training of 20,000 at the Naval Air Technical Training Center (NATTC). The two naval facilities quickly became known as "North Base" and "South Base."

Norman citizens expressed much concern about the morals of the young women at the university and in the town with the effect of so many young men stationed nearby.

The residents of Cleveland County threw themselves fully into the war effort. In July 1940, federal excise taxes to support the nation's defense had been increased. The price of admission at the motion picture theatres jumped three cents, and the cost of a pack of cigarettes was raised two cents. The University of Oklahoma established a Naval ROTC unit on campus.

Once more victory gardens were encouraged. A sugar shortage quickly developed. The citizens of Cleveland County rushed to their grocers to stock up on the precious commodity only to find their grocers rationed. During the spring of 1942, Norman schools collected 37,500 pounds of scrap metal and rubber during a salvage drive to help the war effort. The Surplus Marketing Administration Food Stamp Plan was put into effect in the county.

In April 1941, the Army Air Corps announced that a $14 million air depot would be located at Oklahoma City, which would employ 3,500 workers. Tinker Field was completed within two years and hundreds of Cleveland County men found jobs at Douglas Aircraft Company, helping build the C-47 Skytrains.

Humorist Will Rogers came to Norman twice during the 1930s to present benefit performances for the drought stricken farmers of the Midwest. Courtesy Will Rogers Memorial Museum.

The present Cleveland County Courthouse was another WPA project begun in 1939. Workers constructed the new building in front of the old one, which was later torn down. Courtesy The Norman Transcript.

In November 1932, Democrat Franklin D. Roosevelt won the presidential election and he quickly put his New Deal program into effect. In this photo, former president Harry Truman is shown with Eleanor Roosevelt beneath President Roosevelt's picture during the FDR silver anniversary dinner, on the University of Oklahoma campus, March 4, 1958. From left to right: Paul Butler, Chairman, National Democratic Party, Harry S. Truman, Eleanor Roosevelt, and Senator Mike Monroney of Oklahoma. Courtesy June Benson.

Thousands of sailors, WAVES, and Marines received their training in Norman during World War II. This picture was taken at the Commissioning Day exercises and review at the Naval Air Technical Training Center (NATTC) in 1942. Located on South Base, NATTC operated in conjunction with the Naval Aviation Training Center (NATC) at Max Westheimer Field on North Base, later simply known as the Naval Air Station. Courtesy Pioneer Multi-County Library and The Norman Transcript.

Women joined the workforce, too, and established a new identity for themselves as "Rosie the Riveter." They found new freedom in their dress, adopting slacks and sportswear. When Norman Police Chief Bat Ingram took a dim view of women wearing shorts in public, one woman angrily denounced him, stating in a letter to the editor of the *The Norman Transcript,* "Mr. Chief of Police of Norman, you are not dealing with your sisters of yesteryear."

As thousands of sailors moved into Norman, a severe housing shortage developed. Citizens were urged to make their spare bedrooms available to the hundreds of people pouring into the town.

In November 1942, federal gas rationing plans were completed. The rationing of meat, canned fruits, and vegetables began. Ten thousand Cleveland County citizens registered in Norman for War Ration Book No. 2. Farmers were encouraged to remove all roosters over three months old from their flocks. Infertile eggs would keep indefinitely and dried eggs in large quantities were needed for the armed forces and the allies. Scrap metal and rubber drives continued.

The people kept close to their radios to catch the latest war news. In July 1943, word came that the 45th Division from Oklahoma, including the former National Guard Company of Norman, was fighting in Sicily with the new American Seventh Army under the command of Lt. George S. Patton, Jr.

As the war went on inexorably, feelings ran high on the homefront. When someone mistakenly called a wounded World War II veteran a "4-Fer," in a Norman bar one cold December night, a fight broke out which soon involved marines, sailors, and some 200 civilians before the Norman police and shore patrol could restore order.

In November 1944, more than 330 war casualities arrived at the local naval hospital, bringing the grimness of the war to Cleveland County.

On Thursday, April 14, 1945, a double tragedy shocked everyone. First, a destructive tornado north of Moore struck at 3:32 p.m., knocking out electrical power in the county. Three

Sailors were a familiar sight on the streets of Norman during World War II. The curb before Rickner's Bookstore proved a popular place for girl watching. **Courtesy Pioneer Multi-County Library and The Norman Transcript.**

The U. S. Naval Band from the Naval Training School Aviation Maintenance Center played the national anthem during flag raising ceremonies and commissioning of the naval hospital in Norman. The hospital was one of four Navy facilities in the Norman area during World War II. Courtesy Pioneer Multi-County Library and The Norman Transcript.

Construction at the Naval Air Technical Training Center on South Base continued twenty-four hours a day, barely keeping up with the arrival of new recruits. Courtesy Pioneer Multi-County Library and The Norman Transcript.

The USO sponsored dances for service personnel outside Building 92 at the Naval Air Technical Training Center on South Base. Local citizens were concerned about the morals of the young girls of the area with so many sailors around. Courtesy Pioneer Multi-County Library and The Norman Transcript.

Women joined the work force, too, and "Rosie the Riveter" soon became a familiar term. Courtesy Oklahoma City Logistics Center Office of History.

The citizens of Cleveland County joined together in the war effort, many of them working at Douglas Aircraft Company and at Tinker Field in Midwest City, building the C-47 Skytrains, the "flying mules" of the war. This photo was taken in 1943. Courtesy Oklahoma City Logistics Center Office of History.

minutes later, President Roosevelt died in Warm Springs, Georgia. First news of his death was received by those who had radios in their automobiles, and at the University of Oklahoma, which had its own electric system.

News of Roosevelt's death cast a shadow of gloom over the world that not even the imminence of victory in Europe could completely erase. Harry S. Truman became president, and Cleveland County residents celebrated with the rest of the nation on May 8, 1945, at the announcement of V-E Day in Europe. All attention turned to the Pacific where a final drive was being made to force Japan into submission. On August 6, 1945, the first atomic bomb was dropped on Hiroshima, and shortly after, another atomic bomb was dropped on Nagasaki, and the Japanese surrendered.

On the night of August 14, Cleveland County residents poured into the streets to celebrate the end of the war with impromptu parades, horns tooting, much shouting and prayers of thanksgiving. The lives of ninety-seven men from Cleveland County had been lost in the war, most of them from Norman. But now, with the war's end, everyone's thoughts turned to a new era of peace.

Captain V. C. Griffin, USN, was commanding officer of the Naval Air Technical Training Station in Norman during World War II. Courtesy Pioneer Multi-County Library and The Norman Transcript.

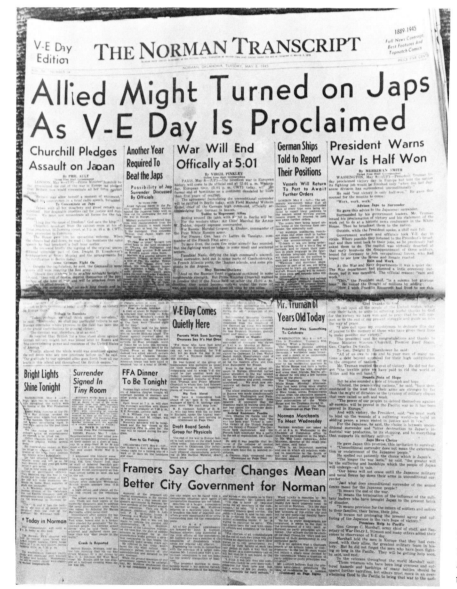

Those in Cleveland County celebrated V-E Day with the rest of the nation then quietly went on to help win the war in the South Pacific. Courtesy Bonnie Speer.

Called "Sooner City," this temporary housing community, erected south of Lindsey Street and on Asp Avenue, housed 450 World War II veterans and their families on the University of Oklahoma campus, immediately following the war. Courtesy Western History Collections, University of Oklahoma.

The Towers, the twelve-story housing complex in Couch Center, changed the Norman skyline when it was completed in 1963 on the University of Oklahoma campus. On the left is Tower No. 1 with the round cafeteria behind it. Tower No. 2 is on the lower right. Adams Center is on the upper right. Courtesy The Norman Transcript.

CHAPTER 9

The Later Years

Dr. George Cross served as president of the University of Oklahoma during WWII and immediately afterwards. During his administration the student body grew from 6,000 to 21,000. Courtesy The Norman Transcript.

With the end of World War II, the University of Oklahoma braced for a vastly increased enrollment. The 1945 graduating class had numbered only 274 members, but prior to the outbreak of hostilities class enrollments had frequently reached over 1,000 students. Now, with large numbers of veterans returning to the campus, enrollment was predicted to be far more than the university could accommodate, and where to house them became the question of the day.

The university owned no student housing except Hester and Robertson Halls, which had provided accommodations for 250 women before the war. The Army and Navy had leased these two buildings, along with the fraternity houses, which could not operate during that time because of the high enlistments and draft.

To help meet the needs of the sudden influx of students in the fall of 1945, University of Oklahoma President George L. Cross leased thirty house trailers from a construction company for student housing, and the Board of Regents approved a $275,000 bond issue to build ninety-six permanent apartments in four buildings on the Neimann Polo Field. True to predictions, the enrollment at OU reached an unbelievable 5,524 students that fall, among them 2,600 veterans, with 1,000 of these veterans married. Every available bedroom in Norman was rented. In desperation, Dr. Cross ordered 500 prefabricated houses at a cost of $1,250,000 from a Dallas firm for temporary housing for university students.

These buildings were erected south of the campus at Lindsey Street and Jenkins Avenue. Called "Sooner City," this temporary housing community, sheltered 450 veterans and their families. Most veterans found the prefabs little better than a foxhole. Their gas heaters could scarcely compete with the elements beyond the thin plywood walls. During subzero temperatures, ice formed on the inside of the walls as Oklahoma experienced its worst cold spell in years.

On March 1, 1946, the Navy announced it was closing the Naval Flight Training Center (NFTC) at North Base. The Navy also said the training programs at the Naval Air Technical Training Corps (NATTC) would be transferred elsewhere in a couple of months.

This was the moment the University of Oklahoma had been waiting for. From the beginning, university officials had been looking forward to the time when the Navy would no longer need these facilities, and the university might be able to acquire them for expansion of the university. The departure of the Navy also would provide more housing for students and classroom and laboratory space. Then word came the Navy might not vacate the bases after all.

The citizens of Norman rejoiced at the news. The presence of the two bases had kept the economy of the area high during the

The 1950s was the era of the big bands. This group is shown performing at the Sooner Theatre in Norman. Courtesy Sooner Theatre of Norman, Inc.

war. Much concern had been expressed about what would happen when the Navy left. When the university voiced its opposition to the Navy's announcement that it might stay, 500 citizens turned out for an indignation meeting at the Armory USO. They discussed plans for keeping the bases in Norman.

All proved to no avail, however. Eventually, university officials convinced the Navy that it should give up the bases. On May 26, 1946, the university took the first step in acquiring title to North Base, valued at over $7 million. The final enrollment at the university for the fall semester of 1946 reached 10,126. Approximately 6,000 of these were veterans, of whom forty percent were married. Many of these families were housed in the barracks on North Base.

The total value of South Base, which included some 200 buildings on 2,200 acres, was approximately $25 million. The Navy retained nominal control of the facility for several more years, reactivating the NATTC on January 15, 1952, at the outbreak of the Korean War, but in early 1959, South Base was declared surplus property. On February 28, 1961, the university received a deed for the water supply on North Base and for several other Navy properties, and the city obtained the drill field east of Jenkins Avenue, which later became Reaves Park. The government kept the remaining land on South Base for later sale for future industrial development.

The veterans who returned to the University of Oklahoma campus and Cleveland County following World War II, found a different world from the one they had left. Gone were the lean days of the Depression and gloomy forecasts. The war had brought full employment and a feeling of togetherness the nation had never known before. In the years immediately after the war, a spirit of progressiveness prevailed in the county. Everyone seemed more relaxed and a period of uninhibited spending began as money, which had formerly been funneled into the war effort, was released for private industry and home building.

Going to the movies was the big entertainment feature of the day. Those in Norman could take their choice of three downtown theatres, Sooner Theatre, University Theatre, or Oklahoma Theatre, or they could attend Boomer Theatre near Campus Corner. If these attractions didn't suit them, they could go to a play at the university, staged by the OU School of Drama where a young man by the name of Bill Weaver graduated in 1948. A decathlon and varsity cross-country track star, Bill later changed his name to Dennis Weaver and starred as Chester in television's "Gunsmoke" series and other productions including "McCloud."

Television hit the Cleveland County scene on the morning of April 26, 1948, when WKY-TV in Oklahoma City transmitted its test pattern at the beginning of its regular programmed day. Soon the citizens were deserting the motion picture theatres and their radios to marvel at this new invention of science that brought the world of entertainment directly into their homes.

The years immediately following World War II brought another kind of independence to the county, as well as to the state and nation. This was a period of social reform and improvement, known as the "civil rights movement."

From the beginning, Cleveland County had been known as a white man's place. The first residents found by surveyor Abner Ernest Norman, during his survey for the railroad in 1872, were Negroes who lived in four huts on a hill east of Choteau Creek, near future Lexington.

Television came upon the Cleveland County scene in 1948, and a decathlon and varsity cross-country track star named Bill Weaver, graduated from the University of Oklahoma that year. Later he changed his name to Dennis Weaver and starred as Chester in "Gunsmoke." Also, he had a leading role in "McCloud," "Gentle Ben," and "Kentucky Jones." Courtesy University of Oklahoma School of Drama.

A tornado struck North Base without warning at 5:52 p.m., April 30, 1949. It demolished a number of buildings and vehicles, and barely missed seventy-five National Guardsmen who were practicing on the rifle range on the west side of the base near Mt. Williams. Forty-eight of the guardsmen were injured. The rifle range has not been used since then. Courtesy The Norman Transcript.

James Garner gained fame for his role as Bret Maverick in television's "Maverick" series. He was nominated for an Academy Award for his starring role in "Murphy's Law" in 1986. A descendant of pioneer businessman L. L. Griggs, Garner was born in Norman on April 7, 1928, as James Scott Bumgarner, and grew up here, graduating from Norman High School. He is shown in this 1958 photo with his father and brothers. From left to right: Charles Bumgarner, James Garner, W. W. Bumgarner, and Jack Bumgarner. Courtesy Charles Bumgarner.

Black cowboys, employees of Chickasaw rancher Montford B. Johnson, were also known to have stayed in dugouts at Norman's Camp, located near what is now the intersection of Parkview Terrace and Fleetwood Drive in Norman. The blacks had come to the Indian Nation with the Indians over the Trail of Tears, and were preferred as cowboys over white men in the cattle country because of their wide acceptance among the trouble making Plains Indians.

During the run, the southern part of the Unassigned Lands was largely settled by whites from the South. They brought with them their prejudices against the Negro. Although a few blacks had settled on undesirable claims in the Cross Timbers area and a number of black construction workers found employment in Cleveland County during those first days of settlement, their presence was not tolerated for long.

Racial problems were reported as early as 1892 when all Negroes in Norman were told to leave the town. Eight months later, a group of rowdy citizens in Lexington attacked and drove the black population in that town across the river to Purcell. The press encouraged the situation. One leading newspaper printed the following in a special promotional issue:

> "One unique and well-known feature of Norman's population is there is not one negro in the city. This has excited considerable favorable comment in sections of the territory where the fact is best known. Laboring men regard it favorable to their class, removing a competition considered dangerous."

Such an attitude resulted in mob action, driving a black construction worker from Norman on June 28, 1898. In 1907, members of the Klu Klux Klan threatened a colony of blacks working on a 220-acre ranch thirteen miles northeast of Norman with murder if they did not leave. The last racial incident occurred in 1922, when an all-black orchestra from Fort Worth was threatened with violence while playing for a Norman High School dance. But the orchestra members continued playing until midnight and then caught the train for Oklahoma City without incidence.

This unwritten code in Norman, that no black person could stay in town after sundown, persisted until World War II when many a black serviceman was seen on the streets of the town. During the war, these black servicemen fought side by side with white servicemen. Afterwards, black citizens determined to fight for their equality.

On September 3, 1945, the National Association for the Advancement of Colored People (NAACP) met in McAlester and decided to test Oklahoma's segregation laws in education. On January 14, 1946, a young black woman by the name of Ada Lois Sipuel applied for admittance to the University of Oklahoma. She had graduated from Langston University, a black school, and wanted to study law at OU. Her transcript was acceptable, but University President George Cross denied her admittance solely because of her race, for at the time, Oklahoma statutes prohibited the mixing of blacks and whites in the state's education system. On the basis of this, the NAACP took the case to court. On January 12, 1948, the U. S. Supreme Court ruled Oklahoma's segregation laws were illegal as they applied to higher education, and the way

This demonstration for racial equality at Green's Drug Store in Oklahoma City led to others including that at the John A. Brown store in Norman on Campus Corner in February 1961. Courtesy Oklahoma Historical Society.

was opened for blacks to study at OU.

Blacks still had a long way to go on the road to freedom though. The late fifties and early sixties were fraught with the struggle for equal housing, educational opportunities, transportation, and voting privileges. On August 19, 1958, black youths staged the first sit-in at Oklahoma City in Green's Drug Store at 200 West Main Street. For three days, the group sat quietly waiting to be served before the first segregation barriers were broken down. Other victories were not so easily won.

The luncheonette in the downtown John A. Brown store in Oklahoma City resisted the sit-ins and demonstrations for three years before blacks could receive service there. Demonstrations at the John A. Brown store in Norman on Campus Corner began on February 1, 1961, in sympathy with these sit-ins.

Although blacks had been admitted to the University of Oklahoma, they had separate restrooms, separate eating areas in the cafeteria, and separate sections in the classrooms. Many people on campus felt this was unfair to the black students. A group of OU students sent a petition to Norman city officials stating that segregation was wrong and they wanted the barriers broken down.

Seven OU professors, a number of graduate assistants, and three faculty wives participated in that first demonstration before the Norman John A. Brown Store, as well as three blacks. A group of pro-segregationists demonstrated across the street, and a large number of students jammed the streets to watch the non-violent activity.

In July, members of the Trinity Lutheran Church in Norman voted to boycott all eating establishments in Norman that practiced segregation.

Justice was a long time coming as the demonstrations and sit-ins continued, but by 1964, civil rights leaders in Oklahoma City announced not one restaurant could be found in Oklahoma County that did not serve blacks. The struggle for equality in other areas continued until the mid-1970s when public and legal segregation was finally destroyed in the nation.

During this time, the period of prosperity in Cleveland

Ada Lois Sipuel Fisher accepts an award for her part in breaking the racial barriers at the University of Oklahoma when she applied for admission in 1946 as the first black person. Denied admittance, the NAACP took her case to the U.S. Supreme Court which ruled in 1950 that Oklahoma's segregation laws were illegal in regard to higher education. Courtesy The Oklahoma Daily.

Norman presented a quiet appearance in this July 30, 1967, photo looking west on Main Street from Crawford Avenue. The T.G.&Y. store on the right was established in 1936, the first T.G.&Y. store in the nation. Courtesy Sports Information Office, University of Oklahoma.

The first proposal for a reservoir on the Little River dates back to 1945 when Norman city manager R. E. "Buck" Clement went to the U.S. Corps of Engineers with the idea. He signed the necessary papers reserving the water supply for Norman, refusing many inviting offers to let it go to Oklahoma City. Courtesy R. E. Clement.

County continued. Many of the returning veterans found employment in nearby Tinker Air Force Base. The base was an air depot maintaining service and providing parts for the nation's air fleet as well as being an assembly plant during the war, and quick lobbying by Oklahoma City leaders had kept the plant in existence following the war.

The 1950s were building years for Norman. The town's population had grown to 29,000 by then. The city pushed westward toward Oklahoma 74 (now Interstate 35). The building boom erupted on campus, too, changing the skyline of Norman with the X-shaped dormitory in Cate Center, Copeland Hall, and the sixteen-building complex for the Oklahoma Center for Continuing Education being built during that decade. The new Norman High School, which opened at Berry Road and Main Street, was hailed as the "Showplace of the Southwest."

By 1960, Norman's population was increasing so rapidly that city officials began worrying about future water problems. News stories of the day spun a pleasing tale of substantial growth and progress in practically all lines of business and community activity, but an abundant water supply was needed to ensure the city's future growth.

Concern over the ground water supply, from which most of the cities in central Oklahoma drew their water, and the possibility of a surface supply was discussed as far back as 1936.

The first proposal for a reservoir on the Little River east of Norman dated back to 1940 when Norman City Manager R. E. "Buck" Clement approached the U. S. Corps of Engineers with the idea. The government agency stated it couldn't be done; there "just wasn't enough water out there." Nevertheless, Clement signed the necessary papers reserving this water supply for Norman.

Local committees in Norman, Del City, and Midwest City

began studying the water situation. In the early 1950s, the three cities joined together in the Central Oklahoma Water Users Association (COWUA). The members drew up statistics for the proposed Little River reservoir and approached the Bureau of Reclamation (BOR) with the idea. The proposed lake was to be used strictly as a municipal and industrial water supply. This was a radical departure from previous practice, for BOR, had only funded lakes used for power or irrigation up to this time. But if the government would put up the cash to initiate the project, the three cities promised to repay it.

The project required approval by the U. S. Congress as well as a vote of the people of the three cities. Thus began the long fight to get the bill past the red tape in Washington, D. C., and into the hands of Congress, and then to obtain the necessary votes.

In 1955, Norman businessman Harold Cooksey became president of COWOA. He began the first of many treks to Washington where he pleaded COWOA's case, that if they didn't get the water, Oklahoma City would.

Finally on May 11, 1959, Senator Robert S. Kerr, termed at that time the most powerful senator in Congress, introduced the bill for the reservoir on the senate floor. In the House of Representatives, John Jarmon led the fight for passage. Eventually, the bill was passed by both groups, and on June 26, 1960, President Dwight D. Eisenhower signed it into law authorizing a $19 million reservoir on Little River east of Norman. Construction began a year later.

In the fall of 1961, Norman annexed 173 square miles to protect the 6,000 acre site of the future Little River Reservoir. This brought Norman's total area to 185 square miles, making the city the tenth largest of any city in the United States with a population of less than 250,000. The move also added an estimated 2,000 rural residents to the city.

Today, Lake Thunderbird draws an estimated 60,000 people a day during its peak season, making it the most heavily used lake in the state for recreational purposes. The name "Thunder-

Norman businessman Harold Cooksey, president of the Central Oklahoma Water Users Association, was instrumental in obtaining congressional approval for the Little River reservoir in 1960. Courtesy The Norman Transcript.

Lake Thunderbird is Oklahoma's most heavily used recreation area, drawing an estimated 60,000 persons per day during its peak season. The name "Thunderbird" means "Giver of the Rain." This photo was taken in 1965. Courtesy The Norman Transcript.

Completed in 1965, Lake Thunderbird provides water for Midwest City, Del City, and Norman. The lake lies thirteen miles east of Norman. The north marina, Indian Point, is visible in the foreground. Courtesy The Norman Transcript.

bird" comes from the mythical Thunderbird—meaning "giver of rain," revered by numerous Indian tribes. The name was selected for the lake in a contest held in August 1965, and was suggested by Mrs. Frankie McKenzie of Del City, who was honored during dedication ceremonies of Lake Thunderbird on October 1, 1965.

Ironically, Lake Thunderbird's water level has risen above its recommended storage level several times, causing numerous problems to area motorists, and U. S. Corps of Engineers predictions that there "wasn't any water out there" have floated away.

With its future water supply assured, Norman experienced its greatest growth period beginning in 1961. The Norman Municipal Hospital expanded again, and the city developed Westwood Park, an 83-acre complex with a municipal swimming pool and golf course at West Robinson Street and 24th Avenue NW. The Holiday Inn built a $750,000 facility at I-35 and West Main Street. Sterr's Foods expanded at Berry Road and West Main Street, and the Downtown Shopping Center opened with six new stores. Southwestern Bell and OG&E each moved into new buildings.

The Acme Fence and Iron Company, Norman's first heavy manufacturing industry, purchased seventeen acres a quarter- mile north of Westheimer Field and began construction of a facility to employ 100 people. Dorsett Electronics, Norman's homegrown electronic producer, mushroomed into a multimillion dollar corporation, employing 600 persons in five states. Gilt Edge Farms became the state's largest independent dairy products producer, employing more than 300 people.

larger and central heat and air conditioning were the attractive features along with an extra bathroom and recreation room.

By 1963, Norman's population had reached an estimated 40,000 people. In January that year, the jet age came to the city when a sleek, white plane lifted smoothly off the runway at Max Westheimer Field, thunder blasting from its twin jets. It was the maiden flight of the Aero Jet Commander, designed and built almost entirely in Norman by Aero Commander, a division of the Rockwell-Standard Corporation. The 500 mph six-passenger jet was the first twin-engine jet designed in the United States without military assistance.

Also in 1963, the city built a 63-acre industrial tract, Norman Industries, Inc., adjacent to North Campus and across U.S. 77 and the railroad tracks, attracting new industrial activity to the area.

The Hollywood Shopping Center was begun at McGee Drive and West Lindsey Street. New housing additions included Colonial Estates and Lincoln Terrace. Final plat approval for Brookhaven North Addition, north of Robinson at 36th Avenue NW, heralded an era of higher quality homes.

By 1964, the city had 488 miles of streets. A major improvement that year was the paving of Berry Road between West Lindsey Street and West Robinson Street. Westheimer Field was upgraded, including a new terminal building.

In 1956, an important era in highway construction began within the state when Congress passed the Federal Aid Highway Act, promising the federal government would underwrite 90 percent of the cost of four-lane, limited access highways. The master plan called for three major highways to pass through Oklahoma,

The Norman Municipal Hospital expanded in 1954, 1961 and again in 1982, increasing the facility's bed capacity to 385. The name was changed to Norman Regional Hospital in 1987. This photo was taken in 1981. Courtesy Bonnie Speer.

The Lloyd Noble Center on the University of Oklahoma South Campus was dedicated in 1975, bringing a new era of cultural and athletic events to the area. The quarter-mile concourse seats 11,000 people. Courtesy Bonnie Speer.

The Sooner Fashion Mall brought indoor shopping comfort and convenience to Norman when it opened in August 1976. The mall is situated on fifty-one acres on Main Street, west of I-35. Courtesy Bonnie Speer.

I-35, I-40, and I-44. Construction on I-35, north of Oklahoma City, began in 1957 utilizing old interurban routes and Highway 74 in Cleveland County. By 1965, I-35 was completed into Norman.

A tight money situation created a slowdown in construction in Cleveland County in 1966. Even so, two major apartment complexes were built in Norman, the Villa de Vey at Lindsey and 24th Avenue SW, and the Yorkshire at Chautauqua and Imhoff Road.

The housing market plunged again in the early 1970s. Yet this slowdown seemed to have little effect on Norman's commercial construction. In 1971, Heisman Square Shopping Center sprang up at East Alameda Street and 12th Avenue SE, and Westinghouse developed a $20 million residential air conditioning plant at I-35 and Franklin Road, employing 750 people.

The Moore-Norman Vo-Tech School opened on August 24, 1976, adding a new dimension to Cleveland County's educational opportunities, with students applying themselves to the occupational trades. Courtesy Bonnie Speer.

Then the Arab oil boycott in 1974 caused the brief economic boom to come to an abrupt halt. Widespread unemployment began to develop in the area. General Motors, which had announced plans to build a large assembly plant northeast of Moore, cancelled its plans. Norman citizens rose up in protest over increased utility rates because of rapidly rising energy costs.

Gradually things settled down and businesses tried to adapt to the new economic conditions. The University of Oklahoma Lloyd Noble Center on South Campus, built in 1975, boosted cultural activities in the area, including performances by top name stars and athletic events. Seating 11,000 people on its quarter-mile concourse, the facility contains four levels.

As cultural and business opportunities increased in the area

After years of planning, Norman's new City Office Building was ready to be occupied in the spring of 1980. The $1.3 million dollar structure was paid for with cash from federal revenue funds earmarked for the purpose since 1975. The building is located on Dawes Street, south of Andrews Park. Courtesy Bonnie Speer.

The 1950s were building years for Norman. The town's population had reached 29,000 and traffic problems were already developing as seen in this March 16, 1959, photo of Main Street. Courtesy The Norman Transcript.

One of Cleveland County's most famous landmarks is "Mount Williams," this dirt embankment as seen from Norman's Robinson Street overpass above I-35. A remnant of the World War II Navy firing range, located on Westheimer Field, the promontory is believed to have been named for Lt. Commander J. W. Williams, Jr., who was in charge of North Base when it was dedicated on July 26, 1942. Courtesy Bonnie Speer.

so did educational opportunities. The Moore-Norman Vo-Tech School opened on August 24, 1976. Located at 4701 12th Avenue NW, Norman, the school was a joint project of the Moore and Norman school districts. Classes here concentrate on the occupational trades, including secretarial, brick laying, carpentry, and welding.

Sooner Fashion Mall also opened in August 1976, bringing a new era in shopping comfort and convenience to Norman. This mall is situated on fifty-one acres on the west side of I-35 on West Main Street.

Providing more employment for the county, in 1978 the Shaklee Corporation developed a $44 million facility south of Norman on Highway 9, to manufacture nutritional foods and supplements. TOTCO, a division of Baker International Corporation, moved into a new $5 million facility on Rock Creek Road in August 1979. The General Motors plant near Moore had

announced in 1977 it would proceed with its automobile assembly plant, and the first front-wheel drive, fuel-efficient cars rolled out in 1979. The plant employed 5,400 workers, many from Cleveland County, and poured $120 million in wages into the area economy.

By 1980, Norman's population had reached 70,000 people, and that long hot summer brought water rationing. The city had an ample water supply at Lake Thunderbird, but its water treatment plant proved inadequate to provide the needed amount. Taking the hint, voters passed an additional one cent sales tax to fund a new water treatment facility.

The 1980s brought more economic problems for the county. The Westinghouse air conditioning plant located between Moore and Norman closed. The York Division of the Borg-Warner Corporation took over the facility. Numerous small businesses shut their doors, unable to survive in this period of high costs. The oil industry and agriculture went into a slump. First one bank and then another in Norman failed, citing large losses in oil and construction loans. In 1987, the stock market tumbled and citizens worried about another Great Depression as experienced by the nation during the 1930s.

Even so, Moore, Norman, Noble, and Lexington continued to grow during these troubled times. The pioneering spirit, which had turned a raw prairie into bountiful farms and cities, was still evident in Cleveland County one hundred years later as an $8 million expansion began on Sooner Fashion Mall in 1988.

From a single weedy street on a barren prairie a century ago, Norman, the county seat of Cleveland County, has become a bustling, tree-covered city, fulfilling the dreams of its founders. Photo taken in 1981. Courtesy Leroy Kratochvil.

Oklahoma Memorial Stadium at Owen Field on the University of Oklahoma campus has a seating capacity of 75,000 persons. The press box on top of the west side was added in 1975. Courtesy University of Oklahoma Sports Information Office.

CHAPTER 10

OU Football

The football game raged up and down the grassy playing field. The University of Oklahoma players took charge of the ball and started their push toward the goal line. The crowd followed along the edge of the marked-off gridiron, cheering. Suddenly a drunken spectator, aroused by the action, ran out of the crowd and stood on the goal line. Drawing his two six-shooters he fired two shots into the ground and hollered, "That Oklahoma bunch won't cross this goal, I'll see to that!"

That's the way football was in those early days. It was rough and ready and fired a certain type of enthusiasm in the spectators. The game came to the University of Oklahoma only two years after the institution opened in 1893, and the University of Oklahoma football and the university grew up together.

The game of football had originated back East at Harvard University in 1874. It was an offspring of soccer and rugby. By the time Oklahoma was settled in the land run and the University of Oklahoma opened, the game was already the rage in eastern colleges and universities.

John A. Harts is generally credited with starting the OU

Bennie Owen came to OU in 1905 as head coach of the University of Oklahoma football team and stayed for twenty-two years, bringing a winning tradition to OU. The team won its first official championship under him. Owen Field was named in his honor. Courtesy University of Oklahoma Sports Information Office.

Construction on a new stadium got underway at OU in 1925. On November 12, 1922, 1,000 people had been hurled to the ground when a bleacher on the north end of Boyd Field collasped during the first half of the OU-Missouri game. A campaign for a new stadium got underway. Two years after this first section was completed, the first portion of the eastside grandstands was built, bringing seating capacity at the stadium to 32,000. Courtesy University of Oklahoma Sports Information Office.

Bud Wilkinson, right, became head coach in 1948. During his seventeen years at OU his teams won three mythical national championships and set a record for 47 straight victories. Halfback Billy Vessels, left, was awarded the Heisman Trophy in 1952, the first for OU. He was named to the National Football Hall of Fame in 1961. Courtesy University of Oklahoma Sports Information Office.

Clyde Bogle was among the early University of Oklahoma football players. When the team played away from home, part of Main Street in Norman was roped off and the crowd gathered in front of Barbour's Drug Store to listen to the returns. Each time a play was received by telegraph, the scorekeeper moved a wooden football up and down a board, marked off to represent a football field. Courtesy The Norman Transcript and Clyde Bogle.

football team in September 1895. A bright, adventurous twenty-year-old, he had come to OU to attend school and to teach a class in elocution. He had played football at Winfield College in Kansas.

Before his arrival, Edwin DeBarr, professor of Chemistry and Physics, and a member of the first faculty, had pooled his resources with several male students and purchased a football. DeBarr had played halfback at the University of Michigan. He and the students booted the ball about campus. In 1893, *The Norman Transcript* noted two football teams had been formed at the university. It was not until Harts arrived on campus, though, that things got serious.

Harts was athletic and could kick the football farther than anyone else. One night in September 1895, in Bud Risinger's barber shop, a couple of doors east of the railroad tracks, on the north side of the street, Harts brought up the idea of forming a regular football team. His suggestion brought instant approval and he was chosen coach and captain.

At that time the university had 148 students, but 121 of them were doing high school preparatory work. No thought was given to eligibility requirements. Harts recruited his team among his friends and the most likely candidates.

Those on that first team included Jasper Clapham, Joe Merkle, John P. Evans, Bert Long, Horace Sommers, Fred Bean, Bernard Reuter, Newt Medlock, Bert Dunn, and Will Short. Few of them had ever seen a football before, let alone played in a game.

The team laid out a gridiron on the prairie north of the lone university building, laying a little northwest of today's Holmberg Hall. The players hauled dirt to fill in the buffalo wallows. Most of the students made their own uniforms, wearing brown overalls cut off at the knees and padded in front. They nailed cleats on their shoes. A committee, consisting of May Overstreet, the only woman on the faculty, and students Ray Hume and Ruth House selected the team colors crimson and cream.

That first game, played in Norman against Oklahoma City, has been compared to "Custer's Massacre." The only difference was there were survivors on both sides. Harts jerked a knee tendon and couldn't play. He recruited Bud Risinger, the barber, to take his place. No matter that Risinger wasn't enrolled in the university.

Football was considerably different those days. The game began with the shot of a pistol. There was no forward pass and the emphasis was placed upon brute strength, the players hammering their way to the scrimmage line. Each team was required to make only five yards in three downs, so turnovers were infrequent. The touchdown counted only four points and the game was played in forty-five minute halves not quarters, and the members took Spartan pride in staying for the duration of the game. If they did withdraw, they could not return to the game.

During this first university game, the playing got rougher and rougher. OU took a drubbing, 34-0. Jap Clapham went home and crawled into bed, too sore to do his evening farm chores. Shortly after this game, Harts left school to hunt gold in the Arctic, never dreaming what he had started at OU.

The team played without a coach the following year, but it was all victorious, playing two games with Norman High School and winning both.

In 1897, Dr. Boyd hired Professor Vernon Parrington to head the new English Department. Parrington had been a scrub quarterback on the Harvard football team and had played at Emporia, Kansas. He was prevailed upon to take over the athletic department with no pay.

Parrington was described as a well-groomed young bachelor, a trifle eccentric, but likable. He wore pressed tweeds with a cap to match and smoked brown paper cigarettes incessantly. In the future he was destined to become a Pulitzer prize winner in English literature.

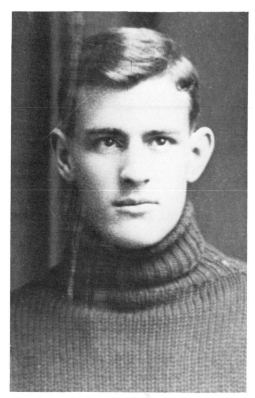

Claude Reeds, Norman fullback who played on the University of Oklahoma team from 1910-13, has been termed the greatest player ever turned out by the Sooner school. He was the first Oklahoma player to be inducted in the National Football Hall of Fame on December 6, 1961. He coached at OU from 1923-29. Courtesy University of Oklahoma Sports Information Office.

The "Rough Riders," the University of Oklahoma's first football team was organized in 1895. The team laid out a gridiron on the prairie north of today's Holmberg Hall. The team posed for this picture in 1899. Courtesy University of Oklahoma and Clyde Bogle.

The University of Oklahoma football team pitted their talents against Arkansas City in this 1899 photo while the spectators moved up down the sidelines with the action. Courtesy University of Oklahoma and Clyde Bogle.

Professor Vernon Parrington, who had been a scrub quarterback on the Harvard football team, took over as coach of the OU football team in 1897. Later, Parrington won a Pulitzer prize in English literature. Courtesy University of Oklahoma Sports Office.

Parrington indoctrinated the Harvard style of playing at OU, which had won the Cambridge team thirty-two of thirty-four games from 1890 through 1892. As a result, during his four years as head of the university athletic department. Parrington's teams won nine games, lost two, and tied one. He was also responsible for instilling an eastern atmosphere into the games with organized cheerleading, display of colors, and ample publicity before the game.

Many still regarded the old game as brutal though. After the team started playing out of town, Joe and John Merkle's father always met the returning train with a wagonload of hay as a makeshift ambulance. He didn't trust the sport. Neither did the parents of Harvey Short, and his mother refused to make him a suit. Short was in a quandary as to what to do until Coach Parrington loaned him his suit which he had worn at Harvard.

Midway between the last half of the first game played against Kingfisher College, December 31, 1897, the Logan county sheriff stopped the game. He had never seen one before and on arriving at the gridiron at the fair grounds in Guthrie, he assumed a drunken brawl was taking place. Dr. Boyd had to add his pleas to that of the other spectators to get the game going again.

It was no wonder the OU team was known as the "Rough Riders" those days, named after Teddy Roosevelt's troops who had just returned from storming San Juan Hill in Cuba.

When playing out of town, university team members paid their own way. They met Texas for the first time at Austin in 1900. Texas beat them 28 to 2, but OU learned much from the team and wasn't scored on in its remaining four games that season.

In 1901, Parrington asked to resign as coach of the football team because of a heavy workload. He stayed on as athletic director though, and Fred Roberts coached one year. Then the university hired Mark McMahan, a tall, sparse young man who had played on the Texas team. A hard driving coach, he didn't hesitate to jump in and scrimmage with his team, and was known as a noisy, brusque man. "He had the kind of voice that made you jump, not once but three times," said one player.

Under McMahan's leadership OU avoided defeat at the hands of mighty Texas for the first time in 1903, 6-6, touchdowns having been raised to five points.

Fred "Buck" Ewing became the coach in 1904. He instituted several new ideas such as not participating in practice or games himself and using only those players who were scholastically eligible.

It was during Ewing's term that OU played its first game against Oklahoma A&M and one of the strangest touchdowns in history occurred. In those days a loose ball went to the first team that could touch it. The game was played on November 5, 1904, at Island Park in South Guthrie.

It was a cold, bitter day, and Cottonwood Creek, which nearly surrounded the playing field, was rolling bankful with red flood waters. Ice was beginning to form along the edges.

On the third down of the fourth play, B. O. Callahan, A&M fullback, punted the ball and it went almost straight up, struck the ground far behind the goal, and bounced into the creek. Immediately, players from both sides charged after the ball. An A&M player reached it first and tried to fish it out of the water with a stick. T. Becker Matthews hit him in the shoulder and knocked him into the creek. Callahan struck out for the ball. Realizing what he had done, Matthews plunged into the icy water after him. Two other OU players and a second from OSU followed. In the melee that followed, Matthews ducked Callahan, who couldn't swim and fought for the bank. Finally Ed Cook of the OU team managed to capture the slippery ball, and touched it down on the shore, giving OU possession.

Cold and wet, the five players climbed out of the water while the crowd laughed, and finished the first half of the game in their water-soaked suits, trading for dry clothes with their substitutes at the half. OU won the game 75 to 0.

Ewing resigned at the end of the year and the university hired Bennie Owen. Bennie was to stay for twenty-two years, bringing stability to the football program. His teams were to establish Oklahoma as a football power.

Born in Chicago on July 24, 1875, Owen had been a quarterback at the University of Kansas where he led the Jayhawks to an impressive 10 to 0 victory record in 1899. He had coached at Washburn College in Topeka, Kansas, at the University of Michigan, and at Bethany College in Lindsborg, Kansas. He

Football fever has always flamed high at OU. These Sooner boosters are bound for Texas in this 1957 photo. Courtesy The Norman Transcript.

Portrayed here by Ron Benally in November 1969, OU's mascot, "Little Red," helped drum up support for the football team during its games. A succession of Native American students represented "Little Red" beginning in the early 1950s, when he danced on the sidelines following every OU victory. He appeared at his last game in 1970 after years of controversy terming him a racial stereotype. Courtesy Electronic Media and Photo Services, University of Oklahoma. Photo by Gil Jain.

Fullback Steve Owens won the Heisman Trophy in 1967 under the guidance of Head Coach Chuck Fairbanks. Courtesy University of Oklahoma Sports Information Office.

emphasized clean playing at Bethany College, where he first came to the attention of OU. Those "Terrible Swedes" played fiercely but with courtesy. There was no slugging or deliberate fouling during the game. These were the same traits he insisted upon in Norman when he began coaching here in 1905.

Owen had first studied to become a doctor. A quiet man, he never shouted or used profane language. The worst he said when something went wrong was, "Gee Cly!" The players liked him at once. Interest in football quickened under Owens.

Owen helped lay out a new football field, Boyd Field, west of the present OU Field House, and erected the first grandstand with room for 500 spectators.

He innovated the use of very little football padding, which was a far cry from Parrington's era when varsity teams went out padded like ice hockey goalies. Owen's theory was that a football player in top physical condition seldom got hurt. Oklahoma players wore only a light shoulder pad of quilted felt sewn in their canvas jacket, with a light pad covering the front of their legs. Owens' first team won seven out of nine games, including its first win over Texas, 2-0.

That fall, Arthur M. Alden, a Norman student, wrote the lyrics to "Boomer Sooner," borrowing the tune from Yale's "Boola."

During the 1905 football season, several players back East were killed during games. This lead to a general outcry from the public to abolish the sport. Several schools did so, including Southwestern Normal at Weatherford, Oklahoma Territory; Bethany College, Lindsborg, Kansas; Stanford; and California. But those who loved the game sought to revise the rules to save it.

Eighteen schools met at Harvard in the spring of 1906 and formed a rules committee. The committee established a new code for football. Most of the new rules were aimed at eliminating some of the brawling aspects of the game. Others stressed eligibility. Tackling out of bounds, hurdling, and piling after the referee had declared the ball dead were forbidden. Tackling below the knee was punishable by a five-yard loss. Before the ball was snapped, only one man could be in motion. The game was shortened to two thirty-minute halves, making it less exhausting. The distance to be gained in each play was extended to ten yards in three downs. Most revolutionary of all was the legalization of a strange thing called a forward pass, but it was seldom used because of its susceptability to interception.

With the inception of the new rules, football increased in favor. Owen's "Boomers," as the team was called at that time, had a tough time adjusting to the rules though, especially that blasted forward pass.

The 1907 football season got off to a bad start on October 16, three days before the Kansas game, when Owen and John Barbour, a Norman druggist, went hunting in the Chickasaw Nation, south of Adkins Crossing. On the way back, Owen accidently shot his right arm, severing an artery. A few hours before the Kansas game, it was deemed necessary to amputate the arm to save his life. Within a few weeks, he was back on the playing field, mocking his own clumsiness.

The three Selmon brothers played for the OU football team during the late 1970s, presenting an awesome defensive field. From left to right, tackle LeRoy, noseguard Lucious, and tackle Dewey. Courtesy University of Oklahoma Sports Office.

The Sooner team always promised plenty of excitement for the spectators. Clendon Thomas is carrying the ball in this 1957 game. Courtesy University of Oklahoma Sports Information Office.

In 1908, the university athletic teams became known as the "Sooners," a nickname that has stuck to this day.

Under Owen's direction the football team continued to grow in power. The 1911 team proved to be the first unbeaten, untied squad since 1898 when only two games were played. Two years later, Claude Reeds, the last of four brothers from Norman to play at OU, was selected by "Outing" magazine to its honor roll of college players. A fullback, Reeds would be inducted into the National Football of Fame in 1961, the first OU football player to receive that honor.

OU became a member of the Southwest Conference in 1915. This included Oklahoma A&M College, University of Texas, Texas A&M, University of Arkansas, Baylor University, and Southwestern University of Georgetown, Texas. OU shared the Southwest Conference title with Baylor that year, thereby claiming its first official championship.

In 1920, the Sooners joined the Missouri Valley Conference, along with the University of Missouri, University of Kansas, Iowa State University, Drake University, Washington University of St. Louis, Grinnell College of Iowa, and Kansas State. Again OU won the conference title its first year.

The gridiron was moved to what is now Owen Field in 1923, and for the first time cars could not park around the playing field. Steel bleachers from Boyd Field stood on the west side of the field, and temporary wooden bleachers were erected on the east side. In 1924, the sale of $650,000 in bonds assured the construction of a new stadium, which was completed in 1925. Two years later, the first portion of the east stands was added, bringing the capacity of the stadium to 32,000.

OU is unique in that the stadium and playing field are known by two different names. Memorial Stadium honors those associated with the university who died in World War I, while Owen Field memorializes Bennie Owen.

Owen resigned as head football coach in 1927. During his twenty-two years at the University of Oklahoma, his teams won 122 game, lost 54, tied 16, and gained its first official championship. Owen was inducted into Helms Foundation Football Coaches Hall of Fame in 1969, a year before his death.

Cecil Samara's Big Red Rocket has been a familiar sight at OU football games since 1950. Samara terms himself OU's Number One Fan. Articles about him have appeared in Look, Life, and Esquire. Courtesy The Oklahoma Daily, University of Oklahoma.

The "Sooner Schooner" has been another familiar sight at OU football games since 1964, racing out onto the playing field following each OU victory in imitation of the Land Run of 1889. The Sooner Schooner is supported by the Doctor and Buzz Bartlett Foundation, Inc., and is manned by members of the RUF/NEKS club. The Sooner Schooner cost the OU team a fifteen-yard penalty for a delayed game at the January 1, 1985, Orange Bowl game when it raced out onto the field without permission of the referees. Washington State won the game, 28-17. Courtesy The Oklahoma Daily, University of Oklahoma.

In 1928, OU dropped out of the Missouri Valley Conference along with the University of Nebraska, University of Missouri, Iowa State University, University of Kansas, and Kansas State to form the Big Six Conference.

A series of head coaches reigned at OU during the next twenty years including Adrian Lindsey, 1927-1931; Lewie Hardage, 1932-1934; Lawrence "Biff" Jones, 1935-1936; Tom Stidham, 1937-1940; Dewey "Snorter" Luster, 1941-1945; and Jim Tatum, 1946. During this period, OU claimed its first Big Six Conference in 1938. The team ranked fourth in the nation that year and received a bid to play in the Orange Bowl against Tennessee. The game soon turned into the "Orange Brawl." There was considerable hitting going on in the game. Tennessee was penalized 130 yards and OU 90. Two Tennessee players and one from OU were ejected from the game. Much of the controversy was over what Tennessee called the angle block and OU referred to as clipping.

During those days there was no athletic dorm at OU. The

Halfback Billy Sims capped his phenomenal career with the Sooners in 1978 when he received the Heisman Memorial Trophy as player of the year. Courtesy University of Oklahoma Sports Information Office.

athletes lived in boarding houses. Scholarships consisted of room, board, books, and tuition, but athletes had to work for that room and board.

Three weeks after World War II started, twenty-two of OU's lettermen volunteered for military duty; and by the start of the 1942 season, all of Coach Luster's assistant coaches had, also, left. Luster built his teams during the war years around the Naval Reserve Officers Corps in training at OU.

In 1947, Coach Charles B. "Bud" Wilkinson took over as head coach and heralded in the golden years of OU football. His accomplishments during his seventeen years here have become legendary.

Under his leadership, OU won almost every honor that existed, becoming one of the football greats. The teams won three mythical national championships, in 1950, 1955, and 1956, establishing an incredible 93 victories, 47 losses, and 2 ties. They set the NCAA record for consecutive victories at 47 straight.

Wilkinson had played at Minnesota during the late 1930s. During World War II, he served as an assistant coach at Iowa Pre-Flight along with Jim Tatum. After Wilkinson's discharge from the Navy, Coach Tatum invited him to help out in the summer tryouts at OU in 1946. Wilkinson decided he liked football well enough to stay on as a full-time assistant coach. When Tatum took a job at Maryland University in 1947, Wilkinson proceeded to his job as head coach.

Wilkinson has been described as a man who was not easy to talk to. Reserved, he never said much when things went wrong, but simply replaced the offending player. Nevertheless, he was a man who inspired devout loyalty and extreme enthusiasm.

Wilkinson's teams employed the split-T formation. In later years, he said he considered his 1949 team the best—with qualifications. All the athletes had been in the service, had combat experience, were mature, and highly competent.

But he felt it unfair to compare this team with a "normal team." He reserved top honors there for the 1946 team which was formed after three years of recruiting and which had no older players.

In 1952, halfback Billy Vessels captured the coveted Heisman Trophy, awarded to the best college player in the nation, the first in OU history.

Vessels had grown up in Cleveland, Oklahoma, a homeless waif, living with first one family then another. A high school track champ, he soon became a formidable player at OU. Though he played only 25 games at OU, he scored an enviable 35 touchdowns, rushed 2,085 yards, and caught 21 passes for 391 yards and two touchdowns.

During the summer of 1956, a momentous event occurred at OU. The football team acquired its first black player. Prentice Gautt had led Oklahoma City Douglass, a black high school, to 75 straight victories and had been named player of the year. Many influential OU supporters opposed the idea of a black playing for OU. But in the end, Wilkinson's choice prevailed and Gautt made the team.

The cold, chilly day of November 16, 1957, will always be remembered as a dark day in Norman. That was the day Notre

The Pride of Oklahoma marching band is a favorite for half-time entertainment during OU football games. Directed by Gene Thrailkill, the band was voted the best college marching band in the nation in 1987 and received the Sudler Award. Courtesy University of Oklahoma Sports Information Office.

Dame brought OU's 47 game winning streak to a halt.

The Sooners had gone into the game as an eighteen point favorite. The 63,800 fans in attendance believed the Sooners could not be beaten. The score remained tied till near the end of the game. Then with three minutes and fifty seconds remaining in the fourth quarter, Notre Dame scored a touchdown and kicked the extra point for a 7-0 lead. Oklahoma reached Notre Dame's twenty-four yard line in the closing minutes, but a pass by OU was intercepted by Notre Dame in the end zone, and the game was over.

The crowd sat stunned, unable to believe the long winning streak had ended.

The players felt bad after the loss, but they confessed in a way they were relieved. Maintaining the record had been a big strain on them. They went on to win the Big Seven Conference Championship that year and to defeat Duke in the Orange Bowl.

The Sooners remained a power in 1958, but during the next three years they were not ranked among the nation's top ten.

Bud Wilkinson resigned in 1963 to enter an unsuccessful race for the U. S. Senate. He had been named Coach of the Year in 1949 by the National Football Coaches Association; Coach of the Year in 1950, by the Associated Press; and was inducted into the Helms Foundation Football Coaches Hall of Fame in 1969.

Following Wilkinson came a series of other head coaches.

Coach Barry Switzer of the Oklahoma Sooners came to the OU campus in 1966, as assistant coach to Jim Mackenzie. Switzer became head coach in 1973 following the departure of coach Chuck Fairbanks. Master of the wishbone attack, Switzer has become one of the winningest coaches in football history. Courtesy University of Oklahoma Sports Information Office.

Gomer Jones, who had been Wilkinson's right hand man during his seventeen years as head coach, served two years, and Jim Mackenzie from the University of Arkansas, was hired in 1966. Mackenzie brought with him two assistant coaches, Chuck Fairbanks and Barry Switzer, both of whom were to have an important effect on Sooner football history.

When Mackenzie died on April 28, 1967, Dr. George Cross, president of the university, appointed Chuck Fairbanks head coach. Under Fairbanks, Steve Owens won the Heisman Trophy on November 25, 1969. The following year, Fairbanks changed OU's offense from the T-Formation to the Wishbone. The formation had been developed by Texas Longhorn Coach Darrell Royal, a former student, player, and assistant coach at OU.

When Fairbanks resigned in 1973, Barry Switzer moved into the top position. Switzer had been the center and captain on the University of Arkansas championship team in 1959. The following year he coached the freshman team there.

Switzer became the master of OU's awesome wishbone attack. His reign ushered in another golden era in Sooner football history. He was destined to become one of the most successful coaches in football history, surpassing even Bud Wilkinson's record.

Entering the 1988 season, in fifteen years Switzer's teams had obtained 148 wins, 26 losses, and 4 ties. They were named mythical national champions in 1974, 1975, and 1985.

Many Sooners have won impressive titles while at OU. Things have come a long way since those first rough and tumble days on the old playing field north of Holmberg Hall. But one thing has remained the same, the spirit and enthusiasm which greets each game.

Who's Who
Past and Present

As our life experience grows older we become more aware of the importance of biography to our culture and the preservation and writing of its history.

We know that someday people will leaf through these pages piecing together the intervening years in the chronicles of Cleveland County.

So, thusly motivated and in a spirit of altruism, we leave here evidence that we lived, trusting the historical value, if any, to you of another generation.

Micah P. Smith, *Editor*
Who's Who section

The Presidents of
The University of Oklahoma

• **David Ross Boyd**, (1892-08) - b. July 31, 1853, Coshocton, OH.; BA, MA, hon. Ph.D., Univ. of Wooster . . . • **Arthur Grant Evans**, (1908-11) - b. Sept. 9, 1858, Madras, India; BA, Borough Rd. Coll., London, Eng.; (DD, Henry Kendall Coll., Muskogee, OK.; LL.D., U. of OK) . . . • **Stratton Duluth Brooks**, (1912-23) - b. Sept. 10, 1869, Everett, MO.; B.Ph., M.Ph., Mich. State Normal Coll.; BA, U. of Mich.; MA, Harvard; (LL.D., Colby).

• **James Shannon Buchanan**, (1924-25; acting 1923-24) b. Oct. 14, 1864, Franklin, TN; BS, Cumberland U., Vanderbilt U., U. of Chicago; (LL.D., Kingfisher Coll., OK). . . . • **William Bennett Bizzell**, (1925-41) - b. Oct. 14, 1876, Independence, TX; BS, Ph.B., Baylor U.; LL.M., D.L.C., IL. Coll. of Law; MA, U. of Chicago; (LL.D., Baylor U.); Ph.D., Columbia U. . . . • **Joseph August Brandt**, (1941-43) - b. July 26, 1889, Indiana; BA, MA, Oxford, Eng.; (hon. LL.D., Temple U.). . . . • **George Lynn Cross**, (1944-68) - BS, MS, D.Sc., S. Dak. St. Coll.; Ph.D., U. of Chicago; LL.D., Oberlin Coll., LL.D., Christian Coll. . . . • **John Herbert Hollomon**, (1968-70) - b. March 12, 1919, Norfolk, Va.; BS, D.Metall., MIT; (hon., Carnegie Tech, Northwestern, Mich. Tech. Univ., Univ. Akron, Worchester Pollytech.

• **Paul Frederick Sharp**, (1971-78) - b. Jan. 19, 1918, Kirksville, MO.; BA, Phillips Univ.; Ph.D., U. of Minn.; LLD, TX Christian U., Austin Coll., Drake U.; L.H.D., Buena Vista Coll., U. of Nev., Towson St. U.; Litt.D., Limestone Coll. Instr. of Minn. . . . • **William Slater Banowsky**, (1978-85) - b. Mar. 4, 1936, Abilene, TX; BA, Lipscomb Coll., MA, U. of N. Mex.; Ph.D., U. of So. Calif. . . . • **Frank Elba Horton**, (1985-88) -b. Aug. 19, 1939, Chicago, IL; BA, Western IL. U.; MS, Ph.D., Northwestern U. . . . • **David Swank**, (acting, 1988-); b. Oct. 11, 1931. Guthrie, OK; BA, Okla. A & M (OSU), LL.D., U. of Okla.

M. C.
Runyan

**Pioneer Businessman
and City Councilman
1855 — 1925**

Well-known, influential businessman, rowdy, impetuous, alcoholic and a roving lover who carried a gun. After first wife d., remarried and settled down. Had driven mail hack, been a Texas prison guard, owned several businesses in Danville, Ark. He and friend planned on making The Run but missed it. He arrived in Norman the summer of 1889 and bought some city lots and a couple of farms and started a store which became a cross roads community named for his eldest son, Denver. Left store to Denver, opened Arkansas Store with L.L. Briggs (store had a picture sign for those who couldn't read). About 1900 went into business with Denver, retired in 1919 and died in 1925. City Councilman 18 years while city gov. was formed, Andrews Park was born, and city paving begun. A Mason, he served on State School Land Comm. under Gov. Williams and twice was a delegate to Democratic Natl. conv. First wife, Ella McClure, bore: Denver, Roy (Brick), Foy, Myrtle, and one d. in infancy. Later he m. Tillie Jackson, Noble, and had: a baby that d. in infancy, and Nadine. Foy was Supt. of Elem. Edu.; Nadine taught history at Norman High School for many years - using theatrical teaching methods at times; and Myrtle, somewhat deaf and with a limp, kept house for her siblings; Denver ran his hardware store on east Main St. until the 1960's and died soon after; Brick (Roy) m. Maud Ard, a Chickasaw woman, and worked for OG&E at Davis, and died in the 1940's. M.C. has distant relatives in Lawton, Ok., eastern New Mexico, and Tenn. He is finally survived by a great great grandson, Brick Autry, who is director of a county library in West Texas.

James Huston
Felgar

**First Dean OU
College of Engineering
1874 — 1946**

b. July 27, 1874, Stuart, IA; d. July 19, 1946, Norman, OK; s. David and Margaret (Huston) F.; m. Etta (Judd), Chicago, IL, 1906, d. spring, 1947. BA (1901), Univ. of KS; BS (1905), ME (1911), Hon. D. Engring. (1929), Armour Inst. of Tech. (Armour Coll. Engring., IL. Inst. of Tech.), Chicago, IL. P.S. tchr., Newton, KS, 1893-1902; tchr., Armour Inst. Tech., 1904-05; dsgn. drftsmn, Featuerstone Fndry. & Mch., Chicago (6-mos. of 1905); instr., mech. engring, (6-mos. of 1906), Ok. A&M Coll., Stillwater, Ok; instr., mech. engr. (1906-07), prof. (1908), dean (1909-37), dean emeritus (1937-46), Coll. of Engr., Univ. of Ok. Phi Beta Kappa (KS, 1901); Sigma Tau; Tau Beta Pi; Ok. Acad. of Sci.; Soc. for Prom. of Engr. Edn.; ASMC; AAUP; NSPE; lic. Ok. engr. Lion's Club; Norman Safety Council; Norman CofC; orig. mem., OU faculty senate (1909); Who's Who in Amer.; campus eng. bldg. and adjoining street named in his honor. Elder, Presbyterian Church. Came to OU in 1906 when the 37 student School of Applied Sci. consisted of civil, electrical and mechanical engring courses, and the School of Mines had an enrollment of six; in 1909 the two schools were merged to create a Coll. of Engring and Felgar was appointed dean; after retirement in 1937, continued teaching and during WWII, at the age of 68, carried an unusually heavy teaching schedule; while at OU he graduated 2,200 young men and a few women. At the May, 1946, commencement, two months before his death, an oil portrait of the dean, painted by Washington, D.C., artist, Borris B. Gordon, was presented to OU by Coll. of Engr. alumna, and hung in Bizzell library.

Carl William
Kuwitzky

**First Secretary
Norman Chamber
of Commerce
1885 — 1970**

Carl William Kuwitzky was born December 23, 1885, in Nerbaska City, Nebraska; son of Paulinus, Jr., and Louisa Appleona (Butzerin) Kuwitzky; married Sarah Tracy (Robinson) (born December 4, 1887; died December 18, 1972 - interred in IOOF Cemetery, Norman, Oklahoma); children: Edward Vernon (born February 24, 1909), Lucy Elizabeth (McDonald) (born January 11, 1911; died May 19, 1979 - interred in IOOF Cemetery, Norman, Oklahoma). / Came to Norman in 1909, was a Praetorian Insurance agent, worked at McGinly & Berry Grocery and Nolan and Martin Hardware; drove a Koch patent medicine wagon, was first secretary of the Norman Chamber of Commerce and first secretary of the Norman Retail Credit men's Association. Mr. and Mrs. Kuwitzky lived at 311 East Hughbert Street in Norman and their telephone number was 818.

Harold Harvey Herbert

Founder OU
School of Journalism
1888 — 1980

b. Dec. 30, 1888, Freeport, Ill.; d. Oct. 1, 1980, interred Waynoka, Ok.; s. Edwin Day & Anna (Mitchell) H.; m. Mary Elizabeth (Baird), Sept. 4, 1923. Nwsp. & yrbk. ed., Freeport HS, 1907. BA (1912), U. of Ill.; MA (1918), grad. stdy. (1923-27), U. of Wis. Staff (1909-10), ed. (1911-12), *Daily Illini;* Chi Beta; co-founder (1912) of Ch. of Sigma Delta Chi; staff, city ed. (1912), *Freeport Journal;* staff (1909), *Freeport Bulletin;* tel ed. (1912-13) *Peoria Journal;* co-owner, ed. (1918), *Norman Transcript.* With OU since 1913, Founder, act. dir. (1916), dir. (1917-1945), OU School of Journalism; founder (1916) *Oklahoma Daily;* obtd. approv. for maj. journ. degrees (1926), MA (1930); founder (1916), Ok. Interscholastic Press Assn.; founder (1920), *University & Editor (Sooner State Press).* Sec.-treas., (1930-40) AAS&DJ; sec.-treas. (1930-40), v.p. (1940-41), AATJ; assoc. ed. (1924-30), *Journalism Bulletin;* pres. (1935-36), SwJC. Mem. (1915-45), pres., Publ. Bd.; pres. (1930-45), Journalism Press, Inc.; advsr. (1913-59), Sigma Delta Chi; dir. (1919-42 & 1947-56), YMCA; sec. (1921-23), pres. (1934-35 & 1946-47), OU AAUP; U. Senator (1942-58); mem., exec. comm. (1945-59), Coll. of A & S. Mem. U. of Ill., (1912), founding mem. OU ch., (1920), sec.-tres. (1920-25), pres. (1925-26), triennial council delegate (1940-61), Phi Beta Kappa. David Ross Boyd prof. (1948-59); OU Kappa Tau Alpha ch. named *H.H. Herbert Ch.* (1951); Gold Key Award (1954), Columbia Scholastic Press Assn.; Okla. Hall of Fame (1959); school named *H.H. Herbert School of Journalism* (1961); Who's Who in Am. (-1945). Presbyterian: elder (1916-1958 & 1959-78), Clerk of the Session (1917-1978).

Julia Beeler Smith

Writer/Genealogist

b. July 31, 1892, Purcell, Indian Territory; d. George Rylie and Georgia Ann (Collins) B.; m. Micah Pearce Smith on July 31, 1910, in Wellington, KS, (d. May 10, 1948); c. Capt. Jay Beeler (USN ret.); Micah Pearce, Jr.; and Naomi June (Lavine); an enrolled Chickasaw Indian (16th blood, No. 3766, Dawes Comm. rolls). **Education:** Industrial Institute & College (OCW, then USAO),Chickasha, OK; Maryville, TN; became interested in history and genealogy, at age 67 enrolled in typing, and at 68 a writing course. **Published:** *Frontier Times, Real Frontier, Prairie Lore, Sunday Oklahoman* magazine section, *Oklahoma Farm & Ranch World, Chickasaw Times;* contributed chapter to James Smallwood's *Gladly Teach,* a volume of teacher reminisces from frontier dugout days to the modern module (OU Press, 1976); researched genealogy, including Indian lineage; father established **Bank of Purcell,** first bank in Purcell, Indian Terr., later **Bank of Commerce;** he made Run of 1889 across River to est. townsite of Lexington for himself and four Kentucky partners; est. Ninnekah, I.T., (south of Chickasha) hdqrs. for ranching business, its bank, mercantile business and post office; chpt. five of Holt's bio. of Geo. Washington Carver, relates how the great Tuskegee Institute scientist (developer of over 100 uses for peanuts, including popular peanut butter) was befriended by her grandparents, John and Martha Beeler, and children, Della and Frank, in KS after he was denied admission to Highland Univ. because "We don't accept Negroes here." Mem., First Presbyterian Church.

John T. Washburn

1892 — 1970

born November 13, 1892, to Rev. Bradford A. Washburn and Sarah (Jockish) W., near Dover, on land homesteaded before Oklahoma became a state. He married Dollie (Rose), December 20, 1914. Children: T.V., Moore, Ok.; Alma Louise (Keating), Norman, Ok.; Wendell, Ft. Myers, Fl.; Dwight, Okla. City; Mary Elizabeth (Whitney), Tulsa; Kenneth George (died in infancy); and Marland Dorr (deceased). He was a prominent and long-time resident of the Lexington community for 68 years. He farmed for a number of years, was active in farm associations, the IOOF Lodge and in church work and served as county commissioner for his district which covered the southern part of Cleveland County from 1930 to 1946. In 1948 he became a state game warden and served for 12 years before retiring. He also served as a substitute mail carrier for 20 years, was secretary of the Farmers' Union Cooperative Gin Company and of the Spring Hill local of the Farmers Educational Cooperative Union. At the time of his death, he was serving as a member of the Cleveland County Equalization and Excise board. He was a charter member of the Lexington United Methodist Church and a Democrat. Dollie Washburn served as Cleveland County's Women's Democratic Party Co-Chairman in 1965-66. John Washburn passed away July 21, 1970 and Dollie died on April 9, 1979. They are both buried in the Lexington Cemetery. John and Dollie Washburn will long be remembered for the many quail dinners they served to their many friends and family through the years.

Dr. Joseph A. Rieger

Doctor of Psychiatry
1894 — 1973

b. June 17, 1894, in the Banner community; d. Feb. 3, 1973; s. Alois J. and Josephine (Amrein) R., (immigrants who were homesteading a 160-acre farm claimed during the Run of 1889, at 120th Ave., SE, and Banner Road, where they reared Joseph and four other children); m. Rose Pauline (d. 1985); c. Joseph A., Henry A., Patricia A., Sister Kathryn Marie, and Mercedes (Skaggs). As a boy he carried milk on a bicycle to Noble each morning to sell. He attended the Banner school and later, St. Joseph Catholic School. B.S. and M.S. in Pharmacy, (1914-23), M.D. (1932), Univ. of Ok. Worked at Norman P.O. while OU student, 1914-23; instructor, OU School of Pharmacy, 1923-30; student asst. in biochemistry and pharmacology while student, OU School of Medicine, 1931-32; graduate work in Psychiatry, St. Elizabeth Hospital, Wash., D.C., 1934; staff member (1934-53), asst. supt. (1948), Central State Griffith Mem. Hospital, Norman, Ok.; assistant prof., Psychiatry and Neurology, OU School of Medicine, Okla. City, 1934-53; staff mem., OU Infirmary, 1957-60. Mem., St. Joseph's Catholic Church, Knights of Columbus, Catholic Order of Foresters. Pope Pius XII made him a Knight of St. Gregory. Besides medicine, he was involved in real estate investments, enjoyed, with his children and grandchildren, performing maintenance on his rental properties, he dabbled in carpentry, farming, oil drilling and the Penny stock market; his family says his only vice was dominoes which he would play with anyone at anytime for hours. He died while shoveling gravel at the age of 78.

Garner Greeson Collums

Director of O.U. Housing
1898 — 1962

b. July 30, 1898, Clinton, Ark., interred in Memorial Park Cemetery, Ok. City; s. Daniel Boone and Dora (Greeson) C.; m. Margaret Terrell (who founded first travel service in Norman, taught in Norman schools), May 30, 1922; children: James Daniel (b. Jan. 5, 1926 at Chickasha, Ok.); grandchildren: Gary Garner (b. Sept. 22, 1950); Christi Doyle (b. June 14, 1954); James Samuel (b. June 15, 1956). **Education:** High School, Stilwell, Ok., 1915; Tulane Univ., New Orleans, La., 1915-17; BA in History, Univ. of Ok., Norman, Ok., 1919. **Special Work:** Military Gov. & Civil Affairs study, Charlottsville, Va., 1945; Japanese Customs & Social Conditions study, Northwestern Univ., Chicago, Ill., 1944-45; Organized the Hdqrts for Air Training at the Hotel Stevens, Chicago, Ill., 1942-45. **Career:** Dir. of Financial & Personnel Affairs, OCW (now USAO), Chickasha, Ok., 1919-42; military service, 1942-46; Dir. of Housing, U. of Ok., Norman, 1946-62. **Military Record:** WWI, Co. D SATC Unit, U. of Ok., 1915; WWII, adjutant, 14th A.F. Flyer Tigers, Chinese-American Composite Wing, China-Burma—India Theater, under Gens. Chiang Kai-Shek, James H. Doolittle, and Claire Lee Chennault, 1943-46; USAF Reserve, 1946-55; retired full Col. from reserve. **Honors:** U. of Ok. Commissary named in honor, 1980; 50-yr. Award, Kiwanis Club, Norman; hon. member, Phi Alpha Delta law fraternity, U. of Ok., 1919. **Affiliations:** Kappa Sigma Fraternity, 1916; Charter mem., pres. (1939), Kiwanis Club, Norman; Mason at Chickasha (1919) and Norman (1946); mem., Amer. Legion Post 54, Chickasha, 1914; mem. Amer. Legion Post 88, Norman, 1946. Methodist. Democrat.

Abe T. Johnston

Retired

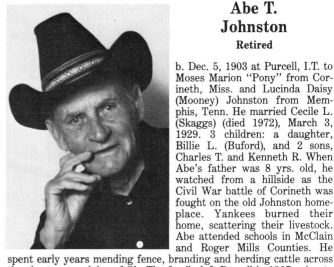

b. Dec. 5, 1903 at Purcell, I.T. to Moses Marion "Pony" from Corineth, Miss. and Lucinda Daisy (Mooney) Johnston from Memphis, Tenn. He married Cecile L. (Skaggs) (died 1972), March 3, 1929. 3 children: a daughter, Billie L. (Buford), and 2 sons, Charles T. and Kenneth R. When Abe's father was 8 yrs. old, he watched from a hillside as the Civil War battle of Corineth was fought on the old Johnston homeplace. Yankees burned their home, scattering their livestock. Abe attended schools in McClain and Roger Mills Counties. He spent early years mending fence, branding and herding cattle across the short grass plains of Ok. The family left Purcell in 1907 going to Roger Mills Co. to work on his grandfather's horse ranch. After 5 yrs. of drought, 30 families formed a wagon train bound for Scott Co., Ark. Abe rode most of the way on a burro, a gift from his grandfather. After a brief stay in Ark., they returned to Purcell, buying a farm SW of town. In the early 30's, Abe's family moved to Catoosa, Ok. where he managed the Sweetheart Inn, a club on Route 66. He later tended bar for Bob Will's brother-in-law, "Bigum House", at his club, The 33 & 66 Junction, near Tulsa. In the mid-30's, they moved to Lexington where Abe was a time keeper during construction of the Lexington-Purcell bridge across the S. Canadian River. He later worked on the Navy Gunnery School east of Lexington during World War II. At the end of the war he worked at the Physical Plant of the Univ. of Ok. At this time he was president of Painter's Local Union 1014 for 10 yrs. Abe is a Baptist and a "card carrying" Democrat. Since retirement, Abe enjoys frequent traveling and volunteers at the Hospital serving 3,740 hours presently. Abe appeared as an extra in the movie "Fast Charlie - Moonbeam Rider" starring David Carradine and Brenda Vaccaro.

Edna M. Couch

Dietition (Retired)
Amateur Historian

b. Nov. 23, 1903, Kickapoo country, east Okla. Co. Walked to 1-rm. sch., later horse-drawn van; only all rural Cons. Sch. in stat. BS in Nutrition & Dietetics, Battle Creek Coll., MI. 40-yrs., hospital dietitian, 9-yrs. site Old Ft. Supply, 4-yrs. OU Goddard Health Cntr. Granddaughter of William L. Couch, 1st prov. mayor of OKC, May 1 to Nov. 11, 1889; Couch claim to history, if any: Wm. L. Couch, b. Nov. 20, 1850, Traphill, NC.; s. Meshach and Mary Bryan C.; rode horse to 1-room log sch.; moved to KS. as teenager, 1867; m. Cynthia Gordon, Feb. 28, 1871, Olathe, KS.; homesteaded in 2-rm. box house; businessman in Wichita, KS., 1877; Winter, 1879-80, joined Payne's Ok. Colony - the "Boomers," tried 10-yrs. to get Ok. lands open; Feb., 1883, wagonmaster for 119 wagons with 600 settlers to Camp Alice, 2½-miles NW of Jones, Ok.; elected colony v.p. summer, 1883; invaded Okla. lands, arrested often, never tried. When Payne d. Nov., 1884, elected Boomer pres. He led 200 Boomers to Stillwater, Dec. 12, 1884; defied US Army and 2 Hotchkiss cannon to 27 Jan., 1885; supply wagons carrying food were turned back, starving Boomers went home. Jan., 1886, to 1889, with Sidney Clarke, went to Washington, D.C., to press for opening Ok. lands to settlers; legislation failed and then attached as rider to Indian Approp. bill and Congress approved. In 1889 the newly opened land had no law or gov. except consent of people. Jan. to Apr., 1890, Sidney Clarke and Wm. Couch, in Washington, working for territorial status. Apr. 4, 1890; shot in knee by irate homesteader; funeral was on 1st anniversary of Run. In 10-yrs. of his less-than-40-yr. life, he had accomplished more than many longlived men.

Ruth Foreman Updegraff

1904 — 1975

b. Jan. 31, 1904, Vian, I.T. (Okla.); d. Apr. 10, 1975, interred IOOF Cem., Norman, Ok.; d. George Bullett Jr. and Maggie (Waggoner) Foreman; m. Paul Updegraff (D. Mar. 16, 1959) Aug. 3, 1930. BA in Eng. (1928), MA (1940), BA Journ. (1960), U. of Ok. Teacher, Vian Schools, 1922-26; Registry Off., U. of Ok., 1928-38; exec. sec., Ok. Outdoor Council, Norman, Ok., 1960-68. Ed., Ok. Garden Clubs newsletter, 1953-63; ed., Okla. Wildlife Fed. newsletter, 1960-68; author, Flower and Garden Magazine column on gardening in SW region. Mem., Beautification Comm. of Norman C. of C., 1955-56; witness before US House of Reps. sub-committee on Fisheries and Wildlife Conservation for Ok. Outdoor Council, Inc., on Wichita Mt. Wildlife Refuge, 1956; chmn., Mayor's Comm. on Dedication of Reeves Park, 1962; chmn., Comm. to Make Norman a Bird Sanctuary, 1964. Life mem., OU Alumni Assn., 1944; life mem., Natl. Council of St. Garden Clubs, 1955; Who's Who in Ok., 1958; life mem., Ok. Garden Clubs, Inc., 1961; Who's Who of Amer. Women, 1968-69; honoree of Ruth Updegraff Park, 1978-79; Gov.'s Award from Ok. Wildlife Federation, 1975. Pres. 3 yrs., Norman Ch., AAUW, 1933-41; mem., Cleveland Co. Am. Red Cross Ch., 1940-59; mem., st. coordinator (1957-62), Theta Sigma Phi (Journ.), 1951-62; mem., Ok. Outdoor Writers, 1961-75; charter mem., Great Rivers Outdoors Writers, 1962-75; charter, life mem., Ok. Ornithological Society, 1975. Pres. (1942-43), Norman Garden Club, 1941-75; pres. (1946-48), Norman Council of Garden Clubs, 1941-75; pres. (1953-55), Ok. Garden Clubs, Inc., 1941-75; reg. dir., Natl. Council of St. Garden Clubs, 1966-67; mem. Natl. Council of St. Garden Clubs, St. Louis, Mo. Episcopalian. Democrat.

Horace Hopkins Bliss

Professor of Chemistry
1904 — 1988

Born Sept. 1, 1904, at Sandusky, Ohio, to Chester Bradley and Henrietta Maude Ittner Bliss. Died at Norman, Okla. on March 17, 1988. He received his A.B. and M.S. degrees in 1926 from the Univ. of Michigan and a Ph.D. in analytical chemistry with a minor in physical chemistry in 1931 from the Univ. of Illinois. He joined the OU faculty September, 1946. In 1957 he became the first director of the summer institutes for science teachers. Ever since his retirement in 1973 from his position as a chemistry professor at the Univ. of Oklahoma, Dr. Bliss had worked the halls and offices of the state Legislature in behalf of legislation to benefit the elderly. He was probably the person most responsible for enactment of the death-with-dignity law, the Oklahoma Natural Death Act. He continued to work until the end of his life for a bill to protect the assets of spouses whose mates are institutionalized. In addition to his lobbying activities, he was involved in many other civic and service projects. Dr. Bliss was a friend of the young also; he had played Santa Claus in the Norman Christmas parade for the last nine years. Memberships included: Am. Chemical Society, Am. Assoc. for Advancement of Science, Am. Society for Metals, National Science Teachers Assoc., Okla. Education Assoc., Okla. Science Teachers Assoc., Am. Assoc. of Retired Persons, Okla. Retired Teachers Assoc., Norman Chamber of Commerce, Norman Lions Club, and the AARP Okla. Legislative Task Force. Many people who never heard of Horace Bliss will benefit from his good works.

George Lynn Cross

University President
(Emeritus)

b. Woonsocket, S. Dak., May 12, 1905; s. George and Jemima (Dawson) C.; m. Cleo Sikkink, Oct. 28, 1926; children: Mary-Lynn, George William, Braden Riehl; B.S. S. Dak. State Coll., 1926; M.S., 1927; D.Sc., 1960; Ph.D., U. of Chicago, 1929; LLD, Oberlin Coll., 1960; LLD, Okla. Christian Coll., 1975; Instr. Botany, U. of S. Dak., 1930-34; Prof. Botany, U. of Okla., 1934-38; head Botany Dept., 1938-42; Acting Dean, Grad. Coll., 1942-44; Acting Dir. Research Inst., 1942-44; Pres U. of Okla., 1944-68; Emeritus, 1968-; Pres. Ok. Health Sc. Found., 1968-80; Chm. Amer. Exchange Bank, Norman, 1964-84; Dir. Friendly Natl. Bank, Ok. City, 1964-; Dir. Central Natl. Bank, Ok. City, 1954-; Public Panel Mem., 8th Dist., War Labor Bd., 1942; Bd. Mem., U. Presidents, William Rockwell Nelson Trust, Kansas City, 1944-68; Trustee, U. of Ok. Found., 1944-; Elector, N.Y.U. Hall of Fame for Great Americans, 1950-58; Fellow AAAS; Mem. Bd., Fed. Home Loan Bank of Topeka, 1957-68; Chmn. of Bd, 1960-68; Mem. Fed. Savings and Loan Adv. Council, 1959; Mem. Natl. Assn. of State U. Pres. (Pres., 1959-60); Inductee, Ok. Hall of Fame, 1951; Amer. Assn. Univ. of Profs.; Torrey Botany Club; Botany Soc. of Amer.; NEA; Ok. Acad. of Sc.; Natl. Geog. Soc.; Amer. Soc. of Naturalists; Ok. History Soc.; Norman C. of C.; Newcomen Soc.; Phi Beta Kappa; Phi Sigma; Alpha Phi Omega. Presbyterian. Author: Blacks in White Colleges; Presidents Can't Punt; The Univ. of Ok. and World War II; Professors, Presidents and Politicians; Letters to Bill; The Seeds of Excellence; The Univ. of Ok. Research Inst. Hm: 812 Mockingbird, Norman, OK.

Odies Lee Primrose

Funeral Director
Semi-Retired

b. February 28, 1906 at Tupelo, Mississippi, to Oscar L. and Minnie (Larkin); married 1st: Blanch (Turner), died Sept. 19, 1984; married 2nd: Rossie (Oliphant) on March 22, 1985; children: Turner Odies, Dr. Stephen P., Ben, Anna Maude (Peters), Guy Sherman, Patricia (Smith) and Vern. **Education:** earned a degree in accounting with a minor in business law from the University of Okla. 1926-30. **Personal certification:** Licensed Funeral Director, State of Oklahoma.

Business Career: Began his career as an accountant for a local funeral home. Joined George Jansing in a partnership in the depression year of 1931 and established the Jansing-Primrose Funeral Home in Norman, Okla. On August 11, 1947 he founded the present Primrose Funeral Service, 1109 N. Porter, Norman, Ok. **Activities:** former member Board of Directors of the City Nat'l. Bank and Trust Co., Norman, Ok.; Life Member Masonic Lodge and the Shriners, Norman, Ok. Awards and Honors: 50-year service pin from Oklahoma Funeral Directors Assn., 1986; deacon in First Baptist Church, Norman, Ok. 1931 to present. Professional Memberships: Honor member of Order of the Golden Rule, April 28, 1982 to present; member of National Funeral Directors Assn., member of the Oklahoma Funeral Directors Assn., 1936 to present; sixty-five year member of Demolay. **Other memberships:** Member of the Norman Lions Club. Office: 1109 North Porter, Norman, Okla., 73071. Phone 321-6000.

Cleo Sikkink Cross

Wife and Mother
O.U. Hostess for 25-Years

b. July 22, 1906, Waubay, S.D.; d. William and Lydia (Long) S.; m. George L. Cross, Oct. 28, 1926; children: Mary-Lynn, George William, Braden Riehl; BS w/honors, S.D. St. Coll., 1928; empl. U. of Chicago, supported family while husband completed Ph.D pgrm. in Bot.; res. Vermillion, S.D., 1930-34; Norman, OK, 1934-. New Sooners (Pres.), 1934-35; PTA; org. Host Family Pgrm. Intl. Students (40's); co-org. Norman Planned Parenthood Chpt.; Campfire Girls (local, regional and 7 yrs. Natl. bd., v.p. 1955, declined pres. due to duties as mother, wife and Univ. hostess); patroness Sigma Alpha Iota (music), 1949-; mem. Norman Juvenile bd.; USO, chrm., WWII, Korean C.; Presby. Trustee, Elder and pres. Untd. Presby. Women; Red Cross, dir. 5 yrs.; PEO, chrm. St. Conv., 1967; mem. Gov. Boren's Inag. Comm.; mem. Okla. Health Systems Bd., 1974-77; mem. Bd. Cleve. Co. Mental Health Agcy., 1983; fdng. mem. and Bd. of Dir. Norman Comm. Med. Lab, 1984-; mem. Sen. Boren's Okla. Foundation for Excellence. Wabunaki (pres.), 1983); Merry Makers (pres., sec.-treas.); Quest Club (sec.); Wed. Bk. Club. Woman of Year, 1951 & 1968; "Cleo Cross Day in Okla.," Apr. 11, 1968; Mortor Bd., 1968, advisor 4 yrs.; Camp Fire Natl. Luther Gulick Award, 1964; hon. mem. Altrusa Intl., 1968; Okla. delegate to Natl. PEO Supreme Conv., twice; hon. life mem. of Natl. Cong. of PTA; Cleo Cross Intl. Student Scholarship Fund establ. by Univ. Women, 1966 (with husband contributed in excess of $100,000 to finance pgrms); recd. U. of O. Distinguished Serv. Cit., 1968. Home: 812 Mockingbird Lane, Norman, OK 73071 (Data from GLC).

Paul Walter Updegraff
Attorney-At-Law
1906 — 1959

b. October 1, 1906 in Birta Yell County, Arkansas; d. March 16, 1959, interred in IOOF Cemetery, Norman, Okla.; s. Walter Everett and Ella (Lawhon) U.; m. Ruth Foreman, August 3, 1930; children: Elizabeth (Mrs. Jerry Loeffelholz, b. Jan. 28, 1940), and Paul Walter, Jr. (b. Jan. 12, 1944). **Education:** Vinita High School, Vinita, Okla., graduated, 1925; pre-law, Oklahoma A&M (now Okla. State University), Stillwater, Okla., 1925-27; LLB, University of Ok., Norman, Ok., 1927-30. **Career:** Cleveland Co. Attorney, Norman, Ok., 1933-34; Attorney-At-Law, Norman, Ok., 1935-59. **Creative Works:** Legal articles in The American Judicature Soc. Magazine, Okla. Bar Journal and Case and Comment; assoc. ed., NACAA Law Journal. **Activities:** pres. (1940), Norman Lions Club, 1933-59; mem., Norman Chamber of Commerce, 1936-59; chrmn. (1940-44), Cleveland Co. Chapter, Am. Red Cross, 1940-59; commander (1947-48), Am. Legion Post 88, Norman, Ok., 1946-59; chrmn. (1956-57), secy. (1946-56), Norman Municipal Hospital Bd., 1946-47; candidate for Lieut. Governor, State of Ok. as an Independent, 1958. **Military Record:** Lt. (j.g.), U.S. Navy, American, European, and Asiatic Theaters with over 80,000 miles of active duty, Feb., 1944-46. **Honors:** Who's Who in America. **Professional Memberships:** vice pres. (1955), Ok. Bar Assn., 1930-1959; mem., House of Delegates (1955-56), American Bar Assn., 1930-59; mem., American Judicature Soc.; Inter-American Bar Assn.; mem., Negligence and Compensation Lawyers. **Clubs:** Phi Delta Phi, Univ. of Ok. Baptist. Democrat.

Savoie Lottinville
O. U. Regents
Prof. (Emeritus) of History

b. Nov. 17, 1906, Hagerman, Ida.; s. Walter J. & Mary E. (Igoe) L.; m. (1st) Rita Higgins, Jun. 15, 1933 (dec. May 22, 1955), c. Marie Therese (Livesay) & Elinor; m. (2nd) Helene Collins (Carpenter), Dec. 18, 1957 (dec. Jun. 28, 1985). / BA, U. of Ok., 1929; BA (1932), MA (1939), Oxford U. / Rep., *O.C. Times,* 1932-33; asst. ed. (1933-35), bus. mgr. (1935-38), dir. (1938-67), U. of Ok. Press; O.U. Regents history prof., 1967. / Sec. (1945-47), v.p. 1947-49), pres. (1949-51), Assn. Am. U. Presses; pres. O.U. Phi Beta Kappa, 1941-42; dir., Econs. Club of Ok., 1968-71; mem., Ok. Advg. Council (1966-67), chrmn. (1963-65), to U.S. Civ. Rights Comm.; advisor (1966-67), fellowships juror (1967), NEH; cons., Natl. Park Serv., 1969-; liason estbl. Norman USN bases, 1942-43; Rockefeller & Ford Founds.; recd. orig. offer, 1st chmn. (1946-48), DeGolyer Col., *History of Sc. & Tech.* / Ed., *Life of Geo. Bent;* co-ed., *A Soldier in the West: Letters of Theodore Talbot;* ed., Duke of Wurttemberg's *Travels in N. Am., 1822-24;* ed., Thomas Nuttall's *A Journ. of Travels into the Ark. Terr. During 1819;* author, *The Rhetoric of History;* contbr., *Essays in Honor of Sir Herbert Butterfield; Integration of the Humanities and the Soc. Scs.;* ed., *Civilization of Am. Indian* series, 1938-67; founder, ed. of *Am. Exploration and Travel* series, 1939-67, *Centers of Civilization* series, 1959-67 and *Western Frontier Library* series, 1953-67. Rhodes Scholar, 1929-32; Phi Beta Kappa, Okla. Hall of Fame; O.U. Disting. Serv. Cit.; D.Litt., SMU, 1952; D. Hum., Coe Col., 1970; Heros Box Klub, Berlin, Germany, 1930-31; Half-Blue Boxing, Oxford U., 1930-31; O.U. Boxing coach, 1934-37.

Joseph Richard Taylor
Sculptor, Rancher, Educator
(Retired)

b. Feb. 1, 1907, Wilburton, Wash.; s. Moses Richard and Lulu Adeline (Killman) T.; m. Elsie Rapier (b. May 2, 1908) on Apr. 19, 1930. B.F.A. (1931), M.F.A. (1932), Univ. of Wash. Prof. of sculpture, School of Art, Univ. of Okla., 1932-69; David Ross Boyd prof., 1963-69; retired from OU, 1969; owns Joe Taylor Ranch, Alex, Ok. Exhibits in all leading art galleries and museums in US, 1932-88; sculptor of Dr. W.B. Bizzell monument, south of OU library, 1952; more than 500 sculptures in major museums, galleries, public and private collections in U.S.; numerous awards; architectural sculptures on countless buildings in the Southwest, including Jim Thorpe bldg., Capitol Complex, Okla. City; DeGolyer collection, bronze screen on 3rd fl., OU Library; numerous bronze plaquets; etc. Taught camouflage technique at OU to US Army personnel (WWII), McDowell scholarship, McDowell Music club, 1940; Phi Beta Kappa; first Governor's award, distinguished lifetime service in the arts, 1978; OU's highest honor, Distinguished Service Citation, 1977; two time winner, Best of Show award, Okla. Sculptors Society, 1983; Okla. Hall of Fame, 1960. Mem., dir., Okla. Sculpture Society, 1986-87; Okla. Artist's Assn.; Who's Who in American Art; Who's Who in the South and Southwest; Who's Who in America, 1960. 12-yr. mem., twice pres., Lions Int., Norman, Ok.; Wabunaki Club; pres., Reviewer's Club; Who's Who in Univ. and Colleges; Democrat, Baptist. Home: 701 W. Brooks, Norman, OK 73069. Phone: 329-1247.

James O'Leary Hood
Physician
1907 — 1961

b. Mar. 9, 1907; d. May 5, 1961; s. James Berry and Maybelle (Paschall) H.; m. Bess Beasley, Sept. 29, 1939; c. James O'Leary, Robert Sidney. B.S. in med., 1929, M.D. 1931, OU. **Career:** Pvt. pract., Norman, 1931-38; co. health off., 1938-40; dir., OU Stu. Health, 1946-60; assoc. prof., Pub. Health, OU, 1950-61; dir., OU Sch. Pub. Health, 1952-55; ch. staff, Ellison Infirm., 1946-60; Norman Hosp. staff, ch. of staff, 1946-47; Mayor of Norman, 1935-38; **Military:** Joined 45th N.G. Inf. Div., 1923; comm. Med. Corps, 1936. Active duty Med. Corps, U.S. Army, 1940-46; 50-52. Overseas WWII (Afr. & Eur.) 45th Inf. Div., regtl. surgeon, 179th Inf.; Div. Artillery, 1943-45; Korean Crisis, 45th Div. surg., 1950-51; cmdr. off. 211th Med. Bat. (Germany) 1951-52; disch. Aug. 1952, Lt. Col. Med. Corps, N.G.; **Awards:** Bronze Star, Purple Heart (both w/Oak Leaf Clusters); Com. Med. badge; EAME medal (6 bronze stars and arrowhead for inv. of Sic.); Def. Serv. medal, Arm. Forces Res. medal. **Memberships:** Am., So., Ok. and Cl. Co. Med. Assns.; Am and Ok. Pub. Health Assns; Am. and Ok. Acad. of Gen'l Practice; Am. Student Health Assn.; Am. Assn. Adv. Sc.; Assn. Mil. Surgeons; 45th Inf. Div. Assn.; 40 & 8 Soc.; Am. Legion; hon. cmdr. OU Thos. C. Reynolds Am. Leg. Post 303; OU & Sch. of Med. Alumni Assns.; Dad's Assn.; chtr. mem., Ok. Med. Research Found., mem. bd. dir. Cl. Co. Red Cross; mem. at lge. Last Frontier Council, Nat'l Council, Sooner Dist. chrmn., Boy Scouts of Am.; council mem., Camp Fire Girls; mem., chrmn., health comm., PTA, 1959-60; Boy's State; adv., Alpha Phi Omega; U. Fund; C. of C., mem. Dem. Central Comm. (chrmn., Clev. Co.) 1934-38; del. 1936 Dem. nat'l. conv.) Who's Who in So. & SW, Phi Chi med. frat. Kiwanis. Mason. Methodist.

Horace Brightberry Brown

College Dean / Professor

b. Aug. 19, 1908, Holly Springs, MS.; m. Dorothy B., Dec. 26, 1932; s. Dr. H. Jack Brown. **Edn.**: BSC, U. of MS., 1931; MBA (1932), Ph.D. (1941), Northwestern U. **Career**: dean, OU Coll. of Bus. Adm., 1949-73; dean, (1941-49), prof. (1932-41), U. of Ms.; visiting prof., Harvard U., 1955-56. **Works**: article of MS. Bus. Bull., 1941-49; book reviews, So. Econ. Jour. and Journ. of Mktg.; Okla. Bus. Bull. **Activities**: const., Natl. Cotton Council of Am.; const., Contr. Gen. of U.S. on Training & Upgrading of Accts. for Gen. Accounting Off., 1955-62; dir., Veterans Edn., U. of MS., 1944-45; chrmn., Price Panel, Lafayette, Co. Price & Rationing Bd.; dir., v.p., C. of C., Oxford, MS., 1942-46. **Honors**: Dean Emer. & Regents Prof. of Bus. Adm., OU Coll. of Bus. Adm., 1973-79; natl. v.p., Beta Gamma Sigma, 1962; Fellowship in Econ., U. of MS., 1930-31; Fellowship in Mktg., Northwestern U., 1931-32; Dist. Serv. Award, U. of MS., 1969; Dow Jones Dist. Serv. Cit., 1971; Who's Who in Am.; Who's Who in Am. Coll. & U. Adm.; Who's Who in the So. & SW.; Who's Who in Am. Edn.; Intern. Who's Who; Who Know & What; Who's Imp. in Edn.; Am. Men and Women in Sc.; Am. Council of Learned Socs.; Directory of Am. Scholars; Leaders in Edn.; Directory of Educational Specialists; Personalities of the So.; Leadership Index; Who's Who in Ok. **Prof. Memberships**: Am. Assn. of Collegiate Schools of Bus., 1955-56; pres., Natl. Council of Profl. Edn. & Bus., 1956-57; Am. Mktg. Assn., Am. Econ. Assn.; dir., Norman Savings & Loan; dir. Friendly Nat'l Bank, Ok. City; mem. Advisory Bd., W. Div. of Sooner Fed. Savings & Loan Assn.; mem., Econ. Club of O.; pres., Rotary Club. **Office**: 307 W. Brooks, Norman, OK.

John Womack

U.S. Postal Employee
Research Historian
1911 — 1987

b. Dec. 22, 1911, Byars, Okla.; s. David B. and Annie (Runyan) W.; d. May 2, 1987, int. in St. Joseph's Cem., Norman, Okla.; m. Agnes Lucille (Schader), Nov. 27, 1935 (d. Jan. 21, 1978); c. John Jr., Gary D., Gayle A. (Smouse), Patricia S. (Collins), Shirley J. (Olivarri). Gr. Norman HS, 1929. WWII: Av. Ordinanceman, 3rd Cl., US Navy, Norman, Ok., Apr. 17, 1944-Oct. 27, 1945. Author: numerous research projects, incl.: *Norman, An Early History, 1929–1900*, 1976; *Cleveland County Place Names*, 1977 (rev. 1981); *Franklin, Oklahoma Territory*, 1978; *1890 Norman, OK., Census*, 1981; *1890 Lexington, OK., Census*, 1982; *Cleveland County, OK., Historical Highlights*, 1982, and numerous other articles in *The Norman Transcript* and *The Warchief* of the Indian Terr. Posse of Ok. Westerners. Outstanding Suggestor Award, USPO (ret. June 30, 1973); Parade Marshall, '89er Celebration, Norman, Ok., Apr. 20, 1985. Mem., Indian Territory Posse of Oklahoma Westerners, Cleveland Co. Historical Soc., Okla. State Historical Soc. A self-described "History Nut"; regarded as top authority on Cleveland County history; his intellectual curiosity lead him to doubt most word-of-mouth, and much printed, information until he personally researched it, but believed there is a bit of truth in all yarns; convinced U.S. Dept. of Interior to add eight County place names to *The Oklahoma Gazeteer*, incl. "Ten Mile Flat;" his papers, if released to a research library, will be the reliable sorce of knowledge about Cleveland County for future historians.

Roy Floyd Valouch

Electrical
Contractor
1912 — 1986

born August 21, 1912, at Norman, Oklahoma, to John Norbet and Mary (Hartman) Valouch; married Evelyn (Greene) on December 24, 1935. children: Marilyn J. (Lassetter), Gloria A. (Moore), Beverly K. (Millstead) and Nancy C. (Peed). / Graduate of Norman high school. / Held one of the first electrical contractor's licenses granted in Norman; learned trade from Bob Palmer. / Served apprenticeship with Bob Palmer, Norman, Okla., 1938-44; electrician with Sheffield Steel, Houston, Texas, 1944-45; journeyman electrician, Bob Palmer Electric, Norman, Oklahoma, 1945-52; owner, Roy Valouch Electric Company, Norman, Oklahoma, 1938-86. / Deacon, First Baptist church, Norman, Oklahoma; member of Josh Lee Sunday school class at First Baptist church, Norman, Oklahoma. / Member of Kiwanis club of Norman. Roy Valouch passed away on June 24, 1986. Democrat. Baptist. Office: 113 West Gray, Norman, Oklahoma 73069. Phone 321-6267.

Ida Sloan Snyder

Communications
1913 — 1988

b. July 7, 1913, Wichita, KS, to Alfred and Caroline (Dohl) S.; d. Oct. 18, 1988. m. Leonard M. Snyder (d. June 18, 1984) on Oct. 1, 1955, at Norman, OK. Interested in journ. while ed. of NHS student paper; torn between careers in education and journ. until father, the late Alfred Sloan, cir. mgr. & part-owner, *The Norman Transcript*, put her to work answering circulation complaints; proximity led the city ed., the late Roscoe Cate, to ask her to cover and report a story he ran with her byline on front page; enrolled in journ. at OU; earned BA degree in 1935. Reporter, (shared the popular "Press Box" column duties), part-time city ed., *The Transcript*, (1934-53); probably best-known woman in city during these yrs. due to her uncanny ability to recognize and report volumes of local news. (Took leave, summer 1944, to be reporter/researcher, *Newsweek Magazine*). Staff writer, public relations assoc. (1953-70), communications director (1970-78), retired editor-writer (1978-79), Natl. YWCA; Who's Who in Public Relations (intern. ed.), 1976. Mem., P.R. Soc. of Amer.; mem., (pres. NYC ch., 1960-62), Women in Communications (formerly Theta Sigma Phi), 1935-; mem., Community Agencies Public Relations Assn., NYC. Retired, 1978. Mem., Corresponding Secy., Cleveland Co. Hist. Soc.; Firehouse Art Ctr.; Jacobson Found.; secy. (1988-89), Cleveland Co. Dem. Women; rep., Galaxy of Norman Writers on NAHC Roundtable. Home: 203 S. Univ. Blvd., since 1981 (a home she and her late husband, Leonard, purchased in 1967 from Mrs. A. B. Adams to become third owners; built in 1911 by Joseph C. Minteer; remodeled by him, 1923, and was the first Norman home converted to apt. living.

Micah Pearce Smith Jr.

Advertising Agency Executive
(Retired)

b. Nov. 13, 1916, Norman, Okla.; s. Micah Pearce and Julia Maud (Beeler) S.; m. Viola Sarajane Hatfield, June 1, 1946 (d. Apr. 10, 1986); children: Julia Annette (Dennis), Carla Marie (Taylor). **Education:** journalism, Univ. of Okla., 1936-41. **Military record:** Aviation Cadets, 1942. **Career history:** adv. staffs, *Ponca City News, Daily Oklahoman & Times, Muskogee Daily Phoenix & Times Democrat, Clinton Daily News,* 1941-47; dir. advt., *Clinton Daily News,* 1947-53; dir., advt., *Great Bend* (Kans.) *Daily Tribune,* 1953-55; ptnr., ex. v.p., mgr., Industrial Printing Corp., Okla. City, Ok., 1956-57; dir., advt., *Daily Ardmoreite,* Ardmore, Ok., 1958; dir. advt., *Norman Transcript,* Norman, Ok., 1959-60; editor/pub., *North Star,* Okla. City, Ok., 1961; acct. exec., J.F. Gelders, Co. Advt. Agency, Okla. City, Ok., 1962-73; ptnr, exec. v.p., Gelders, Holderby & Smith, Inc., AAAA advt. agy., Okla. City, Ok., 1963-73; founder/ed., *The Chickasaw Times,* tribal newspaper, Norman, Ok., 1970-78; state civil defense coordinator, Okla. City, Ok., 1972-73; Okla. fuels allocation officer during shortage, 1973-80; chrm., pres., mgr., Media Marketing Assocs., Inc., advt. agy., Okla. City, Ok., 1981-. **Author:** semi-monthly newspaper column, *Tele-Views,* 1985-; editor/co-author *Genealogy and Autobiography of Micah P. Smith, Sr., and Others,* 1987. **Honors:** sec. Chickasaw Advisory Council, Ada, Ok., 1971-79; coordinator Oklahoma gubernatorial campaign, 1969-70; pres., adv. mgrs., Okla. Press Assn., 1953; Who's Who in the S. & SW (and Mexico), 1982-; Who's Who in the World, 1985-; upcoming Who's Who in Adv. Presbyterian (elder, trustee, deacon). Home: 1525 Melrose, Norman, Ok. 73069. Ph. 321-9632.

Viola Hatfield Smith

Teacher
1917 — 1986

b. Aug. 3, 1917, d. Apr. 10, 1986, interred Norman; d. Carl Mahlon and Georgia Viola (Cecil) H.; M. d. after her birth, reared by Nettie (Thompson) H.; m. Micah P. Smith, Jr., Okla. City, OK., June 1, 1946; c. Julia Annette (Dennis), Carla Marie (Taylor). **Education:** Classen HS; Ok. City Univ.; Univ. of Calif. at L.A.; B.A., Eng. and Gov. majors, Univ. of Ok., 1938. **Career:** Taught at Wanette and Duncan, Ok.; WWII staff of Comm. Office, U.S. Navy, New Orleans, La.; returned to Ok. City; married; residences in Muskogee, Clinton and Ardmore, Ok., Great Bend, Ks. before settling in Norman in 1959; returned to HS teaching; initiatied first gov. classes at Norman HS (srs. only); teacher of year; mem., chmn., HS administrative comms.; instrumental in having students incl. in annual OU Little United Nations; ret. due to rheumatoid arthritis after 20 yrs.; invited to appear before Ok. House of Reps., suprised by Lt. Gov. Spencer Bernard, sub. for Gov. Geo. Nigh, reading proclamation declaring July 2, 1985, "Viola Smith Day in Ok.," stating, in part: "Sen. Lee Cate, Reps. Carolyn Thompson, Nancy Virtue and Cal Hobson have all benefitted from her tremendous dedication, knowledge and talents in the classroom;" family establ. annual "Viola Hatfield Smith Memorial Scholarships" at OU Foundation for funding NHS grads. excelling in gov. (1987 awardee: Matthew Alan Gray; 1988: Thaddeus Mitchell Burr). **Affiliations:** Kappa Tau at OCU, Gamma Phi Beta at OU; Chpt. DZ of P.E.O.; and Delta Kappa Gamma. Presbyterian.

Edward Finley Montgomery

Journalist
Editorial Writer

b. Feb. 6, 1918 at Greenfield, Mo.; s. Edward Philip and Marie Alberta (Finley) M.; m. Constance Ainley, Oct. 31, 1942; c. John Edward (dec.), and Karen Sue (Harpole). B.A. in Journalism, Univ. of Mo., Columbia, Mo., 1938-40; assocs. degree, Muskogee Junior College, Muskogee, Okla., 1936-38. Until his retirement from the *Daily Oklahoman,* his byline stories appeared almost daily on the front page, reporting news from the state capitol; a respected journalist whose professionalism is reflected in the impartiality with which he reported; presently editorial writer for *The Norman Transcript.* Assoc. editor, *Shelby County Herald,* Shelbyville, Mo., 1940-41; news editor, *Bartlesville Enterprise,* Bartlesville, Okla., 1946-48; news editor, *Clinton Daily News,* Clinton, Okla., 1948-50; reporter and city editor, *Daily Oklahoman & Times,* Okla. City, Okla., 1950-64, 1967-81; reporter, State Capitol News Bureau, Okla. City, Okla., 1981-85; news editor, columnist, editorial writer, *Norman Transcript,* 1964-67, 1985-. Author of fiction stories in *The Saturday Evening Post, Argosy, Field & Stream,* western and air war magazines. First Lieut., U.S. Army Air Force, in U.S. and Southwest Pacific, July 1941-Sept. 1945. Inducted into the Society of Professional Journalists' Oklahoma Journalism Hall of Fame, 1986; mem., Sigma Delta Chi. Mem., author of annual show scripts, Oklahoma Gridiron Club. Democrat. Disciples of Christ. Office: The Norman Transcript, 215 East Comanche, Norman, Okla. 73070. Phone 321-1800. Home: 1525 Franklin Drive, Norman, Okla. 73072. Phone: 321-4297.

Wayne Stewart Wallace

Insurance Executive
1919 — 1977

b. Jan. 1, 1919, Cordell, OK., to J.M. and Allie B. (Stewart) W.; d. Apr. 21, 1977; m. Mary Christine (Dillingham) Aug. 16, 1940; c. David B. / HS: Stillwater, all-conf. ftbl. plyr.; mem., bsktbl. & track teams; DeMolay; band; Natl. Honor Soc.; Boys' Quartet; pres., Boys' Glee Club; 1936. / BS & MS, Ok. A&M (OSU); wrk. toward Ph.D., Univ. of Ok.; pres., XI MU (pre-law); Sigma Alpha Epsilon; led first effort to chng. A&M to OSU. / Taught, coahced, Morrison, Ok., Higgins, TX.; history, govern., debate coach, Clinton, Ok. / WWII: decorated combat sgt., Leyte and Okinawa campaigns; spec. agnt., Political Intelligence, Korean Occup. / Mem., Ok. House of Reps., 1948-52; chmn., Ways & Means commn. and Appropriations & Budget sub-commn.; Dem. pres. elector, 1956; mem., Gov. JHE's Commn. on Higher Edu.; aging consultant, HEW. / Founder, chmn., pres. of following: Exchange Natl. Bank, Moore, Ok., Univ. Natl. Life (merged with USLIFE on NYSE), Professional Investor's Life, Tulsa, Ok., Natl. Interstate Life, Norman, Ok., Farmer's & Ranchers Life (Ok. Farmer's Union), and Life Corp. of Amer. (Mark Twain Life); commissioned to reorganize Seaboard Life Ins., Miami, Fla.; at age 39 served concurrently as pres., Seaboard Life, Miami, Fla., Univ. Natl. Life, Norman, Ok., and Jefferson Davis Life, Biloxi, MS.; chmn., pres., Mid-West Creamery Co., (Farm Fresh, Inc.), Ponca City, Ok.; ed. & publ., Midwest City Monitor, Del City News and Ok. City World. / Shriner; 32nd degree Mason; VFW; OU & OSU Alumni Assns.; Ok. Press Assn.; Twin Lakes Golf & Country club; First Christian Church, Norman, Ok. / Past Memberships: Rotary; Jaycees; Elks; and Norman C. of C.

Henry Clifton Easterling
Dentist

b. June 20, 1920, Stigler, Okla.; s. Carl Lloyd and Pearle Belle (Hall) E.; m. Wilma (McGuire), June 24, 1944; children: Susan Alice (Herron), Henry Clifton II; BS Pharmacy, 1942, Univ. of Okla.; DDS, Baylor College of Dentistry, Dallas, Texas, 1945; Registered Pharmacist, Okla. and Texas; Registered Dentist, Okla. and Texas; staff, Norman Regional Hospital, Norman, Okla.; director, Delta Dental Plan; Dentist in USNR (lt.jg.), USN Hospital, Corona, CA., 1945-46 and (lt.dc.), USAF Hospital, Fairbanks, Alaska, 1952-54; Retired from Navy at Lt.Cmdr. rank 1966; Dentist at Norman, Ok., 1946-52 and 1954-. **Activities:** advisory committee, Oscar Rose School of Dental Hygiene, Midwest City, Ok., 1970; advisory committee Univ. of Ok. College of Dental Hygiene, Okla. City, Ok., 1970; Norman Rose Society (pres.), Norman, Ok., 1962 & 1974; Consulting Rosarian, American Rose Society. **Honors:** outstanding graduating senior in Dentistry for Children, Amer. Society of Dentistry for Children, 1945; outstanding Delta Chi Alumnus, 1957; Meritorious Service Award, Delta Chi, 1987; Who's Who in the South and Southwest, 1963-64 & 1973-74. **Memberships:** Amer. Dental Assn., 1945-; Ok. Dental Assoc., 1946-; Amer. Society of Dentistry for Children, 1945-; Academy of General Dentistry, 1978-; Pierre Fauchard Academy, 1946-. Democrat. Methodist. **Affiliations:** Lions Club, Norman, Ok.; 1952; Kappa Psi (Pres.), Univ. of Ok., 1942; Delta Chi, Univ. of Ok., 1941-42; Psi Omega dental fraternity, Baylor Univ., Dallas, Tx., 1942-45; Petroleum Club, Okla. City, Ok. Ofc: 230 E Alameda, Norman, OK 73069, Ph. 321-4060; Hm: 2644 Smoking Oak Rd., Norman, OK 73072, Ph. 321-4326.

Arrell Morgan Gibson
Historian
1921 — 1987

b. Pleasanton, KS., Oct. 1, 1921; d. Nov. 30, 1987; s. Arrell Morgan and Vina Lorene (Davis) G.; m. 1st., Dorothy (Deitz), Dec. 24, 1942, div. 1971; c. Dr. Patricia, Kathleen (Ash), Michael Morgan; m. 2nd., Shirley Black, Nov. 1971, div. Nov. 1972; m. 3rd., Rosemary (Phillips-Newell), July 22, 1973. AB, Mo. So. St. Coll., 1946; BA (1947), MA (1948), Ph.D. (1954), OU; L.H.D., Coll. of ID., 1981; Hon. Disting. Prof., So. China Norm. U., Guangzhou, PRChina; Geo. L. Cross Prof. (1972-), Prof. Hist. (1966-72), Chmn. Hist. Dept. (1970-72), Asst. Prof. (1957-61), OU; H. Curator, Stovall Mus., 1960-87; prof., Phillips U. (1949-57), v. prof. U. of NM. (1975); ASU (1973-74); Goldwater Disting. Prof. of Disting. Inst's., ASU, 1986; grad. cons. & lectr., U. of So. China. Many artls., 26 bks. incl.: *A History of Five Centuries*, 1965 & 1981; *The American Indian: Prehistory to Present*, 1980; *The West in the Life of the Nation*, 1976; *The Chickasaws* (2nd in Pulitzer), 1971; *The Santa Fe & Taos Colonies: Age of the Mses;* ed. of *The Autobiography of E. E. Dale Edward -1900-1942*, 1983; *Where the West Wind Blows*, 1984. Civic lectr. BSA ldr. USN, 1942-45. Who's Who in Amer., 1970-; DSC, OU, 1982; OK Hall of Fame, 1985; Disting. Alum. Award, MO. So. St. Coll., 1972; Award of Merit, Amer. Assn. for St. & Local History, 1974; Honoree for Lit. Contbn., Ok. Inst. of Litts., 1982; 1st Achmnt. Award, Am. Indians Histns. Assn., 1983. Prog. chmn., secy, v.p., pres-elect, 1989, W. Hist. Assn.; dir., Ok. Hist. Soc.; Phi Beta Kappa; mem. adv. comm., Natl. Cowboy Hall of Fame and MS. Choctaw Cultural Center, Phi Alpha Theta; mem., pres. (1987), Yr. of the Book. Mem., sheriff, The Westerners, O.C.; Blue Cord; hon. life mem., Ok. Fedn. of Writers; W. Writers of Amer. Democrat. Christian (onetime lay minister).

Patricia Toothaker Donahue
Psychiatric Social Worker

b. September 6, 1922 at Alamo, Texas, d. Henry Tull and Minnie Elizabeth (Scott) Toothaker; m. Hayden Donahue, (State Director of Mental Health, 1952-59, 1970-78), February 22, 1947. Children: Erin Mathews, Kerry Eckhardt, and Patty Crocker. **Education:** Pharr-San Juan-Alamo High School, Pharr, Texas, 1939-1942; Bachelor of Arts, University of Oklahoma, Norman, Okla., 1973-1977; Master of Social Work, University of Oklahoma, 1977-1978. **Certification:** licensed by State of Oklahoma with specialty in Clinical Social Work. Career: Psychiatric Social Worker, Central Oklahoma Community Mental Health Center, Norman, Okla., 1979-present; private practice (limited basis). **Professional Memberships:** National Association of Social Work, 1978-; vice president, Advisory Council, Cleveland County Aging Services, 1987-; treasurer, Oklahoma Society for Clinical Social Workers, 1986-1987; **Participant Affiliations:** VII World Congress of Mental Health, Vienna, Austria, July 11-16, 1983; member: Cleveland County Mental Health Association; National Alliance for the Mentally Ill; president, Cleveland County Medical Auxiliary, 1970-71; sustaining member, Junior League of Norman, Inc. 1976-; member, past pres., Reviewer's Club, 1965-; member McFarlin Memorial United Methodist Church, 1962-; Office: Central Okla. Community Mental Health Center, 909 Alameda, P.O. Box 400, Norman, Oklahoma, Phone: 360-5100.

Richard Carter Luttrell
Executive V.P.
Hospital Casualty Co.

b. Aug. 6, 1924, Norman, Okla.; s. Robert T. and Gladys (Simpson) L.; m. Doris (Carter), on Jan. 27, 1951; c. Richard Carter, Jr. (b. June 18, 1956) and Anne (Garrett) (b. May 29, 1960). Graduate, Central H.S., Muskogee, Okla., 1946; BBA, Baylor University, Waco, Texas, 1946. Business manager, Hillcrest Hospital, Waco, Texas, 1950-55; administrator, Norman Regional Hospital, Norman, Okla. 1955-85; executive vice president, Hospital Casualty Co., Okla. City, Okla. 1985-. President, Norman Civic Improvement Association, 1969; member, American Hospital Association Council on Government Relations, 1964-65; member, Medical Advisory Board of Okla. Department of Public Welfare, 1963-82; director, Norman Chamber of Commerce 1971-77; chairman, Board of Deacons and Board of Trustees, First Baptist Church, Norman, Okla; Distinguished Service Award (Cleveland Rogers Distinguished Service Award), Okla. Hospital Association, 1971; President, Okla. Hospital Association, 1963; House of Delegates, American Hospital Association, 1966-76; President, Okla. Hospital Council, 1982-83; American College of Hospital Administrators; Blue Cross Assn. Provider Appeal Panel, 1970-74; trustee, Blue Cross/Blue Shield of Okla., 1966-72, 1974-83; trustee, American Hospital Assn. Advisory Bd.; chmn., Region 7, American Hospital Assn., 1977-80. Member, Norman Rotary Club, 1953-85; mem. Norman Sooner Rotary Club, 1988-. Staff sgt., US Army Airborne Engineers, Burma theater, 1943-46. Office: 505 Lincoln Blvd., Okla. City, OK 73216; Phone: 524-0503, ext. 210.

Robert J. Buford

Publisher

Born February 7, 1929, Durant, Okla.; son of Paul N. and Rubye (Simpson) B.; married Billie Louise Johnston, January 28, 1950; children, Jennifer and Christopher. graduated Central High School, Okla. City, 1947; student University of Oklahoma, Norman, 1947-50; employed in production department University of Oklahoma Press, Norman, 1947-1951; production manager *Yukon Sun,* Yukon, Okla., 1951-52; founder, publisher, editor, *The Welch American,* Welch, Okla., 1952-59; production manager, *Oklahoma Livestock News,* Okla. City, Okla., 1959-60; v.p., asst. mgr. The Transcript Press, Norman, Okla., 1960-70; co-founder, president, Executive Type, Inc., Oklahoma City, 1970-86; dr. adv., *Guffey's Executive Journal,* Okla. City, 1970-86; co-founder Type Traditional, Norman, Okla. 1986-; Publisher: *Shades of Gray; Noble County History; Cleveland County, Pride of the Promised Land; Jack Love, Eighty-Niner; Mulhall, Oklahoma, 100 Yesteryears; 1889 etc., A Collector's Cookbook.* Memberships include The Oklahoma Press Association, Oklahoma City Advertising Club, Toastmaster's International (Norman, Okla.); Lion's Club (Norman, Okla.), Junior Chamber of Commerce (Miami & Norman, Okla.), Printing Industry Association of Oklahoma and Southwest Missouri, and Associates of Western History Collections, Westerners International. Methodist. Home address: 338 Collier Drive, Norman, Oklahoma. Office: 457 West Gray, Norman, Oklahoma. Phone: 366-8362.

Bonnie Lue Speer

Freelance Writer and Teacher

born March 2, 1929, at Gage, Okla.; daughter of John E. and Vera A. (Stoner) Stahlman; married Jess Speer, Oct. 26, 1965; children Connie Lue Nelson (Wilson); Donna Mae Nelson (Atnip); Deborah Kay Nelson; Cheryl Ann Nelson (Hanlon). Graduate of Gage (Okla.) High School, 1946; B.A. (1975), M.A. (1976) in Journalism, Univ. of Okla., Norman, Okla. Instructor at following: Moore-Norman Vo-Tech, Norman, Okla. 1984-; Independent Studies Dept., Univ. of Okla. Norman, Okla 1978-; Mid-America Vo-Tech, Wayne, Okla., 1982-84; Univ. of Okla., Norman, Okla., 1978. Author of *Errat's Garden,* a picture book; *Norman United Way,* a documentary film, 1976; *Heck Thomas, My Papa,* a biography, 1988, *Pride of the Promised Land,* a history of Cleveland County, 1988; *Moments in Oklahoma History, a book of trivia,* 1988; and over 300 nonfiction articles for various publications, 1961-. Member, centennial committee, Chamber of Commerce, Norman, Okla., 1986-. Foundation scholarship (1973), Honor Roll (Spring 1975), Kappa Tau Alpha (1976), Univ. of Okla. Vice pres. (1981), pres. (1982-83), member Norman Galaxy of Writers, 1976 to present; member, founder and 1st pres. (1984), Central Okla. Romance Writers, 1984-; member, Romance Writer's of America, 1982-; member, Okla. Writer's Federation, 1976-. Member South Canadian Radio Society, 1980; VFW Auxiliary, 1984-; Cleveland County Historical Society, 1988. Republican. Southern Baptist. Home: 1400 Melrose Drive, Norman, Okla. 73069. Phone: 321-7302.

Charles W. Bert

Benjamin H. Perkinson Prof. (Chair) of Engineering

b. Nov. 11, 1929, Chambersburg, Pa.; s. Charles W. and Gladys A. (Raff) B.; m. Charlotte (Davis), Jun. 29, 1957; children: Charles and David. B.S. in M.E., Pa. St. U., Univ. Park, Pa., 1951, M.S.M.E., 1956; Ph.D. in Engr. Mechs., Oh. St. U., Columbus, Oh., 1961. Registered Prof. Engr., Okla. and Pa. Jr. Design Engr., Am. Flexible Coupling Co., St. Coll., Pa., 1951-52; Proj. Off., US Air Force, Eglin AFB, Fl., 1952-54; Aero. Design Engr., Fairchild Aircraft, Hagerstown, Md., 1954-56; Prin. M.E. thru Proj. Dir., Battelle Columbus Labs., Columbus, Oh., 1956-59, and 1961-63; Instr., Engr., Mech. Oh. St. U., Columbus, Oh., 1959-61; Assoc. Prof. thru Prof., U. of Ok., Norman, Ok., 1963-. Author or Co-author, over 250 papers, Open Lit. Conf. Proceedings, 1958-; Ed., Conf. Proceedings, Dev. in Mechs., 1975; Ed., Symposium Proceedings, Mechs. of Bimodulus Materials, 1979. Weblo Den Leader, Cub Scout Pack 225, Norman, Ok., 1970-71; Publicity Chmn., BSA Troop 225, 1971-73, Chmn. Troop Comm., 1972-73; Mem. Troop Comm., BSA Troop 245, Norman, Ok., 1976-82. Capt., AF Reserve, US Air Force, 1951-63 (active 1952-54). Pressure Vessel & Piping Lit. Award, ASME, 1975; Honor Lectr., Mid-Am. St. U. Assn., 1983-84; Lectr. at 8 U., Midwest Mechs. Lectr. Series, 1983-84; Disting. Alumnus Award, Coll. of Engr., Ohio St. U., 1985. Fellow Membership Grade, ASME, various positions, 1952-; Fellow Mbrship Grade, AAAS, 1974- (Nom. Comm., 1988); Fellow Mbrship Grade, SEM, various offs., 1958-; Fellow Mbrship Grade, AAM, 1970-(Dir. 1979-82); Rotary Club, 1981-. Ofc: 865 Asp Ave., Norman, Ok 73019 (325-5011). Hm: 2516 Butler Dr., Norman, Ok 73069 Ph. 329-4459.

Shiro Takemura

Mfg. Plant President Hitachi Computer Products (America), Inc.

Mr. Takemura was born in Komahashi City, Japan, January 19, 1931, the son of Mr. and Mrs. Shigetake and Misao Takemura. He and Hiroko were married May 3, 1959. He attended Waseda University at Shinjuku-ku, Tokyo, Japan from 1949 to 1953 where he earned a Bachelor of Engineering degree. Mr. Takemura began his career with Hitachi, Ltd., at Hitachi City, Japan at the Kokubu Works in 1953, where in 1971 he was promoted to Departmental Manager; then in 1975 was moved to Dept. Mgr. of Kanagawa Works of the company located at Hadano-shi, Japan. In 1983, he was again promoted, this time to General Manager of the works and in 1984 the company transferred him to its Odawara-shi plant where he remained as General Manager until 1986. That year Hitachi Ltd. made a decision to open a computer products manufacturing plant at Norman, Oklahoma and he was selected as President of the plant. As a business leader he is active in both city and state organizations. He is a member of the Board of Directors of three organizations: The Oklahoma State Chamber of Commerce (1988), the Norman Chamber of Commerce (1988), and the Cleveland County Chapter of the American Red Cross (1987-90). He also holds memberships in the Governor's Chief Executives for OK Team (1988) and the Office of Business and Industrial Cooperation at the University of Oklahoma (1988-90).

Jim Miller
Newspaper General Manager

born Rockport, Missouri, February 20, 1931 to Paul Raymond and Jean Ruth (Larson) M.; married Rosamond, August 3, 1951; children: Tim, Greg, Danny & Jean Ellen. / B.A. Journalism, University of Oklahoma, 1952; post graduate studies, University of Tulsa, Tulsa, Okla., 1955-57. / Advertising manager, *Tulsa World & Tribune*, Tulsa, Okla., 1954-71; assistant advertising director, *Houston Chronicle*, Houston, Texas, 1971-81; national advertising manager, Scripps-Howard, Houston, Texas, 1981-83; General Manager, *Bartlesville Examiner*, Bartlesville, Okla., 1983-87; General Manager, *Norman Transcript*, Norman, Okla., 1987-. / Member of board, Okla. Arts Institute, 1986-88, and the Oklahoma Symphony Orchestra. / Lieutenant Colonel, U.S. Army Reserve (Ret. 1979), Japan and Korea. / President, Ad Club, Tulsa, Okla., 1967; president, O.U. Journalism Alumni Association, 1986; president, Midwest Advertising Executives Association, 1979; member, education committee, Southern Newspaper Publishers Association. / Member, Kiwanis club, Norman, Okla., member of board, United Way, Norman, Okla., 1988-89; member of board & executive committee, Norman Chamber of Commerce, 1988-; member of board, member of board, Salvation Army, Norman, Okla., 1987-; member of board, Juvenile Services, Norman, Okla., 1987-. Democrat. McFarlin Methodist church. Office: 215 E. Comanche, Norman, Okla. 73069. Phone 321-1800. Home: 332 Windbrook Drive, Norman, Oklahoma 73072.

Donald E. Mayes
Center Manager
Sooner Fashion Shopping Mall

b. Dec. 9, 1933, Enid, Okla.; s. Ralph Waldo and Phoebe Lucille (Paulk) M.; m. Diane (Brown), 1961; c. Dion (Cougler) and Arion. / Will Rogers high school, Tulsa, Okla., 1951; U. of Tulsa; Sam Houston St. Teachers Col.; Friends U., Wichita, Kans., Santa Ana Jr. Col., Santa Ana, CA.; U. of Denver, 1967; Mich. St. U., 1971; Notre Dame U., 1972. / Naval aviation cadet (Marine applicant), 1954; Army ROTC, (SHSTC) Huntsville, Texas, cadet major, U.S. Marine Corps Reserve, platoon leader (PLC), 1951-53; Korea, Japan, Okinawa, Formosa, and U.S. / Gen. Mgr.: Tulsa Southland Shop Center, 1965-67, Denver Northglenn Mall, 1967-72, Wheaton (Md.) Plaza, & McLean (Va.) Tysons Corner Center, 1972-73, Hampton (Va.) Coliseum Mall, 1973-75, Hartford (Conn.) Civic Center Shops, 1975-76, Houston (Tx.) Sharpstown Center, 1976-77; dir. prop. mgmt., East Bay Dev. Corp., Boston, Mass., 1977-79; owner, Mayes Mgmt. Corp., NY and Conn., 1979-82; proj. mgr., C.A. Henderson Co., Okla. City, Ok., 1982-84; leasing rep. SW. Reg., Franklin Property Co. and B.F. Saul Realty Service Corp., Chevy Chase, Md., 1984-86; center manager, Sooner Fashion Mall, Norman, Ok., 1986-. / pres., Tulsa Oilers Prof. Football League, councilman and mayor, Northglenn, Colo., charter member, Rotary club, Northglenn, Colo., and Mt. Kisco, N.Y. / Bd. dir. of C of C, American Red Cross, United Way - all of Norman; adv. bd., Salvation Army; member, Norman Kiwanis club; Chairman, 89er Day Parade 1889-1989. / Republican. Catholic. Office: 3301 W. Main, Norman, Okla. 73072. Phone 360-0360. Home: 2104 La Dean Dr., Norman, Okla. 73069. Phone 321-5471.

James G. Harlow, Jr.
Chairman/President
Okla. Gas & Electric Co.

born May 29, 1934, Oklahoma City, OK to James G. and Adalene (Rae) Harlow; married Jane M. (Bienfang), January 30, 1957,; children James G., III and David Ralph. Graduated from Norman High School, B.S. in Engineering, University of Oklahoma, Norman, Oklahoma 1952-57, Doctor of Commercial Letters, Oklahoma City University, Oklahoma City, Okla., 1983; chairman, board of directors and president (1982-); president and CEO (1976-82); president (1973-76); various positions (1961-73), Oklahoma Gas & Electric Co., Oklahoma City, Okla.; president, Allied Arts Foundation, Oklahoma City, Okla., 1982-83; president, Oklahoma City Chamber of Commerce, 1976; president, Oklahoma State Chamber of Commerce, 1980; member, board of directors, United States Chamber of Commerce, 1978-84; president, board of governors, Kirkpatrick Center, 1987-; lieutenant commander, U.S. Navy, 1957-59; inductee, Oklahoma Hall of Fame, Oklahoma Heritage Assoc., 1987; president, Oklahoma Economic Club, 1986-87; president, University of Oklahoma Foundation, Norman, Okla., 1986-; Who's Who in America; member, Beacon Club, Petroleum Club and Oklahoma City Golf and Country Club. Office: P.O. Box 321, Oklahoma City, Okla. 73101. Phone 272-3195. Home: 1713 Pennington Way, Oklahoma City, Okla. 73116. Phone 842-4565.

Harold R. Belknap, Jr.
Physician - Internal Medicine

b. Dec. 13, 1934; s. Harold Raymond and Helen Lucille (Shoemate) B.; m. JoAnn McCauley Evans, Jan. 21, 1984; children, Jamie Lucille (Foor), Harold Raymond III. **Education:** B.A., U. of Okla., Norman, Ok., 1952-56; M.D., Tulane U., New Orleans, La., 1956-60. **Certification:** Amer. Bd. of Internal Medicine, 1967, recertified, 1977. **Career:** Internal Medicine Specialist, Internal Medicine Assn., Norman, Ok., 1967-. **Creative work:** research/author, "Genetic Study of Families in Which Leprosy Occurs." **Activities:** acting chief, Gomer Jones Coronary Care Unit, Owen Sta., Norman, Ok., 1978-; pres., Norman Regional Hosp. staff, Norman, Ok., 1976; pres., Guy Fraser Harrison Acad. of Performing Arts, Okla. City, Ok., 1987; chmn., Profl. Education Com., Am. Cancer Soc., Norman, Ok., 1986; mem., Admission Bd., U. of Ok. Coll. of Medicine, Okla. City, Ok., 1985-; Cub, Boy Scout, Explorer Scout Leader, Boy Scouts of Am., Norman, Ok., 1972-. **Honors:** Geiger Award for Best Sr. thesis for a pub. health problem, Tulane U. Sch. of Medicine, New Orleans, La., 1960; Cert. of Accomplishment, Okla. State Med. Assn., Aug. 5, 1978; Norman's Most Favorite Dr., Norman Transcript Reader Poll, 1987; Award of Merit, Boy Scouts of Am., 1978; Silver Beaver Award, Boy Scouts of Am., 1983; Youth Vol. of Yr. Award, Jr. League of Norman, United Way of Norman, 1987. **Memberships:** Cleveland Co. Med. Assn., 1967; Okla. State Med. Assn., 1967-; Amer. Med. Assn., 1967; Amer. Soc. of Internal Medicine, 1967-. Church of Christ. Republican. Office: 900 N. Porter, Norman, OK 73071, ph. 329-0121. Home: 1111 Fountain Gate Ct., Norman, OK 73072, ph. 360-3124.

Franklin Schaffer Coulter

Superintendent
Moore–Norman AVTS

born May, 10, 1937 at Eldon, Mo., to Oscar Leroy and Nona Marie (Schaffer), was married to M. Sheryl (Breaux) on Sept. 10, 1963; children: Michael, John and Kelly. B.S. in Industrial Education (1958-61), M.S. in Guidance and Counseling (1962-65), Kansas State University, Pittsburg, KS. Certified in Educational Administration, University of Okla., Norman, OK, 1975-77. Drafting teacher & athletic coach, Deerfield High School, Deerfield, KS, 1961-64; director of counseling, Hugoton Public School, Hugoton, KS, 1964-69; director of student services, Liberal Area Vo-Tech, Liberal, KS, 1969-74; assistant superintendent (1974-79), superintendent (1979-), Moore-Norman AVTS. Chairman, Cleveland Co. American Red Cross, Norman, OK, 1988; member of the board of Norman Chamber of Commerce (1980-), Cleveland County Economic Task Force (1987-), Cleveland County Private Industry Council, Inc. (1985-) and Juvenile Services, Inc. (1985); president, United Way of Norman (1983), all of Norman, OK; Served in U.S. Army as corporal, Fort Myer, VA, 1956-58. Member of the following: Oklahoma Vocational Association, 1974-, Oklahoma Council of Local Administrators, 1974-, American Vocational Association, 1969-, Oklahoma Career Guidance Association, 1978-, National Council for Local Administrators, 1988. President (1986), member of board (1985-), Rotary Club (Noon). Catholic. Office: Moore-Norman Vo-Tech School, 4701 12th Avenue, N.W., Norman, OK 73069. Phone 364-5763. Home: 3914 Warwick Drive, Norman, OK 73069.

William O. Williams

Director of
O.U. Publications

born September 1, 1938 at Fairland, Oklahoma, to Lee Owen and Delce (Adams) W.; married Juanita (Stratton) - presently a communications specialist at York International Corporation, on November 29, 1957; children: Tammy and Tracy. / Graduated from Fairland High School in 1957; received the first track scholarship offered and graduated with an Associate Degree from Oklahoma A. & M. Junior College in Miami, Oklahoma; B.F.A., University of Tulsa. / Freelance artist, Tulsa, Oklahoma, 1960-62; Art Director, Sun Oil Company, Tulsa, Oklahoma, 1962-69; Director of Publications, University of Oklahoma, Norman, Okla. 1970-; freelance artist. / Designer of historical books on *The Cherokees, Muskogee, Ft. Smith* and *Guthrie;* guide books on *Mexico;* numerous photo works; water colors in U.S. and Mexico; teacher of photography and water color seminars in the United States and Mexico; did photography essay on *Uganda, Africa,* for Episcopal Church; for 12 years designer and winner of three National awards, United Way materials, Norman, Oklahoma. / Numerous graphic awards both regional and national; University College Designers awards; CASE; Tulsa Art Directors awards. / Past president (1977), member board of directors (1977-84), University and College Design Association. / Member, International Juggler's Association, performing throughout the Southwest. Office: 900 Asp, Room 338, Norman, OK 73019, Phone: 325-1701. Home: 2009 Scott Drive, Norman, OK 73069, Phone: 364-4540.

G. Neal Taylor

Artist
Illustrator

born Feb. 6, 1940 at Sherman, Texas, to Haskell Perry and Rose Mae (Stark) T.; married Coralie (Lewis), July 5, 1968; children: Clinton (b. Jan. 26, 1974). Bachelor of Fine Arts, University of Oklahoma, Norman, Okla., 1960-63. Self-employed freelance artist, Durant, Okla., 1978-; advertising art & sales, Speed Horse Publications, Norman, Okla., 1976-77; lead illustrator, U.S. Postal Technical Institute, Norman, Okla., 1973-76; assistant art director, John Roberts, Inc., Norman, Okla., 1964-73. Creator, oil painting: *"A Run for All Reasons,"* (reproduced as a dust jacket for this volume), 1979; artist, creator: *Oklahoma Bicentennial,* a Silver Medallion, 1973; sculptor: *"The Spirit of '89",* in bronze, 1981. Member, Westerners International, Okla. City., 1979-88; vice president, Durant Art Guild, Durant, Okla., 1988. Sergeant, U.S. Army Reserve, Norman, Okla. 1963-69; military training, U.S. Army, Ft. Polk, La., 1963-64. *$5,000 First Prize,* Franklin Mint, 1973; *$1,000 Award,* Oklahoma Heritage Art Exhibit, Red River Arts Council, 1988; *2nd Place - oils,* Five Civilized Tribes Museum, Muskogee, Okla., 1983; and numerous *Best of Shows* and *1st Place Awards,* various art shows, 1979-88. Republican. Member Church of Christ. Home: 100 Shadowwood Lane, Durant, Oklahoma 74701. Phone: (405) 924-9076.

Carl M. Rose

Bank President

b. June 7, 1942, Wekwoka, Okla.; s. M.T. and Frances N. (Carl) R.; **Education:** B.B.A., Univ. of Okla., Norman, Okla., 1960-64, M.B.A., 1968-69. **Career history:** Pres., CEO, United Bank & Trust Co., Norman, Okla., 1986-; ex. v.p., Allied Okla. Bank, Okla. City, Okla., 1981-86; v.p., 1st Interstate Bank, Albuquerque, N. Mex., 1978-81; developer/builder, Angel Fire, N. Mex., 1976-78; v.p. of finance, W.P. "Bill" Atkinson Enterprises, Midwest City, Okla., 1974-76; v.p., Liberty Natl. Bank, Okla. City, Okla., 1969-74; prof., College of Business, Univ. of Okla., Norman, Okla., 1971-75; prof., College of Business, Okla. City Univ., Okla. City, Okla., 1972. **Author:** *Determining Yields on Construction Loans,* 1980; *Determining a Bank's Cost of Capital,* 1970. **Civic Activity:** trustee, Moore/Norman Vo-Tech Foundation, Norman, Okla., 1987; director, Norman C. of C., 1988-; Asst. Chrm. for Finance division, Okla. City United Appeal, Okla. City, Okla., 1972; director, Mummers Theater, Okla. City, Okla. 1972-73; loan ex. to Oklahoma City United Appeal, Okla. City, Okla., 1969; **Military Record:** sgt. E-5, U.S. Army, West Germany, 1966-68. **Honors:** Beta Gamma Sigma, Univ. of Okla., Norman, Okla., 1969; Who's Who in South & Southwest, 1981-88. **Affiliations:** Petroleum Club, Okla. City, Okla. and Albuquerque, N. Mex., 1978-88; Trails County Club, Norman, Okla., 1986-; Albuquerque Country Club, Albuquerque, N. Mex., 1979-81. Business address: 333 12th Ave., SE, Norman, Okla. 73071, Phone 360-6061.

Larry B. McDade
Photographer

born September 10, 1944, at Del Rio, Texas, to John B. and Agnes R. (Endicott) McDade; married Dana (Crider) on June 10, 1966; children, Kimberly. BA degree from the University of Oklahoma, Norman, Oklahoma, 1962-68. Certified Professional Photographer by the Professional Photographers of America, 1984. Owner, McDade Studio, Norman, Oklahoma, 1968-; dejay, Radio Station KGOU, Norman, Oklahoma, 1986-; photographer, University of Oklahoma, 1966-68; photographer, *Norman Transcript*, Norman, Oklahoma, 1962-68; substitute teacher, Norman Public Schools, Norman, Oklahoma, 1968-70. Member, Norman Rotary club; member, Professional Photographers of America, 1968-; member board of directors, Professional Photographers of Oklahoma, 1985-; past president, Metro Professional Photographers Association, 1986; secretary-treasurer, Certified Professional Photographers of Oklahoma, 1987-. Baptist. Office: 300 West Gray, Norman, Oklahoma 73069. Phone 329-6449. Home: 1011 Thistlewood Drive, Norman, Oklahoma 73072. Phone 329-6717.

Kenneth R. Johnston
Attorney at Law

b. Nov. 24, 1944, Lexington, Ok.; s. Abe Thedford and Cecile L. (Skaggs) J.; div., 1987; c. Kenneth Wesley, and Kendra Louise. Norman HS, 1963; BS, Univ. of Ok., 1969; J.D., U. of Ok, 1973. Adm. Ok. bar, 1974; adm. to prac., US Supreme Ct., US Ct. of Appeals, Tenth Circuit, US Dist. Ct. (W. Ok. Dist.). Abstr., Sw. Title & Trust, Norman, Ok., 1963-69; v.p., Amer. First Abt. Co., Norman, Ok., 1969-70 & 1971-73; Cleveland Co. Dist. Att. off., 1973-74; 1st Asst. DA, Grady Co., 1974-76; Atty., ptnr., Allen, Johnston & Tack, Chickasha, Ok. 1976. Author, *Criminal Justice System*, 1975 & *Oklahoma Indian Land Titles*, 1977. Mem. Crim. Justice Adv. Comm., Duncan, Ok, 1974-76; Ok. Crime Commission (cts. comm.), 1978-81; member in Chickasha of: City Council, v. mayor, 1978-80, chmn., USAO Board of Regents, 1983-90, chmn., Grady Co. Dem. Party, 1977-78. Capt., Transp. Off., Ft. Eustis, Va., and Oakland Army Terminal, Ca., 1970-71. Disting. Mil. Student, OU ROTC, 1969; disting. mil. grad., OU ROTC, 1969; Fellow, Ok. Bar Assoc., 1980; Judge Ct. of Appeals Temp. div., Ok. Supreme Court, 1982; elected 4th Dist. rep. of Ok. Dist. Att. Assn., 1975-76. Mem. of following: Ok. Trial Lawyers Assn., 1974-; Amer. Trial Lawyers Assn., 1974-; (faculties comm.) Ok. Bar Assn., 1974-; (memb. Agr. Comm.), Amer. Bar Assn., 1974-; pres., Grady Co. Bar Assn., 1974-; Ok. Criminal Defense Law Assn., 1974; USAO Foundation, 1974-; Natl. Dist. Att. Assn., OU College of Law Assn. Mem., Rotary Intern., One of the founders of the Civil Justice Foundation in Washington, D.C. Democrat. Christian. Office: Box 1409, Chickasha, OK 73023.

Tommy Joe Bishop
Pharmacist

b. June 18, 1947, Shawnee, Okla., to Henry Austin and Vela Bonneta (Pickens); married: Chris Lynn (Boswell), June 28, 1968; children: Darcy Lynne, Kayla Jo. Education: B.S., Pharmacy, University of Oklahoma; Registered Pharmacist, Okla., No. 8599, 1974. **Career:** president (Mar. 6, 1986-), vice president (Feb. 1, 1975-March 6, 1986), clerk/delivery (July 1, 1971-Dec. 31, 1973), Central Pharmacy, Norman, Ok.; pharmacist (Aug. 1, 1974-Feb. 1, 1975), pharmacist intern (Jan. 1, 1974-Aug. 1, 1974), Hyde Drug, Norman, Ok. Author: Newspaper Column, *Pharmacy Footnotes*, April 29, 1978-. **Activities:** Mem., dir., treas., Norman Campfire Council, 1983-87; mem., Sunday school teacher, pres. adult class, McFarland Methodist Church, 1978-; Basketball Coach, Optimist Club, Norman, Ok., 1987-88; Softball Coach; United Way, Norman, Ok., 1988. **Military:** US Army Sgt. E-5 (combat medic), So. Vietnam & Ft. Devins, Mass., US Army hospital, Aug. 4, 1969-June 3, 1971. **Awards:** Combat Medal Badge (1970), Commendation Medal (1970), Expert Rifleman (1969), US Army; Eagle Scout Award, B.S. of Amer., 1961. **Memberships:** mem., Amer. Pharmacy Assn., 1974; charter mem., v.p., Cleveland Co. Pharmacists Assn., 1988-; mem., Okla. Pharmacy Assn., 1974-; mem., Natl. Assn. Retail Pharmacists; 1980-; mem., Amer. Coll. of Apothecaries, 1978-. Affiliations: pledge trainer, Kappa Psi (Pharmaceutical frat.) OU, 1973-74; Hon. mem., Lambda Chi Alpha, 1977; Democrat; mem. McFarlin Memorial United Methodist Church. Office: 222 Alameda, Norman, Ok., 73069. Phone 321-2838.

Bob Usry
Plumbing Contractor

born September 18, 1950, Norman, OK; son of Kermit Elwood and Ruby Marie (Phelps) Usry; married Lou Ellen (Sudduth), December 26, 1968; children: Robert Carl and Jaime Lee; attended Norman High School and later obtained high school equivalent. He served on the *USS Bon Homme Richard* in the U.S. Navy from 1968-70 during the Vietnam crisis. A singer, he performed in the Norman area with his own band for several years while working full time in the daytime as a plumber. Although he gave up singing to pursue his career, he still sings at weddings and fund raisers. He began his own plumbing business in 1973 as Usry Plumbing Company; in 1974 he joined with a partner in B & B Plumbing, Inc. In 1987, he started a new company, Bob Usry Plumbing Co. He graduated from the Dale Carnegie Human Relations Course in 1983, was elected president and has received many awards including the Leadership Gavel, and has since graduate assisted 8 classes. He became a charter member of Sooner Rotary Club in 1987. He was elected to the Executive Board of Directors for the Sooner Theatre in 1987 and elected Vice President in 1988. He is a member of the Norman Chamber of Commerce. He began coaching little league in 1976 and coached for 10 years. He coached two years of Optimist basketball. He served on the City of Norman Gas Advisory Board 1975-79. He helped sponsor the Lakeview Gymnastics team in three years of national competition, and was responsible for fund raising for that team for as long as they were in existence. Member of First Freewill Baptist Church of Norman. Home: 2247 60th Ave. N.E., Norman. Office: P.O. Box 703, Norman, OK 73070.

Nathan Glen Veal

Pharmacist

born March 24, 1948 at Norman, Okla.; s. Ralph Leon and Mary Francis (Stufflebean) V.; married Jennifer Lee (Buford), September 20, 1969; children: Bradley Clifford (born May 20, 1973), and Brent Corey (born April 19, 1977). / B.S. in Pharmacy, University of Oklahoma, Norman, Okla., 1971-75. / Registered pharmacist, Oklahoma #8904. / Pharmacist, Central State Hospital, Norman, Okla., 1977-80; director of pharmacy, Oklahoma Veteran's Center, Norman, Okla., 1980-85; staff pharmacist, Veteran's Administration Hospital, Oklahoma City, Okla., 1985-87; inpatient pharmacy supervisor, Oklahoma Medical Center, Oklahoma City, Okla., 1987-. / Military: Aviation Ordinanceman, E-5, U.S. Navy, VA-145 Squadron, Whidbey Island, Washington, 1967-70; *U.S.S. Enterprise,* Viet Nam, 1968-69. / Awards: National Defense Service Award (1970), Vietnam Service Medal (1969), Armed Forces Expeditionary medal (1969), U.S. Navy; letters of commendation from Cmmdr., *U.S.S. Enterprise* and Commanding Officer, V.A. 145, 1969. / Memberships: chaplain, Kappa Psi, 1973-76; mem., program committee, Oklahoma Society of Hospital Pharmacists, 1972-; mem., American Society of Hospital Pharmacists, 1988-; mem., American College of Healthcare Executives, 1988-; mem., Oklahoma Public Health Assn. / member McFarland United Methodist Church. Office: Oklahoma Medical Center, 800 N.E. 13th Street, Oklahoma City, OK 73072. Phone 271-4606.

Jerri L. Culpepper

Editor/Writer

Until September 1988, Jerri L. Culpepper (writer of the business biographies featured in the "Partners in Progress" section of this book), was employed as a reporter/columnist for *The Norman Transcript.* At the Transcript she produced a weekly column on the Arts, "Arts Beat." She is currently employed at the University of Oklahoma, where she serves as editor of *OU Update,* an in-house magazine serving Oklahoma University's Norman, Oklahoma City Health Sciences Center, and Tulsa Medical College Campuses. She is also a free-lance writer. Her articles have appeared in such national magazines as *Nation's Business* and also locally in the Norman Chamber of Commerce's 1988-89 Visitor's Guide. Born September 20, 1958, in Tulsa, Oklahoma, she is the daughter of William Franklin and Betty Joene Culpepper, also of Norman. She has two sisters, Lori Culpepper of Norman, and Gina Barker, of Vancouver, Washington, and also one niece, Lindsey Nicole Culpepper of Norman. Jerri received her bachelor of arts degree in journalism from OU's H. H. Herbert School of Journalism and Mass Communication in 1981. Memberships include the Norman Galaxy of Writers, and the Oklahoma Womens Political Caucus.

Partners
In Progress

Commerce is not only an economic necessity in a successful community, it also serves as a cohesive force to improve the lives of its citizens.

The histories of the following Cleveland County Partners in Progress prove a devotion to this ideal as well as sucess in attaining that goal.

Allard Cleaners

Jim Allard has been in the dry-cleaning business for a long time — since he was 14, in fact. That was the year his father died and he began working toward the day he could buy his father's cleaning establishment back. (His father died without leaving a will.)

In 1968, he attained his goal of buying the business.

But Allard Cleaners' history goes way back before the sixties. The business was started in 1923 by an uncle of Jim Allard's. They set up shop in their current location — 305 East Main — on Feb. 15, 1934. The Allards took over the space formerly occupied by Pentax Cleaners upon the death of the cleaners' owner.

Today, computerization and more modern dry-cleaning equipment have drastically changed the face of the business. In addition, Allard has doubled the number of employees since becoming owner.

But not everything has changed.

Allard still strives for customer satisfaction, for one thing.

Noting that "business is good," Allard attributes part of his success to his insistence on keeping up with developments in dry-cleaning equipment and materials.

"I think I know more about it (the dry-cleaning business) than most people," he said. "I have completed seminars by the New York Neighborhood Dry Cleaners Association and the International Fabricare Institute in Illinois.

Although Allard is involved in virtually every aspect of the business, from the actual cleaning to customer relations, he specializes in performing challenging cleaning tasks. Recently, for instance, a woman brought him an approximately 100-year-old wedding dress that was to be displayed in the Plains Museum in Altus. Because starch would have turned it yellow eventually, Allard used simple soap and water to clean it, then used plastic sizing to keep it from yellowing.

Cleveland County Record

A veteran Oklahoma newsman once said southern Cleveland County is to newspapers what the Bermuda Triangle is to airplanes. It chews them up and no one ever hears from them again. With that advice in hand, newspapermen John A. "Andy" Rieger and Jerry A. Laizure opened the *Cleveland County Record* in 1984 with the first edition of the newspaper published Jan. 2, 1984.

The *Record* followed the *Cleveland County Reporter* which closed its doors in the summer of 1984. The *Reporter* was a merger of the *Noble News* and the *Lexington Sun*.

Rieger was a reporter and later an editor at *The Daily Oklahoman and Times* in Oklahoma City before leaving to launch the venture. Laizure was a former newspaper production employee in Bartlesville and Pawhuska.

He was production supervisor at *The Oklahoma Daily,* the OU student newspaper, prior to setting up shop in Noble. The two met in college where Rieger edited *The Daily.* Their wives, Karen S. Rieger and Peggy S. Laizure, as well as their children are active in the business.

The weekly paper is qualified to publish legal notices and is a member of the Oklahoma Press Association. It serves Noble and southern Cleveland County and has begun to build an east Norman audience. The newspaper, located on Main Street in Noble, was one of the first in the state to be typeset entirely on computer.

The general-circulation newspaper covers Noble school and government news, county news, sports news and current events. Their mailing address is Box 1564, 106 S. Main, Noble, Oklahoma 73068. The phone number is 872-3000.

Central Pharmacy

Central Pharmacy was founded by Ralph Reed, whose first pharmacy, located closer to downtown Norman, was called Reed's Prescription Shop. Reed's father, Fred Reed, was co-founder of Reed and Foster's Drug Store, one of Norman's oldest drugstores. It was located at the corner of Main and Peters.

Tom Bishop, a Cleveland County resident since 1965, began working at Central Pharmacy, 222 Alameda in Norman, July 1971 as a delivery boy. Having just returned from Vietnam, where he served as a combat medic, he was enrolled in the school of Pharmacy at the University of Oklahoma. He later became a pharmacy intern.

After graduating in December 1973, he left Central Pharmacy in order to work as a pharmacist at Hyde Drug. But a year later, when he was offered the chance to work as a pharmacist at Central Pharmacy, he jumped at the chance. Today Bishop is the head pharmacist and pharmacy owner.

Half jokingly, Bishop, who is the first member of his family to become a pharmacist, said he went into pharmacy because his father, an oilfield "roustabout," wanted him to go into a "clean work environment."

"Also," Bishop said, "I had admired the pharmacists in my hometown of Wewoka. They seemed to be very wise men."

Bishop noted that Central Pharmacy is a "prescription-oriented shop." Hours are 9 a.m. to 6 p.m. weekdays and 9 a.m. to noon Saturdays. It is closed on Sundays, although the pharmacy does have an answering service. Other features are a drive-up window, computerized records and free delivery.

Also available at Central Pharmacy are an assortment of medical equipment, including wheelchairs and walkers for rent or sale, and a variety of cold remedies and vitamins.

Gordon's Specialty

Gordon's Specialty is no johnny-come-lately. The business, today located at 101 W. Gray in Norman, has roots that go back to the '40s, explained Allen Morain, son of Gordon Morain, who founded the business.

Here's how it all began: Morain, a chief projectionist and air conditioning maintenance man with Griffith Theaters (now Commonwealth) first came to Norman in 1940 to work for the theater chain's five Norman theaters.

At that time, Morain noted, Norman was a small town of 5,000-plus, so it wasn't surprising that he quickly became known about town for his expertise as a repairman.

In fact, Gordon (everyone called him by his first name in those days) was granted a draft exemption by the commander of the two Navy bases here because of his mechanical expertise.

Between maintaining the equipment at the five Naval theaters and the town's five theaters—there were four

downtown and one on campus—he was kept working seven days a week, noon to midnight.

But Morain didn't waste his mornings sleeping. Noting that during the war "people didn't throw away things and buy new things; they fixed them," Morain said his father began getting swamped with orders from people who needed repairs on everything from Christmas tree lights to water coolers.

"Soon," Morain said, "he was making more money in the morning, just walking around downtown, than he was working for the theaters."

In 1947, Gordon Morain resigned his job with Griffith Theaters and went in-

to business for himself full time. The late Cecil Brite, an accountant, suggested that he name the fledgling business Gordon's Specialty.

The next year, he moved from his garage shop to 217 W. Main. It was at that address that several lines of home appliances were first added. In 1950, the growing business moved to the newly completed Hale building at 400 W. Main and, in 1955, they moved to their current location on West Gray.

In the ensuing years, the savvy, mechanically minded entrepreneur expanded his business to include setting up the public address system at all University of Oklahoma athletic games and for public officials who were running for office. Gordon Morain also took numerous movies of the Sooners and Coach Bud Wilkinson, as well as the OCU football team.

Gordon Morain has since retired, and the former one-man operation today employs 35 persons in the sale and service of residential, institutional and commercial air conditioning and heating systems, major home appliances, and mechanical contracting work.

Hitachi Computer Products (America) Inc.

Hitachi Ltd. made its first direct overseas investment in computer activities with the establishment of Hitachi Computer Products (America), Inc. in November 1985. In April 1987, one year after the groundbreaking, the $14 million, 73,000-square-foot Norman factory, located on 69 acres of land, began production.

In November 1985, Hitachi set up temporary offices on Alameda in Norman, and the first employee was hired in March of 1986.

In opening the facility at 1800 E. Imhoff Drive, Hitachi Computer Products (America), Inc., president Shiro Takemura noted a global trend toward cooperation between countries. He said Hitachi is attempting to serve market needs of manufacturing products where they are to be sold, and said this policy lay behind the decision to start production of large-capacity magnetic disk subsystems in the United States.

Also, in opening the facility, Katsushige Mita, president of Hitachi Ltd., stated that Oklahoma was chosen "because of its excellent workforce and because we were extremely encouraged by the enthusiastic invitations from the Oklahoma state government."

Up until very recently, Hitachi Computer Products (America), Inc. has been in the business of manufacturing large-capacity magnetic disk subsystems ex-

In 1910 Namihei Odaira, an electrical engineer, founded Hitachi, Ltd. He also created its trademark, which has won worldwide respect as a symbol of quality and care. That trademark was based on two characters. The first "hi", meaning "sun". The second was "tachi", meaning "rise", represented by a man with his feet planted firmly on the ground.
Freely combining the two characters, Odaira expressed his vision of man looking toward the sun, toward a better life for man himself and a brighter future for mankind.

ternal storage devices that play an important role in determining a computer system's overall performance.

Currently, the Norman plant is phasing in a new product line and easing out of computer disk drives. The new product, called MT400, is a cartridge magnetic tape substance, as opposed to the outdated open-reel tapes. The new magnetic subsystem provides a savings in both floor space and media storage space over current systems.

Plans call for an additional building to be built in the next year or so to accomodate the new product.

When Hitachi Computer Products (America), Inc. first opened in 1987, there were 80 workers. As of the fall of 1988, there were 160 workers employed at the Norman plant.

Hitachi Ltd. was established by Namihei Odaira in 1910 as an electrical repair shop for a mining operation. The company continued to expand, becoming one of the world's leading integrated electrical and electronics manufacturers.

Hitachi's current product line ranges from power generating, heavy electrical and industrial equipment to consumer products, electronics products and industrial components and materials.

Among Hitachi's diverse activities, electronics is marked as an area of high growth potential. In this sector, focus is on computers and semiconductors.

Founded in 1962, Hitachi's computer division is a mainstay of the company's electronics activities.

Hitachi's corporate policy for the future attaches a high priority to basic research. As a corporation operating on a global scale, Hitachi strives to be a responsible member of the local community, Hitachi Computer Products (America), Inc. has awarded a number of grants to local organizations, including recent gifts of $5,000 each to the Norman Public School Foundation and Pioneer Library System.

Shiro Takemura, president of Hitachi Computer Products (America), lives in Norman with his wife, Hiroko.

Interurban Restaurant

"The old Interurban ain't what it used to be." — Now an excellent restaurant, the old trolley station was renovated and opened its doors to diners October 23, 1976.

If a building could talk, the structure that now houses the Interurban Restaurant, 105 W. Main, could probably fill up enough pages for a full-length novel.

The first trolley left the Norman station in November 1913. (The Interurban line, which originally ran from Oklahoma City to Moore, was started in 1912; Norman was picked up in 1913.) The final run was made Sept. 27, 1947. A black-draped car No. 227 was the last to roll into the station, according to newspaper accounts. In an article running in the Sept. 28, 1947, edition of the *Norman Transcript,* it was noted that the last riders—mostly members of the Oklahoma Railway Employees—struck up a rousing chorus of "The old Interurban ain't what she used to be."

Rusty Loeffler, who owns the restaurant along with his longtime friend Robert Ross, recalled that the old Interurban building during its heyday claimed a small restaurant called the "Terminal Cafe."

When the Interurban was shut down, Loeffler said, the building became a bus station and operated as such until about 1972. In 1976 he, Ross and Loeffler's father, Frank, acquired the building. (Loeffler observed that his father used to ride the Interurban

trolley from Norman, where he attended the University of Oklahoma, to Oklahoma City, where he worked.)

Loeffler noted that they had a lot of help in getting the project off the ground. Wayne Curtis, of Curtis Restaurant Supply, helped them acquire the loan for equipment, while Norman attorney Bill Hall bought the building and then leased it back to them.

Still, the fledgling restaurateurs had their work cut out for them. With the help of local architect Paul Henthorne, who served as job supervisor, Loeffler and Ross renovated the building, going so far as to chip the plaster off the walls and doing demolition work on their own. "And we added a fireplace and a combination office-storeroom in the back—all on a shoestring," Loeffler recalled.

The building again rang with the sounds of a booming business on Oct. 23, 1976, when the Interurban first opened its doors for business. (Loeffler vividly recalls the date: it was the last time that OSU beat OU.)

In 1985 they purchased the building and began further work on the building, including expanding the kitchen by 1,300 feet. A little later, they closed the restaurant for about three weeks in order to refurbish the

entire place. They put in new floors, added on a patio, and landscaped the front. Other new changes including leasing the adjoining lot in order to expand parking.

Changes also have been made to the menu. In 1976, Loeffler recalled, they had "a half dozen hamburgers, fries, prime rib, homemade soups and salads, nachos, a couple of steaks, two or three sandwiches, crab legs and omelettes. The big items," he said, "were our french onion soup, omelettes and spinach salad."

"The most significant change," Loeffler said, "was probably the addition of a wide range of Mexican food, barbecue and pasta. We also expanded our sandwich selection. And lately we've added our 'Heart Healthy' items."

"In the seventies," Loeffler said, "people ate mainly burgers and steaks. Now, it's chicken and soup and salad."

Evidently Loeffler and Ross have been doing something right. After opening the Norman restaurant, other Interurbans followed. Today Ross and Loeffler have restaurants in Edmond Tulsa and Oklahoma City in addition to Norman.

One reason the Norman restaurant has been so successful, Loeffler theorizes, is that its locally owned. This holds several advantages, one of the most obvious being that they can keep better track of local tastes. It also means that they can get involved in the community. Interurban hosts an annual golf tournament to benefit Big Brothers/Big Sisters of Cleveland County and also hosts an annual beach party to raise funds for Young Life, a non-denominational Christian organization for young persons in 9th through 12th grade.

Also, Loeffler said, "You have to pay attention to the basics. Stick with the same concept of serving good food at a good price. Beyond that, one thing that separates us from some restaurants is our high service standards. We do a good job of training our waiters and waitresses. They do more than just serve food; we emphasize sales and taking care of the customer.

IOOF Cemetery

The IOOF Cemetery, located in northeast Norman at 1913 N. Porter, just may be the longest continually operating business in Norman, according to manager Ernest Waggoner.

In any case, records show that IOOF was the first "official" cemetery in Norman. The first burial occurred September 25, 1891 — only two years after the '89er Land Run. Before that, according to *Norman — An Early History, 1820-1900,* by the late Cleveland County historian John Womack, burial sites were located on school land. (The first burial site in Norman, according to Womack, was located on 10 acres at the southwest corner of what is now West Main Street and Berry Road.)

Originally, the cemetery covered about 10 acres. Today, IOOF owns 119 acres, with about 65 acres of that as yet undeveloped. The cemetery is bounded by Porter on the west and Rock Creek Road on the north.

The Norman cemetery has accum-

mulated about 12,000 burials, and Waggoner said they estimate that there is enough land remaining for about 100 years worth of operation.

Waggoner noted two facts of which many persons are unaware: first, that the IOOF Cemetery, owned by the Independent Order of Odd Fellows, is a non-profit cemetery and, second, that one doesn't have to belong to the lodge to be buried there. He also noted that the cemetery does not serve Norman only, but also the surrounding communities.

There are currently six persons

employed at IOOF and the Norman Monument Co., which IOOF purchased in 1981, including Waggoner and his wife, Louise, who does office work. Both granite and bronze memorials can be ordered at the Norman office, although the engraving is done elsewhere.

The Waggoners, both of whom were born and reared here, came to work at IOOF Cemetery 24 years ago. Waggoner said he started out mowing the grass when he was 18, becoming manager in 1971.

The couple have two sons,

Don James Co.

Donald Lovett James lives north of Norman, where he produces the animal sculptures that have made his Don James Co., Inc. an international success.

He was born in Wilmington, Delaware, October 1, 1957, son of Thomas and Elizabeth (Lovett) James. He graduated from Mt. Pleasant High School in Wilmington, Delaware in 1975. Don came to Norman in 1979 in pursuit of a dream — independence and an opportunity for self-expression. With only limited formal education but with talent and faith in God, he began to build a career in art. After two years of working at odd jobs and sculpting animals on the side, Don created and produced one of the most popular art products in America — the Don James Animals. Sold throughout the United States and abroad, the sculptures have become a favorite with animal lovers and art collectors.

Mr. James has contributed significantly to the economic and cultural welfare of Cleveland County. Despite

the temporary decline in Oklahoma's economy, Don's company has continued to grow and presently employs more than 50 people. A member of the Norman Chamber of Commerce, Don contributes materials and supplies to the crafts activities of several nursing homes and children's programs sponsored by the Chamber. Concerned

about preserving the environment, Don is a member of the Oklahoma Sierrans and the Oklahoma Wildlife Foundation.

Don anticipates the continued growth and prosperity of Cleveland County and believes his decision to build his career here was indeed fortunate.

Mayes Funeral Directors

Mayes Funeral Directors was founded in 1900 by the Meyer family. Operated by Henry Meyer Sr., it was originally located in the 200 block of East Main Street in Norman, in the space now occupied by Blair Furniture Store.

In 1927 the Meyer family built one of the few funeral homes specially designed for use as a funeral home in Oklahoma. (Most funeral homes at that time operated out of the back of furniture or hardware stores or other businesses.) That funeral home, at 222 E. Comanche, continued to be run by Meyer Sr., until his death in 1929. It was then operated by his widow, Dixie, and their son Henry P. Meyer Jr. They continued to manage the business until 1945, when Henry Meyer died.

Then, Meyer and Meyer Funeral Home, as it was called until 1964, was bought by George Jansing, Boss Lindsay and Earl Willard. They operated the business as a partnership until 1956, when Pat Mayes acquired it from

Pat Mayes

Lindsay, Willard, and the estate of Jansing.

In 1964, a new funeral home was built at 500 Alameda. At that time, the name was changed to Mayes Funeral Directors.

The business continued to operate as a single entity until 1981, when it was incorporated with two Guardian funeral homes in Oklahoma City. In 1982 Mayes acquired Gaskill Funeral Home in Shawnee. Other acquisitions followed: Hutchins-Maples Funeral Home of Bristow in 1982, Smith Funeral Home of Ada in 1983, Roberts Funeral Home of Westville and Stilwell in 1984 and Memorial Park Cemetery in Ada in 1985. In May 1987 another funeral home was built: Guardian Northside, located at 115th North Pennsylvania in Oklahoma City.

Currently, the Norman funeral home has six employees. According to owner Pat Mayes, "Mayes offers every option for post-death activities that the public would want or need, including arrangement of services and cremation.

"We also," he added "operate the largest pre-paid funeral trust plan in Oklahoma."

Mayes is past president of the Oklahoma Funeral Directors Association and the National Funeral Directors Association.

McDade Studios

What started out in 1968 as a part-time venture has since grown to become one of Norman's best-known photography studios.

Larry McDade, owner of McDade Studios, 300 W. Gray in Norman, said he and Greg Taber established McDade-Taber Inc. in 1968 at 106 S. University Blvd. At the time, McDade was a student at the University of Oklahoma, where he was studying foreign languages with a minor in journalism.

After six months, McDade bought Taber out and went into business on his own.

Currently, McDade has two full-time photographers who also serve as manager and assistant manager respectively; Lori Yunice and Shelia McGaha.

Although McDade Studios has always specialized in wedding photography, now they specialize in video

photographing weddings.

"The majority of our weddings are now done in video," he said. In fact, McDade could be said to be a crusader in the video movement locally. "To my knowledge," he said, "no other photography studio in Norman does what we do."

McDade gives the couple a lot for their money. Not only are the couple's wedding vows captured on tape, thanks to a wireless microphone, but so are comments made beforehand in the groom's dressing room and at the

reception afterward.

"Sometimes, you get the cute, off-the-cuff comments that way," McDade said.

Although wedding photography and video photography comprise the majority of work done at McDade Studios, they also do school, family and children's portraitures. McDade specializes in "environmental" portraitures — portraits taken out-of-doors, in the subject's home, or other location outside of the studio. McDade Studios also does commercial and industrial photography, passport pictures and old-time copy and restoration work. They also will produce videos of birthday parties and other special events.

Although they have somehow come to be thought of as "high-priced," McDade said they try to keep their prices competitive. Couples, for instance, may opt to have one of McDade's assistants produce their wedding video, or have McDade make the arrangements personally. (A minimum order is $750, he said, noting that most packages run about $1,500.)

Moore-Norman Vo-Tech

What began in the early 1970s as a goal to expand the job skills training opportunities for high school students through the formation of a vocational and technical school district has grown by the late 1980s into a valuable resource to individuals of all ages and to businesses.

Moore-Norman Vo-Tech School began with a referendum in 1972 called by the boards of education from Moore and Norman public school districts. They asked voters to give approval to the formation of an independent vocational and technical school district.

The school now plays a vital role in the economic life of the two communities through its two-pronged approach to job skills training for the workforce.

Not only does the school offer the training programs for high school students and adults which lead to entry-level jobs, many of the programs offer highly specialized skills in the new technologies.

Plus, the school has been a leader in the state in serving new and existing firms with a variety of specially designed programs ranging from pre-employment training to leadership and management skills.

The school operates in a $13 million facility on a beautiful 75-acre campus.  State-of-the-art equipment is used by students in each of the 24 full-time programs. Each year about 700 adults and 500 high school students enroll in programs which meet each weekday. The school has achieved a national reputation for the development of individualized curriculum materials which facilitate a variety of styles and paces, as well as make possible the open entry-open exit concept.

About 11,000 adults enroll each year in programs offered through the Business and Industry Services Division. Included in that division is Adult Training and Development, which offers several hundred short-term courses each year meeting primarily on evenings and weekends.

Hundreds of individuals are served each year through the economic development section within the Business and Industry Services division. Business and Industry Services also provides pre-employment training offered in conjunction with the State Department of Vocational and Technical Education utilizing money made possible through the state appropriation for new or expanding businesses.

Moore-Norman Vo-Tech School is also designated as the state's training facility for asbestos abatement workers, supervisors, contractors and inspectors. The Oklahoma Asbestos/ Safety Center is operated in a leased facility and is accredited by EPA to provide a variety of training programs to meet the state's stringent regulations related to the safe removal of asbestos from public buildings.

Norman Chamber of Commerce

The Norman Chamber of Commerce was recently the host of a number of activities to celebrate Norman's 99th birthday. The activities were, of course, the annual 89'er Week. But Norman isn't the only one turning 99 this year.

The Norman Chamber of Commerce also began in 1889 when it was established as a commercial organization called the Board of Trade. Activities of this board were not much different than those of the chamber today.

According to records, one of the priorities of the early day organization was the improvement of roads and the construction of bridges across roads leading into Norman. The chamber currently has an active Transportation Committee.

In the frontier days, Norman was known for its low prices on lumber and staple goods and the Board of Trade served as "rustlers" for business, according to transcripts. There were no tax revenues. Road work was accomplished by labor donations of the rural settlers and cash donations from the residents.

The Board of Trade later became known as the Commercial Club and was located in the 200 block of East Main. In 1907 and during the war years, however, the group was practically abandoned.

A re-organization took place in 1919. As the organization got underway, H.L. Muldrow was chosen as president.

In 1933, the organization was chartered and incorporated under the leadership of T. Jack Foster. At this point, the organization embarked on a substantial undertaking of goals and programs.

At this time, there was also a 50 percent increase in dues, from $6 to $12 for professional organizations and a minimum of $12 for each small business.

Committees added or continued during the reorganization included community, finance, organizational cooperation, advertising, transportation, membership, agriculture, industrial and commercial development, education, beautification and government relations.

Also during that year, downtown parking was cited as a continuing problem, 12 new businesses were added to the community and 300 chamber members attended the banquet and annual membership drive. The cost of the banquet was 25 cents.

In 1940, the chamber was relocated to 129 E. Main. The population of Norman had grown from 500 in 1889 to over 11,000 in 1940.

In 1955, the chamber moved to its permanent location at 115 E. Gray. And in 1984 a new building was built at this location and paid for almost entirely by the membership.

Some of the "non-traditional" programs at the chamber today include an arts and humanities program, an education program with the Norman Public Schools and a crime prevention program.

Norman Regional Hospital

January - 1989.

Norman Regional Hospital takes a "high-tech, high-touch approach" to patient care.

That means patients at Norman Regional get more than just the latest in medical care: they get quality care.

"Consumers measure care, not necessarily by our equipment but by the attitude of our staff, the appearance of the room, the quality of food. They don't see all the behind-the-scenes work.

"We have to see what the consumers need, so we do a lot of long-range and strategic planning," said Craig Jones, administrator.

Norman Regional Hospital is a cross between a small-town and a large city hospital, Jones said. Whereas Norman Regional Hospital's investment in high-tech medical equipment makes the hospital anything but "small-town," much of the staff has worked and lived in Norman for many years, and they have a commitment to the community in which they live.

"From the time a person comes in the door and throughout their stay the staff exudes a customer orientation," said Jones. "It's the amenities, the special attention to providing a warm, caring atmosphere which are tangibles to our patients."

The hospital is accredited by the Joint Commission on Accreditation of Health-care Organizations, which set the standards for quality. Both physicians and other health care personnel serve on quality-related committees such as the Patient Care Committee and the Quality Assurance & Utilization Review Committee. In addition, Norman Regional is affiliated with Voluntary Hospitals of America, an association of not-for-profit hospitals.

"The medical staff is another way in which we interpret quality," Jones said. "Our active medical staff numbers about 100." In addition, a broad range of medical and surgical specialties is offered in more than 20 areas represented by the active, courtesy, consulting, oral surgery, podiatry and dental staffs.

Another, more tangible, indication of

Norman Regional's commitment to quality can be seen in the hospital's expansion of services and capabilities.

Take, for instance, Magnetic Resonance Imaging. Jones explained that it works on the principle of reconstructing atoms in the body and then reproducing a copy. The MRI, he said, gives especially good detail of the spine and brain, and is used in conjunction with X-rays and other equipment.

Laser surgery, an area that also lies on the cutting edge of technology, is another service offered at Norman Regional. Used primarily in gynecology and opthalmology surgery, these lasers enable physicans to perform certain types of surgery with fewer complications and for less cost.

Cancer patients will soon benefit from the hospital's comprehensive cancer management center, expected to open by the summer of 1989. The new facility, which is being built on the hospital's east side, will feature a linear accelerator which creates radiation in a direct beam, enabling unhealthy tissue to be treated with fewer side effects. A computer simulator which will be used to help cancer patients plan an individualized treatment program.

Other services offered at the 280-bed hospital include several specialty units. The hospital's Coronary Care Unit houses one of the most sophisticated computerized arrythmia monitoring sys-

1927 - Original American Legion Hospital.

tems in the state, plus there is a maternal-care health area and a Surgery Department, complete with Day Surgery Unit. Other specialized services include a 20-bed mental health unit, home health, an 18-bed chemical dependency unit and a physician referral service.

Another focus is the education and wellness classes for the community and patients. Through a closed-circuit television system patients can view the latest programs on wellness and health care. The staff also has access to advanced programming on a hospital satellite network.

Norman Regional Hospital, located at 901 N. Porter, is owned by the City of Norman and operated by an 11-member Board of Trustees comprised by community leaders and physicians. The hospital receives no tax monies, and operates independently of the City of Norman. The NRH Foundation coordinates fund-raising activities to support capital improvements and special program funding.

A quick note about the hospital's history: In 1925 Norman physician John L. Day interested the Pledger-Allen Post of the American Legion in establishing a hospital. The legion secured the Whitwell property at Johnson and Ponca streets as the location for their hospital and, in 1925, the legion conducted a fund-raising campaign. The following year, the American Legion Hospital, built as a memorial to the 16 Cleveland County men who died during World War I, opened with 14 beds.

The American Legion Hospital was sold to the city in 1944. The City of Norman has owned and operated Norman Municipal Hospital — the hospital later changed its name to Norman Regional Hospital to reflect its wider area of coverage — since June 1, 1946. The original American Legion Hospital was demolished in 1954.

The Norman Transcript

The Transcript had its beginning in 1889 when Indian Territory was first opened for settlement. Newspaperman Ed P. Ingle stepped off a Santa Fe train that year in April, strode through the prairie grass to a spot near the train station and staked his claim on a piece of land.

That land, now at the intersection of West Main Street and Santa Fe Avenue, became the first home for *The Transcript,* the oldest business in Norman. The first issue of *The Transcript* rolled off the press July 13, 1889, with a salutatory note from Ingle which read:

> It will ever be a champion of the people and will be found ready to investigate both sides of any question of importance for the welfare of our people.

Ingle continued to have an interest in *The Transcript* until 1903 when he sold out to J.J. Burke. Burke had come to Oklahoma City in 1889 where he assisted in publishing the *Oklahoma City Times.* Burke continued to make newspaper history in Norman, and *The Transcript* was always a booster for the fledgling city and its institutions.

A familiar headline in the paper for many years was "Another Norman Boy Makes Good," used by Burke in conjunction with articles about the success of some young man who grew up here and made a name for himself elsewhere. One hometown boy who "made good" in Norman began his distinguished career in 1916 as a carrier for *The Transcript.* The carrier was Harold T. Belknap, who remained with *The Transcript* until his death after more than 68 years of service.

In 1918, Burke sold his interest to H.H. Herbert, director of the School of Journalism at the University of Oklahoma, and Tucker E. Miller. Through a variety of transactions and sales, by 1927 *The Transcript* was owned by R.H. Parham, Fred E. Tarman, Alfred Sloan and Belknap.

Tarman became editor and publisher in 1929 upon the death of Parham.

Belknap was named business manager. Tarman remained as editor until his retirement in 1969 when Belknap became editor and publisher. Don M. Frensley, who joined the staff in 1957, became co-publisher. During his 15 years as editor and publisher, Belknap helped guide *The Transcript* — and Norman — through a period of intense growth.

Belknap is best characterized as a "shirt-sleeve" executive who exerted strong leadership and kept the newspaper in the forefront of business growth in the community. Belknap was also active in local affairs and supported efforts he thought would benefit the city and the university. Several years before his death in January 1985, the university presented Belknap its Distinguished Service Citation, the highest honor it can bestow.

Frensley became publisher after Belknap's death. *The Transcript* was purchased by the Donrey Media Group in 1985 from the Belknap family and Frensley.

The Transcript has been in six buildings since Ingle staked out his claim near the train station. The next home of the paper was in the first brick building constructed in Norman, on the site of the Sooner Theater. The newspaper stood next door to the fire station with its horse-drawn fire engine.

The paper moved in 1925 to quarters on Peters Avenue. At that time Norman was a growing city of 10,000. The newspaper had a staff of 32 with a monthly payroll of $4,000, one of the largest in the city. In 1946 a building was erected on the newspaper's present site to house the mechanical departments of the paper.

That facility was remodeled and enlarged in 1956 to provide approximately 14,500 square feet of space. Another expansion in 1975 doubled the size of the building again. The expansion brought *The Transcript* into the age of offset printing and computer typesetting with the installation of a 64-page, eight-unit Goss Urbanite offset press.

Other equipment includes a Mycro-Tek computer system in the news and classified departments, and the latest in photocomposition typesetters an equipment.

Oklahoma Electric Cooperative

Hand made is a term that signifies quality today, but back in the 1930's on the farm, "hand made" was just the way it was done . . . the way everything was done. Hand labor made young men and women old before their time, but that all began to change with rural electrification.

By 1930, electric power was already having a profound effect on life in Oklahoma's towns and cities. Thomas Edison built the first central station electric system in 1882. Electricity was one of the key attractions of city life and contributed to the exodus of many rural residents. However, only the most affluent of farmers or farms near towns could get "the electric". Over 90 percent of Oklahoma's farm families lived and labored in a darkened land that is hard to remember in today's age of microwave ovens and satellite TVs.

A few electric companies were willing to extend service to rural customers, but the price usually was prohibitive. As a rule, farmers had to pay from $2,000 to $3,000 per mile for construction of the lines to their homes and that was in the 1930s. On top of that, rural customers usually had to pay more for the electricity, between 10 and 40 cents per kWh.

It all began to change starting on May 11, 1935 when President Franklin D. Roosevelt signed Executive Order 7037, creating the Rural Electrification Administration (REA). Norman's Oklahoma Electric Cooperative received it's first REA loan on November 13, 1936. The first lines were energized May 13, 1938.

OEC's history actually started in May, 1936, when farmers in the western part of Cleveland and eastern part of McClain counties were approached by a promotion agency regarding rural electrification. They asked for $10 from each farmer with the promise that service would be provided out of Oklahoma City within a short time. The farmers were a little skeptical and turned to a trusted leader in the community, D.B.R. Johnson, dean of OU's school of pharmacy, for advice. Johnson also operated a farm near Newcastle. He along with E.E. Hardin, early organizer and first president of the Cooperative, sought to "find out what was up." They advised the farmers not to pay the promoters, that the federal government had money for the project and was ready to make it available upon presentation of satisfactory project plans.

A meeting of the interested parties was called and held at Short's filling station where a committee to work on the project plans was formed. The project would not be funded until a sufficient number of families had signed up and paid a $5 membership fee. In the 1930s that was not a sum to be taken lightly. The signup teams got wiser as they went along. They found that it was better to have both members of the farm couple present when they talked about the benefits of electricity. Often the wife would pay the signup fee before the organizers had finished arguing with her husband.

On October 1, 1936 approximately seven hundred farmers of Cleveland and McClain counties had filed application for the rural electrification project and a request for a government loan was made. Dedication ceremonies were held May 20, 1938, in the Norman High School Auditorium and at that time fifty homes were already using the Co-op's electricity.

In Cleveland County, local backers of the Cooperative were Mr. Frank G. Higginbotham and Horace M. Sheff. Many farmers were instrumental in distributing survey forms, which were compiled by Sheff, who also drew up tentative maps for the project.

Others who assisted in the early work of building the Cooperative were V.I. Poe, Emile Fontenier, J.H. Redman, M.D. Sewell, H.H. Smith and Henry Sheff. Ben Huey of Norman was elected to provide legal advice for the young cooperative. Original board of directors were E.E. Hardin, president, Henry C. Sheff, vice-president, Horace M. Sheff, secretary-treasurer, Horace H. Smith, and George Nemecek. Nemecek was the original project manager. His duties included all preliminary procedures and supervision of the program. He contacted consumers and advised them on house wiring and plumbing. He later resigned and became a member of the board. His position was assumed by E.W. Cralle a former Norman electrical contractor.

By the end of 1938, the Cooperative had 260 miles of line and served 428 members. These members each used an average of 42 kWh per month and were billed an average of just $3.46. Today, OEC has over 4,000 miles of line and over 26,000 meters.

In 1939 the Oklahoma Inter-County Electric Cooperative became Oklahoma Electric Cooperative. Line construction had to be suspended during World War II since all available materials had to go to the war effort, but member participation was continued in 1942 along with support of Western Farmers' Electric Cooperative, OEC's power supplier.

The first office was located at 229 West Main in Norman. It was then moved to 316 East Main. In 1949 an office was built at 101 E. Gray and served the Co-op until 1973 when the present office was built at 242 24th Avenue N.W.

Rural economic development has always been a part of OEC's mission. OEC employees are involved in their communities and working hard to bring new industry and jobs to the rural towns and communities served by the Cooperative. Today, OEC provides more than just electricity to its members. A number of "Good Neighbor" programs are offered such as free energy audits, water heater and heat pump rebates, extended office hours and a rural crime watch program. The services offered may change over the years, but the cooperative spirit behind them will not.

The 1st trainload of OEC poles - 1937.

Oklahoma Gas & Electric Company

Back in 1917, Oklahoma Gas and Electric Company bought the electric distribution system in Norman. The same year, a transmission line was built between Oklahoma City and Norman.

That line, along with a transmission line built to El Reno the same year, marked the beginning of the enormous network of interconnected transmission lines in the OG&E system

Ever since that time, OG&E has grown and expanded its service to a large part of Cleveland County.

For many years, Norman has been a District Headquarters in the Western Region, which included Norman, El Reno, Guthrie and Oklahoma City.

OG&E office and field personnel for the District numbered up to 54, depending on the era and the situation.

In OG&E's organization, a district has served both administrative and operational functions. The District Headquarters itself takes care of the accounting and administrative duties.

The Operating Headquarters includes the line and service crews who actually maintain, repair and operate the electrical equipment itself.

Over the years, the tendency has been for more centralized control, particularly in administration and accounting. However, the Districts still form the grass roots base of OG&E's structure. Local work is done by OG&E people who are part of the community.

Artist's rendering of how OG&E's new Western Region Headquarters office will appear when remodeling is completed. The former Carey-Lombard Lumber Company building at 128 East Main, Norman, dates back to 1894.

In 1987, OG&E reorganized the Regions, and Norman, while remaining a District headquarters, also became headquarters for the new Western Region. This vast area of 140 cities and towns stretches from Kansas to Texas and includes Ardmore and Durant in the south and stretches all the way to Woodward, Enid and rural areas over much of western Oklahoma.

Though the Oklahoma City metro area is now a separate Region, Norman's central location and status as a Region Headquarters assures an expanded role in OG&E's operations.

In fact, the number of OG&E per-

sonnel has more than doubled with the formation of the new Western Region, so that there are now 109 company positions in Norman.

To serve as a home for the new Region, OG&E picked the 1894-vintage Carey-Lombard Lumber Company building, more recently known as the old First National Bank building, at 128 East Main.

Work got under way in 1988 to restore the exterior of the building to its original appearance.

Energy saving features and interior remodeling assure that the building will be an efficient office facility as well as a restored historic site.

The Region Operating Headquarters was initially located at the old Totco Building, 600 Rock Creek Road. The permanent facility, destined for extensive remodeling, is in the former Prince Valve Company site on 36th Street N.W.

The District office remains at 130 East Eufaula and the District Operating Headquarters on Rock Creek Road just west of the temporary Region facility also remains in operation.

Although OG&E's presence and service to Cleveland County have lasted over seven decades, OG&E officials predict that it's just the beginning of a long and mutually beneficial relationship.

G.W. Hanley and Garland Council pause for a mid-day break by their truck in Norman, 1951.

Pab Personnel

The Professional Adjustment Bureau, a collection agency begun by Seth Millington, first opened its doors at 132 W. Main in Norman in August 1962.

By 1968, it had outgrown its offices and re-established itself at 119 S. Santa Fe.

The following year, the business was incorporated and began doing business as PAB Inc. and PAB Personnel Agency.

In May 1977, Millington purchased the Credit Bureau of Norman. At that time, it was computerized with the national entity and also purchased two collection agencies: Doctor's and Merchant's Account Service and Oklahoma Collection Bureau. It also purchased two credit bureaus: the Credit Bureau of Purcell and the Credit Bureau of Clinton.

In 1986, all divisions with the exception of PAB Personnel were sold to Associated Credit Services of Houston, Texas. PAB Personnel then moved to its current location at 118 W. Main.

Now, in addition to its services as a permanent employment service, PAB Personnel provides a temporary help service.

At PAB Personnel, Millington said, "We interview people and try to place them with employers, and we take job orders from employers and try to match them. We also do employee leasing — a situation in which an employee has his own employees, but elects for someone else to do the payroll, etc., so that, in effect, we're leasing back their own employees to them." There are now five full-time employees at PAB Personnel, plus about 50 temperory employees who are out on either full-or part-time employment assignments.

Millington, a native of Edmond, has lived in Norman since 1962. He majored in accounting at the University of Oklahoma, where he received his bachelor of business administration degree in 1956.

He served in the United States Marine Corps, as an M.C. aviator, from 1956 to 1961.

He is a past president of the Oklahoma Collectors Association and the Associated Credit Bureaus of Oklahoma. He is also a past member of the Lions Club, has served on the board of directors of the Norman Chamber of Commerce, and served on the Oklahoma State Department of Corrections for seven years.

He and his wife, Ellen, have five grown children: Sharon, Will, Douglas, Jeff and David.

Primrose Funeral Home

The personal touch.

That's what Primrose Funeral Home, 1109 N. Porter Avenue in Norman, strives to offer.

The philosophy of generating goodwill in the community comes from founder Odies Primrose, who opened the funeral home in 1931.

Primrose, who at 82 remains active in the business, can recall many of the families he helped through hard times. And what's more, they remember him, often calling for his "personal touch" when the death of a loved one occurs.

Primrose and an assistant, George Jansing, opened Jansing-Primrose Funeral Home in a Norman house in 1931. After several years in business with Jansing, Primrose opened his business at its current location.

"We (he and Jansing) converted an old two-door Buick sedan into an ambulance," Primrose recalled, adding, "In those days, funeral homes ran the ambulance service, too."

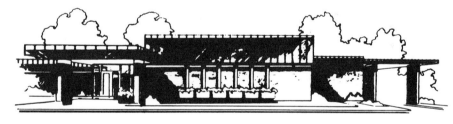

The Depression saw the fall of many businesses in Oklahoma. Many, like Primrose, that survived did so by calling on the resources of the whole family. Primrose's wife, Blanch, for instance, drove an ambulance from Norman to Oklahoma City — a $5 call. (Norman at that time did not have a hospital, Primrose explained.)

The same economic conditions that forced wives and even children to help out with the business made it difficult for family members to come up with the funds for funerals. Sometimes payment was made with chickens or eggs. In one instance, a woman sent small amounts for 20 years to pay for her mother's funeral. This, even though a funeral cost only $150.

Ben Primrose, one of Primrose's seven children, said that the goodwill generated by his father through the years was the catalyst for the success the company enjoys today. A concrete example of that success is the new $1 million funeral home built recently at 13313 N. Kelly. The new facility, located in front of the main entrance to Memorial Park Cemetery, serves north Oklahoma City and Edmond.

Now remarried (Blanch passed away), Primrose and his wife, Rossie, live in Norman, where Primrose continues to serve as a longtime deacon of First Baptist Church. A Mason, he is also a member of the Lions Club, Oklahoma Funeral Directors Association and other civic groups.

Shaklee Corporation

Billed as "the largest private commercial development in Norman's history", the $50-million dollar, 300,000-square-foot, state-of-the-art Shaklee facility officially opened in South Norman in October of 1979, it is located on a 200-acre-site south of Oklahoma 9.

Oklahoma was chosen as the location for Shaklee's first plant outside of California for several reasons; one being the state's central location; and secondly many of the substances and ingredients used in the manufacturing of Shaklee's nutritional products can be found in this region. Norman plant manager, Larry Clark, noted that Shaklee wanted to locate where there was clean industry. Shaklee was one of the first of the large high-tech industries to settle into Norman (the others are Westinghouse, which began operations in the early seventies, and TOTCO, which began operations just months after Shaklee).

Clark noted that the Norman plant primarily manufactures nutritional supplements in tablet form, although powdered drink products and Energy Bars are also manufactured there. "We are the worlds leading manufacturer of nutritional products", said Clark. "Nutrition is our major business. We pride ourselves in being in harmony with nature. We steer away from synthetics".

The Norman plant was honored in July 1988 by the American Veterans of World War II, Korea, and Vietnam (AMVETS) as **Employer of the Year** for 1987. The plant was cited for its outstanding results in hiring veterans and for its overall excellent participation in community activities. "Shaklee is very involved in the community, and we make corporate responsibility an important commitment. We feel that, as a company, we owe something to the community'" said Mario Nunez, Personnel Manager. "We encourage management and employees to get involved with the United Way, the Chamber of Commerce, Big Brothers/-Big Sisters, the Red Cross, and other community service organizations." The extensive grounds of the Norman plant has a ParCourse which is open to the public during daylight hours. The ParCourse has a one-mile jogging trail and several picnic tables. Shaklee has also contributed to projects at the University of Oklahoma, Cleveland County 'Y' and now sponsor the "Science Screen Report" for the Norman School District.

Shaklee Corporation has divisions in the U.S., Japan and Canada, and is the parent company of Bear Creek Corporation of Medford, Oregon. Shaklee also makes household, personal care products and the BestWater Purification System. Co-founded in 1956 by Dr. Forrest C. Shaklee Sr. and his sons, Forrest Jr. and Lee, Shaklee has been publicly owned since 1973. It is a Fortune 500 Company with stock traded on the New York Exchange. Shaklee's goals are:

(1) To enhance the quality of life and well-being of people and the environment through healthy, natural products, (2) to provide a high level of personal service, and (3) to be a specialty marketer of differentiated products with exclusive attributes.

Sooner Fashion Mall

In the midst of an $8 million expansion/renovation program, Sooner Fashion Mall also has an eye on Oklahoma's past.

The mall will put the emphasis on the first part of its name — "Sooner" — next year with a series of Centennial-related activities. Among other things, said mall manager Don Mayes, there will be a "Gold Mine," a quilt show and an antique toy exhibit and sale. Mayes also is involved in the celebration of the 1889 Run on a personal basis; he is serving as chairman of the 89er Days Parade.

But back to the present.

The expansion/renovation project entails several changes. When the project was first unveiled, Michael F. Kelly, chairman of The Center Companies, a Minneapolis-based company for the property, said: "Plans call for not only the renovation of the overall interior and partial exterior, but we will be adding approximately 132,000 square feet of shopping space, including a new 102,000-square-foot Dillard's building."

Dillard's now operates a 68,000-square-foot store at the mall. The present Dillard's location will be reoccupied by J.C. Penney's in 1989, and a new tenant (as yet unknown) will locate in the current J.C. Penney space.

Plans also call for the addition of new parking space, the redesigning of the traffic flow pattern, improvement of access roads and complete resurfacing of areas not presently paved.

"With the widening of West Main Street in front of the center to six lanes last fall, and with the addition of signal lights at the center's main entrance, the parking lot and traffic flow improvements will make Sooner Fashion Mall a much more comfortable and accessible place for our customers to shop," Kelly said. He also noted plans for landscaping to beautify the area and further enhance the mall's appearance for passers-by on Interstate 35 and Norman.

Kelly noted that "many exciting features" will be added to the mall, including space for over a dozen new retail specialty shops. The expansion also will provide new locations for existing tenants. Landscaped fountains and seating areas, a new tile floor and new sky lighting will capture the center's new, modern mood and brighten

the overall motif.

The Sooner Fashion Mall opened on Aug. 12, 1976. This marks the second expansion since that date. J.C. Penney's and the H.J. Wilsons department stores (the latter is now occupied by Service Merchandise) opened in October 1978.

With the addition, the center will exceed 600,000 square feet in gross leasable space on the 51-acre site.

Noting that the mall is visited by some 15,000 people per day, according to rough estimates, Mayes stated: "We do, in dollars per square foot, as well or better than any other mall in the state."

The largest mall in Cleveland County, the Sooner Fashion Mall also services the counties of McClain, Garvin, Grady and Pottawatomie. It is the last regional mall located on I-35 South between Oklahoma City and Dallas.

Currently, the mall generates more than $55 million in gross sales. Following completion of the expansion — which is set for April 1989, to coincide with the state's Centennial — projected sales are expected to exceed the $70 million mark.

The mall is owned by The Equitable Life Assurance Society of the United States.

Transcript Press

Before it was incorporated in 1950, the Transcript Press was a department of the Transcript Company, publishers of *The Norman Transcript,* from 1889 through 1985. For many years the operation was housed on the second floor of a building located one-half block south of Main Street on Peters Street. In 1960 the firm moved to a building specially designed to house printing operations at its current location, 222 E. Eufaula.

Today the firm has 30 full-time and part-time employees who produce newsletters, magazines, brochures, programs and advertising inserts as well as printed business materials, forms, letterheads, envelopes and business cards.

The Transcript Press is equipped with two large two-color offset presses, a large one-color offset press and two small one-color offset presses with the capacity to print anything from a business card to a multivolume book with color plates. The press also has kept its letterpress capacities, although the greatest volume of today's production is through the use of offset equipment.

Typesetting is achieved through the use of sophisticated video display terminal CRTronic equipment. Camera work is done on a large press camera and film is processed in a self-contained Log E Tronic processing unit. Litho plates also are processed in an automated unit. Perfect binding, comb binding, and saddle stitch binding also are done in the plant, while larger volumes are bound out-of-house.

President and manager of the Transcript Press is Ron Minnix. Other members of the coordinating staff are Bob Rice, assistant manager; Gene Moser, sales associate; Tom Hodge, production superintendent; Chuck Bacon, business manager, and Jean Hill, office coordinator.

A graduate of the University of Oklahoma School of Journalism Minnix has more than 20 years of experience in the fields of selling, management, buying and customer relations. Currently, he is Visiting Associate Professor in the advertising Department of the H. H. Herbert School of Journalism and Mass Communications at OU.

Minnix joined the Transcript Press sales staff in 1970, was named manager in 1980, and purchased the printing operation in 1985 from the heirs of Harold R. Belknap and from Mr. and Mrs. Don M. Frensley.

Before coming to the Transcript Press, he had been in advertising sales at the *Dallas Times-Herald* and the *Norman Transcript.* He served two years in the U. S. Army, with a nine-month stint in Vietnam as a reporter for *Stars and Stripes.*

At the Transcript Press, Minnix produces several newsletters. He also supervises the production for the Oklahoma State Medical Associations' Journal, the Sooner Magazine and the Oklahoma Interscholastic Press Association publications, and is involved in the production of eight-page advertising supplements for Gundaker Realtors. In addition, he coordinates the preparation and production of Mikasa dinnerware advertising brochures for clients all over the United States.

Minnix also supervises printing for major and minor sports for Oklahoma State University, Tulsa University, Oral Roberts University and the University of Oklahoma, producing media guides, recruiting materials, posters, brochures and individual game programs.

Assistant manager Rice, whose father was employed as assistant advertising manager at *The Norman Transcript* before embarking on a 25-year career as an advertising professor at OU, literally grew up in the printing area.

Rice began his service at the Press as a deliveryman and printer's helper while still a student at Norman High School. In 1964, Rice received a printing-lithography certificate from Oklahoma State Tech, Okmulgee, and began full-time employment with the Transcript Press as a photo engraver and cameraman making zinc plates for the Press and *The Norman Transcript.*

He left the Press in 1969 to become preparation foreman for John Roberts Co. of Austin, Texas, where he worked with printing and award plaques. He returned to the Press in 1971 as a photo engraver and camera operator until 1975 when he began customer sales. He became assistant manager in 1980.

Experience in a variety of areas of printing production helps sales associate Moser provide efficient and effective service to his customers.

The Cyril native worked for the *Cyril News* as a student in high school before studying printing at Oklahoma State Tech. He received a printing technology certificate from Oklahoma State Tech in 1960, shortly before joining the Transcript Press staff as a compositor. He stayed at the Press until 1968, when he went to work for OU's University Printing Service.

Moser returned to the Press as art department supervisor after 10 years with University Printing Services, becoming a sales associate in 1981.

Bacon, the business manager, also has spent virtually all of his life associated with the printing industry. A member of a newspaper family, he worked at the *Sayre Journal* following graduation from OU's journalism school in 1973. At the Journal, Bacon was publisher, editor and general manager.

He joined the staff of *The Norman Transcript* in 1980 as reporter, later becoming office manager, controller and business manager. He joined the Transcript Press staff in 1986.

Hodge holds more than 25 years of service at the Transcript Press. As production superintendent, he supervises typesetting, printing, camera and bindery operations.

The Weleetka native studied a year at Eastern A & M Junior College at Wilburton before receiving a printing technology certificate from Oklahoma State Tech.

He came to work for the Press in July 1959 from Tech as linotype operator and floorman. He worked in that capacity for nine years before accepting a position as pressman in his hometown at the Mid Continent Container Company. He then worked a year each at Southwest Stationary and the *Oklahoma Journal,* both in Oklahoma City, before returning to the Press in 1971.

Tarver Construction

J. D. Tarver, founder of Tarver Construction Company Inc. of Norman, began not in the construction business but as a milk hauler. As a rural milkman, J. D. picked up raw milk from area dairies and delivered it to Gilt Edge. His business flourished and by the '50's he had acquired a fleet of three trucks. J. D. ran the business until 1952, at which time a milk association was formed and he decided to go into another line of work.

In 1952, J. D., with a few pieces of equipment, began doing excavation work. His wife, Arlesa, helped in the business by doing the bookkeeping in their "office" located in the Tarver home. By 1959, the business had expanded and began laying asphalt. In 1970, the business incorporated.

Despite the oil bust and subsequent hard economic times in the Sooner state, the business continued to thrive. With a gross sales of about $5 million, Tarver Construction Company is in-

The Tarver Family - (seated): J.D. and Arlesa. (back row, left to right): Jerry, Jill and Jack.

volved in everything from State Highway projects to commercial and private projects.

J. D. retired in 1982, but all three of his children remain very much involved in the business. Jerry is chairman of the board, Jack is president, and Jill is vice-president.

Recent projects have included laying the asphalt on Interstate 35 over the South Canadian River and doing the excavation and asphalt work for the expansion of the Sooner Fashion Mall in Norman. The company also was

contracted to do all of the asphalt overlay on Norman streets in preparation for the upcoming Olympic Sports Festival and Centennial celebrations.

Other recent projects include laying asphalt on 11 miles of Highway 9 to Lake Thunderbird and doing the first phase of work for the new Postal Services' Technical Training Center.

About 20 persons are employed at Tarver Construction Company. For the last five years, the business has been head-quartered in Corporate Plaza, 2420 Springer Drive.

Type Traditional

Type Traditional . . . with its hope in the future — and its roots in the past . . . was founded by Robert J. Buford and his daughter Jennifer Lee Veal, in January 1986 at 457 West Gray, Norman, Oklahoma.

Both Bob and Jennifer attended the University of Oklahoma and both have lived in Norman for the past 28 years; Bob with his wife Billie, and Jennifer with her two sons, Brad and Brent and husband Glen, who is also an OU graduate. He is presently employed as a pharmacist at the Oklahoma Memorial Teaching Hospital in Oklahoma City.

Bob and Jennifer have been involved together with the printed word, in various ways over the past years.

Bob's publishing interest took him into the weekly newspaper business at the age of 21 as founder/editor/publishter of the *Welch American*. At that

time little Jennifer (three years old), was filling the ink well of the big newspaper press with a little shovel from her sandbox (much to her father's horror!), she undoubtedly got ink into her veins equal to Bob's.

In 1975, Jennifer again was working admirably, side by side with Bob (Look Dad, no shovel!), on production of *Guffey's Executive Journal* a real estate publication in Oklahoma City.

During this time Bob had rekindled a keen interest in book publishing after doing the production on several county and city history books over the state. Seeing the potential for great success in this area, Bob and Jennifer decided to continue in this exciting type of publishing.

Their work has been widely acclaimed due to high standards of design and quality workmanship. The typesetting is done with dedication, knowing that these histories will become family heirlooms to endure with time.

Most recent publications have been *Cleveland County, Pride of the Prom-*

ised Land, An Illustrated History, by local author Bonnie Speer; *Jack Love, Eighty-Niner,* by Sharon, Oklahoma author Grace Adams; *Mulhall, Oklahoma, 100 Yesteryears,* by Mulhall authors Kathryn and Max Stansbury; *1889, etc. A Collectors Cookbook,* edited by Ann Champeau and illustrated by Jonnie Witt; written by the Norman Senior Citizens Writing Class and sponsored by The Norman Galaxy of Writers; *Shades of Gray,* by Robert M. Gray; a series on *Mananging the Church* by authors Robert N. and Gary M. Gray; *In Spanish Or In English,* by local poet Myriam Bevers.

Type Traditional has also done production on University of Oklahoma Press books, as well as the following: *Lincoln County, Oklahoma History; Pottawatomie County, Oklahoma History, Noble County, Oklahoma History,* and *Writers of The Purple Sage.*

Traditional Publishers is the publishing and marketing division of Type Traditional.

The University of Oklahoma

In 1890, seventeen years before Oklahoma became a state, the Territorial Legislature established The University of Oklahoma. The University opened its doors in 1892 in a rented rock building on Norman's Main Street. To the south, the first University building was under construction on the wind-swept prairie.

On that first September day, 57 students were in class. An early day faculty member said they were "products of pioneer life" who felt they were "facing a great opportunity."

The early years were marked by slow growth in terms of enrollment and physical facilities. The 1893 administration building burned in 1903. A second structure, completed soon after the first fire, burned in 1907. In the meantime, the University had acquired a Carnegie Library building and the building now known as Old Science Hall.

The sports programs of the University began in 1895 with the organization of a football team. The team played only one game — with the Oklahoma City Town Team — and lost 0-34.

The first two degrees — pharmaceutical chemist — were awarded in 1896. The first two graduates of the regular college course received their Bachelor of Arts degrees in 1898.

In the early 1900s, OU was organized into schools and colleges and the fine arts program was begun. The medical school was developed, joining existing programs in liberal arts, engineering, and law. Business administration began in 1913.

World War I brought the addition of 13 courses to train soldiers and their civilian counterparts. Following the war, the Reserve Officers Training Corp (ROTC) was established on campus.

In the 1920s, enrollment reached 3,500. The Women's Building was completed and the first dormitory, now Whitehand Hall, provided men's housing. Hester-Robertson, a women's dormitory, was completed in 1926.

William Bennett Bizzell served as

Evans Hall, the University's Administration Building, constructed in 1912. The large elm tree in front is believed to be one of those planted by OU's first President, Dr. David Ross Boyd.

President from 1923 until 1941, a period of great progress for the University. The University Press and the alumni *Sooner Magazine* were established. The first doctor of philosophy degree was granted in 1929. The College of Education was established and the medical school was moved to Oklahoma City. Construction included the original library, Buchanan Hall, the Union, and Oklahoma Memorial Stadium.

The tenure of Joseph A. Brandt was brief but marked by innovation. He established University College, the academic unit for freshmen; created the Research Institute, the foundation for today's significant programs, and encouraged faculty participation through the Faculty Senate.

Brandt was succeeded in 1943 by George Lynn Cross who served until 1968. He guided the University through the difficult post war years from the 1945 graduating class of 274 to the skyrocketing enrollment of the late 1960s. It was a time of expansion with new physical facilities and new land with the acquisition of two former bases, the current North and South Campuses.

In the late 1940s, black students sought admission to OU, succeeding in 1948. In the 1950s, the first full-fledged fund-raising campaign was conducted. The University developed Max Westheimer Field and acquired the Biological Station at Lake Texoma. During this time the University's football program achieved national prominence.

The brief tenure of J. Herbert Hollomon was marked by an inaugural year of celebratory events and the student unrest of the late 1960s. While Hollomon received criticism for his handling of events, the University escaped the chaos seen on a number of campuses.

Paul F. Sharp guided the University from 1970 to 1977. He placed a new emphasis on private fund raising with dramatic results including the first $1 million gift from the Noble Foundation for construction of Lloyd Noble Center. Sharp also emphasized scholarly achievements and facilities for students.

OU's next president, William S. Banowsky, also emphasized private fund-raising, expanding the 100-person President's Council into the OU Associates with more than 1,400 who contribute $1,000 each year for academic programs. He also oversaw construction of the first phase of the Catlett Music Center, the doubling of the library with the Doris W. Neustadt Wing, and the beginnings of the Energy Center.

Most recently, during the tenure of Frank E. Horton, the University has emphasized the recruitment of outstanding students, and increased quality and quantity of sponsored research. A $9 million federal grant for Energy Center construction was sought and received.

Currently a search for a new president has begun. Until that time, the University is being led by Interim President David Swank.

In 1990, the University will observe its 100th year. The Centennial will celebrate the accomplishments of the past 100 years and, more importantly, will serve as the cornerstone for a second century of progress.

A Centennial Commission has been appointed to plan the year-long observance. The Centennial Campaign, a $100 million fund raising drive to provide academic excellence, has begun.

Much has changed since those 57 young men and women met in 1892 to plan their course work with President David Ross Boyd, but that long ago frontier spirit is still very much a part of OU. The University of Oklahoma is still a place of great opportunity.

BOB USRY PLUMBING, INC.

Bob Usry and long-time employee Walter Rowe.

Bob Usry Plumbing first began doing business in the Norman area in 1973. In 1974, he and a partner formed B&B Plumbing Inc. However, he still kept his own individual yellow page ad. On June 14, 1987, the partnership dissolved and Usry went back to the original name.

Today, Usry operates his business east of Norman. Although his business has taken off fast since he set out on his own again and he can afford to re-locate in a more central location, he prefers not to. The reason is simple: Keeping his overhead down will offer his customers more cost savings. His prices are very competitive. He now has eight employees: two secretaries, three plumbers and three apprentices.

Usry stays involved in all aspects of the business, from making weekend and evening calls to advertising. Being a graduate of the Dale Carnegie Human Relations Course, he believes in keeping his name in front of the public. He runs ads in the University of Oklahoma's football program, Norman High School athletic program, *The Norman Transcript,* and also runs spot advertising on the Al Eschback Show, to give examples.

Usry noted that his business area includes not only Norman, but also Moore, Noble, Oklahoma City and Blanchard. He does everything from commercial and industrial work to repair, remodeling and residential work. He especially likes challenging jobs.

He says, "There is no job too large or too small. If no one else can do it, we probably can."

Bob Usry Plumbing is radio-dispatched, on 24-hour call seven days a week. A range of repair service is offered, including (but not limited to) unstopping sewers, sink lines, sanitary sewers and washing machine lines; fixing frozen and/or broken pipes in the winter, and installing garbage disposals and all major brand faucets. He also sells plumbing fixtures of all brands.

Valouch Electric

Roy Valouch Electrical Co. Inc., a family-run business started by Roy Valouch in 1938, has weathered a lot of hard times — not the least of which was the oil bust of recent years.

But things are beginning to look up, according to Valouch's widow and longtime partner, Evelyn.

The story of Valouch Electric is a study in changes and constants.

As from the beginning, Valouch Electric is a family-run business. Officially retired but still involved in operations is Mrs. Valouch. Two of her daughters — Marilyn Lassetter and Beverly Millstead — take care of day-to-day business. Two other daughters have moved and no longer are involved in the business. Gloria Moore now lives in Honolulu; Nancy Peed resides in Orange Park, Fla.

There have also been some changes.

When Valouch first set up shop out of his home, the business consisted of electrical contracting work. It wasn't until he moved his headquarters to a white frame house in downtown Norman in 1956 that he also began selling fixtures. He moved to his current location at 113 W. Gray two years later.

In 1980, Valouch sold the contracting part of the business to some of his former employees, and Valouch Electric then concentrated on selling fixtures.

Today, Valouch Electric carries a wide variety of lighting fixtures, ceiling fans and lamp shades. "We try to keep a wide variety to suit every taste," said Mrs. Valouch.

In addition to lamps of every color and shape — including a popular computer model — they sell track lighting and even light bulbs.

Valouch Electric also offers a lamp repair service through a local repairman. And, they provide in-home consultation upon request.

What is the secret of their success?

Modestly, Mrs. Valouch replied: "We try to keep quality products at a good price. And, we offer years of personal service. It's comforting to know that you can serve the public."

Valouch Electric, a member of the Norman Chamber of Commerce, is open 8:30 to 5:30 Monday through Friday and 9 to 4 Saturday.

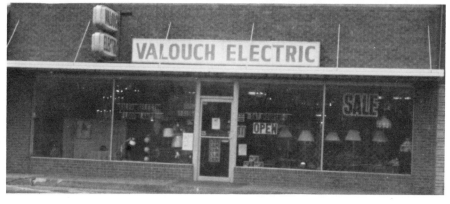

Wright's IGA

The first Wright's IGA store, which opened on Eufaula Street in Norman 1976, had a short history: it burned a year later. But 30 days later, the replacement store was in operation at 1440 N. Porter.

When it first opened, the store on Porter was 10,000 square feet; however, within six months it had expanded into the 4,000 ft space vacated by a drugstore next door. Two years later, it expanded yet another 1,000 feet giving the store a total of 15,000 feet.

But further expansion was on the mind of owner Coy Wright. On Oct. 16, 1981, a new 20,000-square-foot store was opened on West Main. In 1986, it also was expanded, making the store 27,500 feet, the largest of Wright's stores.

A third new 26,200-square-foot store located on East Alameda opened July 18, 1984, and in May 1988, Coy Wright opened a fourth store, this one located at 120 South Fourth Street in Purcell.

Wright attributes part of his continued success to the fact that his is in large part a family-run operation. His son, Larry, and sons-in-law Tom Wilson and Rick Alexander serve as vice presidents and store managers. His wife, Lou, is secretary/treasurer; while his daughter, Diana Wilson, is bakery and deli supervisor for all the stores. His other daughter, Peggy Alexander, is assistant secretary and treasurer. Lori Wright is in charge of our Profit Sharing Plan.

Not that non-family members can't climb the ranks, too. Manager of the new Purcell store is Jason McGee, who has worked his way up since 1976 from checker.

Wright's father, an oil-field worker who farmed in the Wayne area, was killed in an oil-field accident when Coy was only seven. When he was in the seventh grade, Coy, one of six children, supplemented the family income by working at a small supermarket. Wright worked his way up at Humpty to vice president and general manager (1973) of the company's Cleveland (Ohio) division: He briefly left Humpty in 1962, to work as produce merchandiser and buyer for the Dallas division of the Kroger Co. Two years later he returned to Humpty.

"At the time I came to Norman I felt that there was a big vacuum for a good supermarket in Norman," Wright recalled. "Safeway had dominated the town, and we came here because we felt Norman had some of the highest prices in the state. They really had no competition in town."

Wright quickly earned a niche in the community, not only because he offered competitive prices, but because of his dedication to the community. Since the beginning, Wright was committed to giving something back to the community. Over the years, Wright's IGA has helped sponsor many ball teams and school projects, helped with various non-profit groups' drives and supported the Cleveland and McClain counties' Christmas stores, to name just a few examples. He is also the only supermarket in town to give senior citizen discounts.

"Our objective is to help the community in every way that we can," Wright said. "We've gotten involved in the Chamber of Commerce and the Family Y," he said, also noting that several Wright's employees also have gotten involved in community causes on an individual basis.

"I think that our involvement in community affairs has something to do with our success.

Of course, since the first Wright's IGA opened in Norman more than a decade ago the competition has increased. Where there was only Safeway, now there are many supermarkets. But Wright feels that the competition is a good thing. "I like competition," he stated. "I tell our people every time we get a new competitor, we must get sharper and better to survive. That's the American way of life."

It was that competition, for instance, that spurred our effort to come up with a better bakery.

"We've developed the strongest bakeries in Norman featuring the best in cake decorating." Wright said with pride. "Our delis are very successful," he added.

In futher efforts to keep the store competitive, Wright has modernized his stores. That includes the installation of the scanning, which "read" the bar codes found on virtually every product sold in stores today.

Wright also keeps abreast of the latest fads and tries to offer those products he thinks his customers will most like. For instance, he recently added frozen yogurt machines to two stores. "Have you tried it yet?" he asked. "Better not, you'll get hooked," he said grinning.

"But," he added, "I'm probably most proud of our front-end service. And, we deliver sacks to the car for the customer."

Wright's future plans? We will replace the North Porter store "nearby" within the next five years. Other new stores are on the drawing board.

Other plans include further updating the check-cashing program. By offering our customers a range of new check-cashing privileges. "Norman is our home and we will always be a part of this fine city for generations to come or until our Lord returns."

BIBLIOGRAPHY

Books

Blackburn, Bob, *Heart of the Promised Land, Oklahoma County,* Windsor Publications, Inc., Woodland Hills, California, 1982.

Buchannan, James Shannon, *History of Oklahoma,* Printed for the Authors, Chicago, 1924.

Carter, L. Edward, *The Story of Oklahoma Newspapers,* Heritage Association, Western Heritage Books, Inc., Oklahoma City, 1984.

Chagler, Allison, and Stephen D. Maguire, *When Oklahoma Took the Trolly,* Interrubans, Glendale, 1980.

Cleveland County Historical Society, *Pioneers of Cleveland County 1889-1907,* Laird Printing Co., Norman, 1973.

Cleveland County Historical Society, *Pioneers and Early Settlers of Cleveland County,* 1889-1925, Laird Printing Co., Norman, 1973.

Cosby, Hugh E., Editor, *History of Moore,* Oklahoma, Cosby Publishing, Inc., Moore, OK 1977.

Cross, George Lynn, *A Personal Account, 1941-1946, the University of Oklahoma and World War II,* University of Oklahoma Press, Norman, OK 1980.

Cross, George Lynn, *University Presidents Can't Punt, OU Football Tradition,* University of Oklahoma Press, Norman, OK 1977.

Faulk, Odie, *The Making of A Merchant, Raymond A. Young and TG&Y Stores,* Western Heritage Books, Inc., Oklahoma City, 1980.

Forest Trees of Oklahoma, State Board of Agriculture, Forestry Division, and U.S. Department of Agriculture, Washington, D.C., August 1955.

Franklin, Jimmie Lewis, *Born Sober, Prohibition In Oklahoma 1907-1959,* University of Oklahoma Press, Norman, OK 1971.

Franks, Kenny A., Paul F. Lambert, and Carl H. Tyson, *Early Oklahoma Oil, A Photographic History, 1859-1935,* Texas A&M University Press, College Station, 1981.

Gibson, Arrell M., *The Chickasaws,* University of Oklahoma Press, Norman, 1971.

Hicks, John D., Mowry, George E., Robert E. Burke, *A History of American Democracy,* Houghton Mifflin Company, Boston, 1970.

History of Oklahoma, 1924.

Johnson, Neil, *The Chickasaw Rancher,* Redlands Press, Stillwater, Oklahoma, 1961.

Keith, Harold, *Oklahoma Kickoff,* University of Oklahoma Press, Norman, OK 1979.

League of Women Voters. *This Is Norman: 1955.*

Luper, Clara, *Behold the Walls,* published by Jim Wire, 1979.

National Guard of the United States. State of Oklahoma: 1938.

Norman Council of State Garden Clubs. Norman: 1971.

Smith's Directory, Norman, I.T., 1890-1891, courtesy of Edna Couch.

The University of Oklahoma 1980 Football Guide, University of Oklahoma Printing Services, Norman, 1980.

Weeks, Jim, *The Sooners, A Story of Oklahoma Football,* The Strode Publishers, Huntsville, Alabama, 1974.

Womack, John, *Annals of Cleveland County,* published by the author, Norman, OK March 21, 1981.

Womack, John, *Cleveland County Historical Highlights,* Noble, OK November 1982.

Womack, John, "Cleveland County, Oklahoma, Place Names, published by the author, Norman, OK 1977.

Womack, John, *Norman - An Early History, 1820-1900,* published by the author, Norman, 1976.

Newspapers

Cleveland County Reporter, "Lexington and Sandtown, the Wet Years," by John Womack, edited by Larry Colbert, April 17, 1980.

The Norman Transcript, numerous issues, July 13, 1889 to 1987.

"Put Your Duds In Our Suds" was the motto of the Norman Steam Laundry, which was built in 1902 by John Williams. This photo was taken in 1912. Courtesy Multi-County Pioneer Library and The Norman Transcript.

Few young people lived in Norman during the months immediately following the run. John Black, 15, (left) and his stepbrother Alfred Ayers, 17, were popular with the builders around the town. John made the run with his father, Hugh Black and Alfred drove their wagon across the Canadian River to join them later. Courtesy Pioneer Multi-County Library and Western History Collections, University of Oklahoma.

This section of the Norman business district on Main Street, shown in 1901, burned in a disastrous fire in September 1924. Courtesy The Norman Transcript.

The Daily Oklahoman, "The Daddy of OU," February 8, 1931.

The Daily Oklahoman, "South Canadian River Traces Historic Boundary of Oklahoma County," January 13, 1967.

The Daily Oklahoman, "Her Birth Beats City's," May 11, 1971.

The Daily Oklahoman, "OU Fan Cecil Samara - Sooner Born, Sooner Bred and When He Dies . . .," November 7, 1982.

Purcell Territorial Topic, May 14, 1891.

The Sunday Oklahoman, " 'Norman Camp' Now Modern, Busy City," November 25, 1973.

The Sunday Oklahoman, "Window On the Past, Grog Plentiful," November 13, 1977.

Magazines

Allison, Rose, "Carey Lumber Celebrates 100 Years in Business," *Hardhat,* April/May 1981.

Foreman, Carolyn Thomas, "Albert Rennie," *Chronicles of Oklahoma,* Vol. 27, pp. 124-125.

Sandstrom, Eve, "The Mascots," *Oklahoma Today*, September October, 1987.

Sieg, Will, "Sandbar Saloon," from unidentified magazine and unknown date.

Sooner Magazine, "A History of the University of Oklahoma," Paul Galloway, Editor, Vol. 38, No. 1, September 1965.

Sooner Magazine, "First Ten Years of the University, 1892-1903," reprint 1912 *Sooner,* Vol. 8, University of Oklahoma.

Southern Living, "An Oklahoma Alp?", November 1977.

Film Script

Rodgers, Wilma Wickizer, "Early Day Houses, Norman, OK, 1890-1918."

Folders

"Noble," Oklahoma State Historical Society, "A Symposium of Noble, OK.", by Noble Future Homemakers of America, May 1957.

"Lexington," Oklahoma State Historical Society.

"Lexington," vertical file, Purcell Public Library.

"Mount Williams," The University of Oklahoma, OU Information News Media.

Various, Pioneer Multi-County Library, including "Norman Chamber Of Commerce," "*Transcript* Photos,'" and "Norman History."

Miscelleanous

1980 Lexington, Oklahoma Census, compiled by John Womack, 1982.

Transcript, "Lexington-Purcell Toll Bridge," talk by Pearson Woodall, Cleveland County Historical Society, October 7, 1975.

Typescript, "Story of Norman - Surveyor and Site," by John Womack, June 1974, courtesy of Edna Couch.

INDEX

Abernathy, Morgan, 86
Absentee Shawnee Indians, Big Jim's Band, 49, 51
Acers, A. D., 19, 36
Adair, Samuel E. Lt., 15
Adair, W. C., 40, 90, 92
Adams, A. B. Mrs., 155
Adams, Grace, 179
Adkins, Art, 33
Adkins, Betty, 61
Adkins, C. D., 16, 34, 61
Adkins, Columbus D. (C.D.), 33
Adkins Crossing, 23, 57
Adkins Ford, 94
Adkins, Frank, 33
Adkins Hill, 23, 34
Adkins, Hughell, 33, 61
Adkins, James, 33, 61
Adkins, John, 16, 33, 61
Adkins, L. F. Sr., 61
Adkins, Lewis F., 16
Adkins, Oliver, 61
Adkins, Pryor V., 13, 16, 18, 33, 34, 39, 45, 61, 90,
Adkins, Sarah Janes, 61
Adkins, W. A., 61
Agnes Hotel, 94
Alden, Arthur M., 142
Alexander, Peggy, 92
Alexander, Perry, 182
Alexander, Rick, 182
Allard Cleaners, 164
Allard, Jim, 164
Allen, Etta, 92
Allen, Willie, 92
Ambrister, Samuel A., 29
American Legion Post, 111
Amos, F. S. E., 92
Amos, French S. E., 94, 95
Anderhub, John H., 105
Anderson, Judge Mrs., 104
Andrews, Fred, 66
Applegate, Henry, 75
Arbuckle Trail, 6
Ard, Maud, 150
Ark, The, 84
Arline Hotel, 90
Army Air Corps, 117
Army ROTC, 111
Athens of Oklahoma, 49
Atnip, Donna Mae Nelson, 158
Autrey, Myrtle Lee, 111
Autry, Brick, 150
Avants, _____, 84
B&B Plumbing Inc., 181
Bacon, Chuck, 178
Baird, Mary Elizabeth, 151
Baker, John Jerome, 56
Banks, D. F., 29
Banowsky, William Slater, 150, 180
Barbour Drug Store, 102
Barbour, Ed, 92
Barbour, Jennie, 92
Barbour, John, 92, 143
Barbour, Kathryn, 92
Barker, Gina, 161
Barrett, Theodore H., 8
Barrow, Ona, 92
Barry, Bob, 69
Barry, Bob Mrs., 69
Bean, Fred, 138
Bean, Jesse Capt., 4
Beeler, Frank, 86
Beeler, George, 86, 87
Belknap, Harold R., 178
Belknap, Harold R. Jr., 159
Belknap, Harold Raymond, 159
Belknap, Harold Raymond III, 159
Belknap, Harold T., 172

Belknap, Helen Lucille (Shoemate), 159
Belknap, Jamie Lucille (Foor), 159
Benally, Ron, 142
Bernard, Spencer, 156
Berry, Addie, 49
Berry, Alpha, 49
Berry, Avo, 49
Berry, Bob Mrs., 104
Berry, R. C., 110, 113
Berry, Ray, 49
Berry, R. C. Mrs., 49
Berry, Roy, 60
Bert, Charles, 158
Bert, Charles W., 158
Bert, Charlotte (Davis), 158
Bert, David, 158
Bessent, Charles N., 39
Bettes, Grandma, 88
Bevers, Myriam, 179
Big Jim Crossing, 110
Bishop's Creek, 39
Bishop's Spring, 19
Bishop, Darcy Lynne, 161
Bishop, Henry Austin, 161
Bishop, James, 19, 23, 51
Bishop, Kayla Jo, 161
Bishop, Tom, 165
Bishop, Tommy Joe, 161
Bishop, Vela Bonneta (Pickens), 161
Bixler, Mort L., 40, 66, 67, 90
Bizzell, W. B. Dr., 154
Bizzell, William Bennett, 150
Black, Herbert, 84
Black, Shirley, 157
Blake, George, 13, 15, 18, 36, 39, 50
Blake, Tyler, 13, 15, 36
Blakeney, B. B., 55, 66
Blakeney, R. Q., 37
Blakeney, Robert Q., 55, 66
Blakenship, Lester, 24
Bliss, Chester Bradley, 153
Bliss, Henrietta Maude (Ittner), 153
Bliss, Hoarce Hopkins, 153
Bobo, Mrs., 104
Bodine, Christine, 44
Bodine, May Miss, 44
Boggs, Miss, 44
Bonaparte, Napoleon, 2
Bond, L. R., 92
Boomer Sooner, 142
Boone, Nathan Capt., 6
Booze Capital of Southern Oklahoma Territory, 84, 85
Borjes, Diedrich "Dick," 59
Boshers, A. W., 61
Boshers, Stella Adkins, 61
Boston, _____, 37
Boudinot, Elias C., 6, 7
Bowlan, Clay, 110
Boyd, David Ross Dr., 92, 93, 94, 98, 99, 150, 180
Boyd Field, 137
Boyd, William, 114
Bob Usry Plumbing Inc., 181
Braman, E. R., 110
Branden, Hillie, 92
Brandt, Joseph August, 116, 150, 180
Braynt, Ruth, 84
Briggs, L. L., 150
Brockhaus Nursery,, 80
Brooks, Stratton Dr., 98
Brooks, Stratton Duluth, 150
Brown, Dorothy B., 155
Brown, H. Jack Dr., 155
Brown, Harry, 92
Brown, Hoarce Brightberry, 155
Brown, Jimmy, 84
Bryant, _____, 84

Buchanan, James Shannon, 150
Buckhead Saloon, 47
Bucklin, George, 96, 97
Buford, Billie, 179
Buford, Christopher, 158
Buford, Jennifer, 158
Buford, Paul N., 158
Buford, Robert J., 158, 179
Buford, Rubye (Simpson), 158
Bugher, L. B., 112
Bullett, George Jr., 152
Bumgarner, Charles, 126
Bumgarner, Jack, 126
Bumgarner, James Scott, 126
Bumgarner, W. W., 126
Bureau of Reclamation, 129
Bureau of Aeronautics, 117
Burke, J. J., 66,172
Burns, Mrs., 44
Burr, Thaddeus Mitchell, 156
Butcher, Nahum E., 97
Butler, Paul, 118
Butterfield, R. A., 59
Callahan, B. O., 141
Campbell, Charley, 78
Campbell, Walter, 2
Camp Holmens, 5
Capshaw, Madison T. J., 26
Carder, Frank, 105
Carey, W. P, 36
Carey Lombard Lumber Co., 19, 36, 51, 93, 103, 174
Carmon, Jim, 84
Carnegie Library, 43, 98, 99
Cate, Roscoe, 155
Central Oklahoma Water Users, 129
Central Pharmacy, 164
Central State Griffin Memorial Hospital, 101
Chamberlain, Charles M., 12, 34, 72
Champeau, Ann, 179
Chastain, Earl, 22
Chastain, J. M., 22
Cheadle, Mrs., 104
Chennault, Claire Lee, 152
Chesney, Dr., 26
Chesney, Samuel O. Dr., 88
Chevalier, Maurice, 114
Chicago Times, 7
Childs, Darwin, 84
Chisholm, Jesse, 5, 6
Chouteau, A. P. Col., 5
Citizens Bank, 42
City National Bank, 36, 46, 110, 111
Civilian Conservation Corps, 114
Clapham, Jasper, 138
Clark, Frank E., 18
Clark, Larry, 176
Clarke, J. C., 5
Clarke, Sidney, 152
Clement, Daisy Armstrong, 65, 66
Clement, R. E. "Buck", 128
Cleveland County Courthouse, 17, 54, 114
Cleveland County Record, 164
Cleveland County Historical House, 48
Cleveland, Grover President, 40
Co. C 120th Engineers, 106
Co. D. 179th Infantry, 106
Collins, Helene (Carpenter), 154
Collums, Christi Doyle, 152
Collums, Daniel Boone, 152
Collums, Dora (Greeson), 152
Collums, Garner Greeson, 152
Collums, Gary Garner, 152
Collums, James Daniel, 152
Collums, James Samuel, 152
Commercial Bank, 41, 42
Compton, Maud, 92

Compton, Rose, 92
Cooksey, Harold, 129
Cook, Ed, 141
Cook, Teen, 49
Cooley, Ben Dr., 111
Coronado, Francisco Vasquez de, 2
Cottrell, Bud, 74, 75
Couch Center, 122
Couch, Edna M., 152
Couch, Mary (Bryan), 152
Couch, Meshach., 152
Couch, William, 7, 8, 40, 152
Coulter, Franklin Schaffer, 160
Coulter, J. N., 92
Coulter, John, 160
Coulter, Kelly, 160
Coulter, Michael, 160
Coulter, Nona Marie (Schaffer), 160
Coulter, Oscar Leroy, 160
Coulter, Sheryl (Breaux), 160
Cox, Charles, 37
Craddock, Vema, 84
Cralle, E. W., 173
Cralle, Edgar, 62
Cronkite, Walter, 68
Cross, Braden Riehl, 153
Cross, George Lynn Dr. 64, 167, 123, 127, 148, 150, 153, 180
Cross, George William, 153
Cross, Jemima (Dawson), 153
Cross, Mary-Lynn, 153
Cross Timbers, 1, 24
Culpepper, Betty Joene, 161
Culpepper, Jerri L., 161
Culpepper, Lindsey Nicole, 161
Culpepper, Lori, 161
Culpepper, William Franklin, 161
Curtis, Wayne, 167
Dale, Edward Everett Dr., 65
Day, Anna (Mitchell), 151
Day, Edwin, 151
Day, John L. Dr., 110
Day, John L., 171
DeBarr, Edwin C., 92, 94, 95, 104, 138
Delay, E. W. Mrs., 37
Depue, Will, 92
Dickard, Alma, 92
Dickerson, Tol, 69
Dilbeck, Gracie, 84
Dilbeck, Tom, 89
Dill, Lucy, 92
Doctor and Buzz Bartlett Foundation, Inc., 145
Dollarhide, Mattie, 42
Donahue, Erin, Mathews, 157
Donahue, Hayden, 156
Donahue, Henry Tull, 157
Donahue, Kerry Eckhardt, 157
Donahue, Minnie Elizabeth (Scott) Toothaker, 157
Donahue, Patricia Toothaker, 157
Donahue, Patty Crocker, 157
Donehue, Marion, 92, 93
Donrey Media Group, 172
Doolittle, James H., 152
Dora, Lucille Dr., 104
Dorr, Marland, 151
Dorrance, Lem, 92
Douglas Aircraft Company, 117, 120
Don James Co., 168
Drake, Bruce, 58
Dreesen, H. P, 76
Dunn, Bert, 138
Dunn, John, 68
Dunscomb, Pearl Mrs., 111
Dyer, Lester, 75
Dyer, Sam G., 75
Easterling, Carl Lloyd, 157
Easterling, Henry Clifton, 157

Easterling, Henry Clifton II, 157
Easterling, Pearle Belle (Hall), 157
Easterling, Susan Alice (Herron), 157
Easterling, Wilma (McGuire), 157
Eastside School, 44
Edison, Thomas, 173
Edwards, Lewis J., 41
Edwards Park, 41
Edwards, Winnie, 92
Eisenhower, Dwight D., 129
Elledge, Ike, 47
Ellinger, R. F. Jr., 84
Emery, Walter, 68
Endicott, Martin, 37
Endicott, Van, 66
Engleman, Emma, 111
English, Vic Mrs., 71
Etowah, 71, 88
Evans, A. Grant, 100, 150
Evans, Arthur Grant, 150
Evans, JoAnn McCauley, 159
Evans, John P, 138
Evans, Mrs., 104
Ewing, Fred "Buck", 140
Fairbanks, Chuck, 142, 148
Farmers National Bank, 46
Federated Women's Club, 111
Felgar, David, 150
Felgar, James Huston, 150
Felgar, Margaret (Huston), 150
Felgar, Mrs., 104
Field, Walter, 97
First National Bank, 174
First National Bank of Moore, 76
Fishburn, L. R., 24
Fishburn, Tim, 24
Fisher, Ada Lois Sipuel, 126
Fontenier, Emile, 173
Ford, Hyla Miss, 105
Foreman, Maggie (Waggoner), 152
Foreman, Ruth, 154
Fort Gibson, 4
Foster, T. Jack, 170
Foy, Roy (Brick), 150
Franing, John Mrs., 104
Franing Opera House, 103
Franklin, 49, 71, 88
Fred, Dutch, 50
French, Miss, 92
Frensley, Don M., 172
Frensley, Don M. Mrs., 178
Ft. Holmes, 5
Fulkerson, Boise, 104
Fulkerson, Grover, 104
Fulkerson, Malcom, 3, 104
Fun City, 84
Garee, C. E., 52, 57, 59, 78, 79
Garee, Elizabeth, 84
Garee, Elva, 79
Garee, F. A., 57
Garner, James, 39, 126
Gautt, Prentice, 146
General Motors Corporation, 77
George, Kenneth, 151
Gibbons, Floyd, 112
Gibson, Arrell Morgan, 157
Gibson, Dorothy (Deitz), 157
Gibson, Kathleen (Ash), 157
Gibson, Michael Morgan, 157
Gibson, Patricia Dr., 157
Gibson, Rosemary, (Phillips-Newell), 157
Gimeno, Harold, 111, 115
Goodrich, Ed M., 37
Gordon, Borris B., 150
Gordon, Cynthia, 152
Gordon's Specialty, 165
Gorton, Charles T., 13, 15, 18, 19, 34, 35
Gorton, Charley, 93, 94

Gossett, Maude, 92
Gould, Charles E. Dr., 55
Graham, Ike, 82
Graham, "Okie", 82
Graham, R. A., 19
Grand Central Hotel, 113
Gray, Gary M., 179
Gray, Matthew Alan, 156
Gray, Robert M., 179
Green, Amos, 86
Gregg, Josiah, 6
Griffin, D. W. Mrs., 104
Griffin, David W. Dr., 101
Griffin, Jeff, 66
Griffin, V. C. Capt., 121
Griggs, L. L., 126
Grissom, Buck, 84
Grissom, George, 55
Grissom, Margie, 84
Hadsell, S. R. 96
Hall, Bill, 39
Hall, E. C., 167
Hanlon, Cheryl Ann Nelson, 158
Hardage, Lewie, 145
Hardie, Ralph, 89
Hardin, E. E., 173
Hardy, John Mrs., 104
Harlow, Adalene (Rae), 159
Harlow, David Ralph, 159
Harlow, James G., 159
Harlow, James G. Jr., 159
Harlow, James G. III, 159
Harlow, Jane M. (Bienfang), 159
Harrison, Benjamin President, 9, 12,40
Harts, John A., 137
Hayes, Will Mrs., 104
Hays, Mrs., 44
Heck, Homer, 68
Hefley, Belle, 13
Hefley, Harold, 13
Hefley, Henry, 13
Hefley, Jefferson Lehmanowsky "Lem", 12
Hefley, Jess, 13
Hefley, Jesse, 92
Hefley, John, 13
Hefley, John T., 92
Hefley, Lem, 13, 18, 34, 35
Hefley, Lem Mrs., 13, 35
Hefley, Nellie, 13, 16, 35
Hefley, Nora, 13
Hefley, Orna, 13
Helvie, John, 13
Helvie, Roscoe, 92
Hendry, Mary, 83
Henthorne, Paul, 167
Herbert, Harold Harvey, 151
Herbert, H. H., 172
Hico, 88
Higbee, B. L. Sr., 85
Higginbotham, Frank G., 173
Higgins, Rita, 154
Higgins, W. J., 105
High Gate College, 95, 97
Hillsdale Free Will Baptist College, 73
Hill, Jean, 178
Hine, R. V., 154
Hitachi Computer Products (America) Inc., 166
Hobaugh, John, 84
Hobson, Cal, 156
Hocker, Bill, 86
Hodge, E. L., 64
Hodge, Tom, 178
Holcraft, Charlie, 95
Hollomon, 180
Hollomon, John Herbert, 150
Hollywood Shopping Center, 130
Hood, James Berry, 154
Hood, James O'Leary, 154
Hood, Maybelle (Paschall), 154
Hood, Robert Sidney, 154

Hoover, Herbert, 114
Hoover, Mead, 50
Hoover, Mert, 50
Horton, Frank E., 180
Horton, Frank Elba, 150
Hotel Norman, 37
Houghton, Otis, 92
House, Ruth, 138
Hover, _____, 84
Hughes, Mr., 89
Hume, Carleton Ross, 97
Hume, Ray, 138
Hunt, Ollie, 92
I.O.O.F. Cematery, 39, 168
Ille, Adolpf, 86
Ille, G., 86
Ingle, Ed P, 13, 27, 43, 54, 66, 172,
Ingram, Bat, 118
Innis, R. E. Dr., 26
Interurban Eating House, 62
Interurban Restaurant, 167
Iowa Hotel, 76
Irvin, Tom, 24
Irving, Washington, 4
Jackson, Tillie, 150
Jacobs, Hattie, 92
Jacobs, Wallace, 92
James, Donald Lovett, 168
James, Elizabeth (Lovett), 168
James, Thomas, 168
Jansing, George, 169, 175
Jarboe, Jennie, 92
Jarmon, John, 129
J.C. Penney, 177
Jefferson, Thomas President, 3
Jefferson School, 42, 44
Jennison Brothers, 29
Jennison, W. R., 28
Jensen, Theo, 47
Jepson, _____, 56
Johns, Alice, 92
Johnson, D. B. R., 173
Johnson, Dr., 16
Johnson, Edward B., 11, 12
Johnson, Montford, 12
Johnson, Montford B., 78
Johnson, Montford T., 11, 14
Johnson, T. J., 67
Johnston, Abe Thedford, 152, 160
Johnston, Billie Louise, 158
Johnston, Cecile L. (Skaggs), 160
Johnston, Kendra Louise, 160
Johnston, Kenneth R., 160
Johnston, Kenneth Wesley, 160
Jones and Berry Cotton Yard, 28
Jones, Craig, 171
Jones, Gomer, 148
Jones, Lawrence "Biff", 145
Judd, Etta, 150
Jury, William C., 75
KFJF, 69
KIMY, 69
KNOR, 69
KOMA, 69
KRXO, 69
KTOK, 69
Kahoe, Jack, 38
Kai-Shek, Chiang, 152
Keating, Alma Louise, 151
Kelly, Michael F., 177
Kendall, Edwin H., 66
Kendall, William, 96
Kerr, Robert S., 129
Kingkade, 36
Kingkade, Andrew, 12, 18, 35, 39
Kingkade, Martin, 12
Klinglesmith, Mary Anne Miss, 79
Klu Klux Klan, 103, 104, 126
Kraettli, Emil R., 64
Kurkendoll, Roy, 84
Laizure, Jerry A., 164

Laizure, Peggy S., 164
Lake Thunderbird, 129
Larsh, Delbert, 13, 15, 17, 18, 35, 39, 41, 93
Larsh, Harold, 61
Larsh, _____, 61
Lassetter, Marilyn, 181
Leavy, George T., 92
Lee, Cate, 156
Lenby, Don, 61
Leslie, Gus, 82
Leslie, Louisa, 82
Lindeaux, Robert, 15
Lindsay, Boss, 169
Lindsay, H. G. Mrs., 104
Lindsay, Joe, 11
Lindsey, Adrian, 145
Lindsey, L. C., 89
Lindsey, J. L., 64
Lions Park, 42
"Little Red", 142
Lloyd Noble Center, 132, 133
Loeffler, Frank, 167
Loeffler, Ross, 167
Loeffler, Rusty, 167
Longwell, Elbert, 92
Long, Bert, 138
Long, Stephen H. Major, 4
Lottinville, Elinor (Denham), 154
Lottinville, Marie Therese (Livesay), 154
Lottinville, Mary E (Igoe), 154
Lottinville, Savoie, 116, 154
Lottinville, Walter J., 154
Louisiana Purchase, 3
Lowther, R. D. Dr., 26
Lowther, Mrs., 104
Lumper, Lola May, 84
Luper, _____, 84
Luster, Dewey "Snorter", 145
Luttrell, Anne (Garrett), 157
Luttrell, Gladys (Simpson), 157
Luttrell, Richard Carter, 157
Luttrell, Richard Carter Jr., 157
Luttrell, Robert T., 157
Luttrell, Tom, 37
Mackenzie, Jim, 148
Manley, Cora, 84
Manley, Ruby, 84
Marquart, D. W., 40
Marr, Helen, 92
Martin, Mamie, 92
Mary Sudick No. 1, 112
Matthews, T. Becker, 141
Mayes, Don, 159, 177
Mayes Funeral Directors, 169
Mayes, Pat, 169
Mayfield and Bellamy, 36
Max Westheimer Field, 65, 116, 118
McCall, Sam, 101
McClure, Ella, 150
McClure, Myrtle, 150
McCredy, E. D., 79
McDade-Taber Inc., 169
McDade, Agnes R. (Endicott), 160
McDade, Danna, 160
McDade, John B., 160
McDade, Kimberly, 160
McDade, Larry, 169
McDade, Larry R., 160
McDade Studios, 169
McFarlin Memorial Methodist Church, 110, 114
McFarlin, R. M. Mr. and Mrs., 114
McFarlin, Robert, 110, 113
McFerron, ————, 84
McGaha, Shelia, 169
McGee, Jason, 182
McGinley, M., 36
McKenzie, Frankie Mrs., 130
McKim, Jay, 144

McKinney, Sarah Jane, 33
McMahan, Mark, 140
McQuire, Grace King, 97
McQuire, J. D., 47
Medlock, Newt, 138
Mefford, Alvin, 84
Mefford, Ethel, 84
Merkle, Joe, 92, 138, 140
Merkle, John, 90, 140
Merkle, Priscilla, 90
Methodist Episcopal Church, 42
Methodist Episcopal Church
   South, 48, 95
Methodist High Gate College,
   100
Meyer, Henry Jr., 169
Meyer, Henry Sr., 169
Meyer and Meyer Funeral
   Home, 169
Meyers, Frank, 49
Miller, Gus, 61
Miller, Jim, 159
Miller, Marvin, 92
Miller, Tucker E., 172
Millington, David, 175
Millington, Douglas, 175
Millington, Ellen, 175
Millington, Jeff, 175
Millington, Seth, 175
Millington, Sharon, 175
Millington, Will, 175
Mills, Kid, 50
Mills, Lottie Mae, 84
Minnix, Ron, 162, 178
Minteer, Joseph C., 155
"Minute City", 77
Mita, Katsushige, 166
Monroney, Mike, 118
Montgomery, Constance Ainley,
   156
Montgomery, Edward Finley, 156
Montgomery, Edward Philip, 156
Montgomery, John Edward, 156
Montgomery, Karen Sue
   (Harpole), 156
Montgomery, Marie Alberta
   (Finley), 156
Mooney, _____, 56
Moore, 72, 118
Moore First Baptist Church, 73
Moore, Gloria, 181
Moore High School, 73
Moore Methodist Church South,
   73
Moore, Mildred, 77
Moore-Norman Vo-Tech School,
   133, 134, 170
Moore Police Department, 76
Moore, S.M., 93, 94
Moore, Seth M., 13, 18
Moore Volunteer Fire
   Department, 76
Moore, W. S. Mrs., 104
Morain, Allen, 165
Morain, Gordon, 165
Morgan, William "Bill", 68, 69
Morris, Charles, 84
Moser, Gene, 178
Moses, Charles, 26
Mt. Williams, 125, 134
Mueller, Herman, 92
Muldrow, 68
Muldrow, H. L., 170
Munsell, C. G., 65
Murphy, _____, 105
Murray, William H., 112
Naill, George, 61
Nail, C. C. Dr., 77
National Association for the
   Advancement of Colored
   People, 126
National Guard Armory, 106, 114
Naval Air Technical Training
   Center, 117, 118, 119

Naval Air Technical Training
   Station, 121
Naval Air Technical Training
   Corps, 123
Naval Flight Training Center, 116,
   123
Naval Air Station, 118
Naval Air Technical Training, 119
Naval Aviation Training Center,
   118
Naval ROTC, 117
Naval Training School Aviation
   Maintenance Center, 119
Nelson, Deborah Kay, 158
Nemecek, George, 116, 173
Nemecek, Wilneth, 84
Nesbit, R. J., 90
Nesbitt, R. J., 40
Nigh, George, 156
Night Riders, 104
No. 1 Bugher, 112
Noble, 78
Noble Academy, 79, 95
Noble Church of Christ, 80
Noble Farmers State Bank, 83
Noble First Methodist Church,
   79, 81
Noble First State Bank, 83
Noble, John, 78
Noble Methodist Church, 79
Noble Nursery, 80
Noble Presbyterian Church, 80
Noble School, 83
Noble School District, 79
Nolan, James, 36
Nolan, John, 36
Nolan, Tony, 36, 50
Norman, Abner E., 8, 35, 125
Norman Advance, The, 66, 92
Norman Chamber of Commerce,
   113, 170
Norman Cornet Band, 49, 50
Cotton Gin and Cotton
   Seed Mill, 28, 29
Norman First Christain Church,
   90
Norman Galaxy Writers, 179
Norman Milling and Grain Com-
   pany, 43, 48, 101
Norman Municipal Hospital, 111,
   130, 171
Norman Public Library, 42, 111
Norman Regional Hospital, 171
Norman Senior Citizens Center,
   111
Norman Station, 12, 35
Norman Townsite Company, 17,
   18, 34, 46
Norman Transcript, The, 27, 39,
   43, 51, 66, 67, 172
Norman Telephone Exchange, 65
Norman's Camp, 5, 8, 23, 35
North Base, 117, 123, 125, 134
Nunez, Mario, 176
O'Conner, John, 29
O'Halloran, Bessie Merkle, 90
O'Haver, William, 24
Odaira, Namihei, 166
Oder, Major, 61
Oklahoma Call, The, 67
Oklahoma City Daily Times, 92
Oklahoma City Mill & Elevator
   Company, 76
Oklahoma City Oil Field, 112
Oklahoma Electric Cooperative,
   173
Oklahoma Gas & Electric
   Company, 174
Oklahoma Memorial Stadium,
   136
Oklahoma Station, 34
Oklahoma Territory Municipal
   Corporations Act, 41
Oklahoma Town Company, 34

Oklahoma Transportation
   Company, 63
Oklahoma Radio Engineering
   Company, 68
Oklahoma Sanitarium Company,
   100
Oklahoma State Hospital, 101
Oliver, Sam, 84
Old Fort Arbuckle, 4
Osceola, 4
Owen, Bennie, 67, 137, 141, 143,
   144
Owen Field, 136, 137, 149
Owens, Steve, 142, 148
Parham, R. H., 172
Parrington, Vernon, 100, 138, 140
Patton, George S. Jr. Gen., 118
Payne, David L., 7
Payne, Miss Nell, 84
Pab Personnel, 174
Peed, Nancy, 181
Petty, Nora, 84
Phillips, J.D., 65
Phillips, Joe, 89
Pickard, Claude, 60, 89
Pickard, Clyde, 89
Pioneer Drug Store, 36
Pioneer Multi-County Library,
   77
Pioneer Telephone Company, 66
Planters Hotel, 28, 45
Pledger, Fletcher, 108
Pledger Post, 108
Pledger-Allen Post, 171
Poe, V. I., 173
Polk, William, 23, 29
Pool, Agnes, 92
Pool, Lizzie, 92
Prescott, Maurice L., 68
Prichett, Mrs., 104
Primrose, Ben, 175
Primrose, Blanch, 175
Primrose Funeral Home, 175
Primrose, Rossie, 175
Prince, Scott, 47
Professional Adjustment Bureau,
   174
Public Works Administration,
   114
Pucker, Mrs., 104
Purcell Bridge and Transfer
   Company, 87
Purcell, City of, 85
Purcell Register, 14, 27, 66, 85
Purcell Station, 11
Rapier, Elsie, 154
Reach, Cliff, 61
Redman, J. H., 173
Reeds, Armstead, 28
Reeds, Armstead M. Mr. and
   Mrs., 26
Reeds, Artie, 28
Reeds, Claude, 139, 144
Reed, Fred, 50
Reed, Ralph, 165
Regime Club, 104
Reid, W. J., 78
Reiger, Henry A., 151
Reiger, Joseph A., 151
Reiger, Josephine (Amrein), 151
Reisinger, R. L., 49
Renfro, William Governor, 100
Renner, S. P. Mrs., 104
Rennie, Albert, 14, 17, 39, 78
Rennie, James, 78
Reserve Officers Training Corp,
   180
Reuter, Bernard, 138
Rice, Bob, 178
Rice, W. N., 92
Rice, William N., 94, 95
Richardson, Oliver, 90
Rieger, Alois J., 151
Reiger, John A. "Andy", 164

Rieger, Joseph A. Dr., 151
Rieger, Karen S., 164
Rieger, Kathryn Marie Sister, 151
Rieger, Mercedes (Skaggs), 151
Rieger, Patricia A., 151
Reiger, Rose Pauline, 151
Rigg, M., 57
Rigg, N. C., 57
Riggs, Clara Mae, 84
Risinger, Bud, 138
Ritter, Minnie, 92
Robers, Will, 117
Roberts, Attie, 92
Roberts, Fred, 140
Roberts, James, 84
Roberts, Worth, 84
Rock Building, 94, 95, 99
Rockefeller, Carrie, 92
Roosevelt, Eleanor, 118
Roosevelt, Franklin D., 114, 118,
   121, 173
Rose, Carl M., 160
Rose, Frances N. (Carl), 160
Rose, Johnson Mrs., 44
Rose, M. T., 160
Ross, C. D., 71
Rough Riders, 139
Roy, Cook, 60
Royal, Darrell, 148
Ruedy Lumber Co., 76
Runyan, Denver, 88, 150
Runyan, M. C., 88, 89, 150
Runyan, Nadine, 150
Rural Electrification
   Administration, 173
Russell, George, 84
Salisbury, K. B. Capt., 116
Samara, Cecil, 144
Sandel, Wilma, 84
Sand Bar Saloon, 84
Scott, W. J., 82
Seawall Opera House, 49
Seawell Opera House, 103
Security National Bank, 110
Selective Service Act, 108
Self, R. C., 59
Selmon, Dewey, 143
Selmon, LeRoy, 143
Selmon, Lucious, 143
Seminole Townsite and
   Development Company, 34
Service Merchandise, 177
Seven Oil Company, 110
Sevier, Fred, 39
Sewell, M. D., 173
Shaklee Corporation, 176
Shaklee, Forrest Jr., 176
Shaklee, Forrest Sr. Dr., 176
Shaklee, Lee, 176
Sharp, Paul F., 180
Sharp, Paul Frederick, 150
Shears, Charles Irving, 101
Sheff, Henry, 173
Sheff, Henry C., 173
Sheff, Horace M., 173
Short, Harvey, 140
Short, Will, 138
Sikkink, Cleo, 153
Sikkink, Lydia (Long), 153
Sikkink, William, 153
Silk Stocking Row, 43, 45
Sims, Billy, 146
Sims, Mildred, 75
Sims, P. R., 75
Sipuel, Ada Lois, 127
Skaggs, Ed, 61
Slaughterville, 71, 88
'Sloan, Alfred, 155
Sloan, Alfred, 172
Sloan, Caroline (Dohl), 155
Smalley, Edwin, 62
Smalley, Edwin W., 59
Smith, Albert J., 75
Smith, C.J., 74

LEGEND

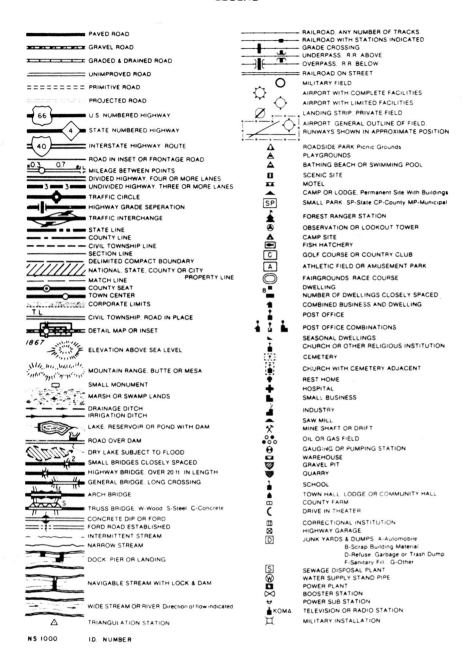

	PAVED ROAD
	GRAVEL ROAD
	GRADED & DRAINED ROAD
	UNIMPROVED ROAD
	PRIMITIVE ROAD
	PROJECTED ROAD
66	U S NUMBERED HIGHWAY
4	STATE NUMBERED HIGHWAY
40	INTERSTATE HIGHWAY ROUTE
	ROAD IN INSET OR FRONTAGE ROAD
0.3 0.7	MILEAGE BETWEEN POINTS
	DIVIDED HIGHWAY, FOUR OR MORE LANES
3 3	UNDIVIDED HIGHWAY, THREE OR MORE LANES
	TRAFFIC CIRCLE
	HIGHWAY GRADE SEPERATION
	TRAFFIC INTERCHANGE
	STATE LINE
	COUNTY LINE
	CIVIL TOWNSHIP LINE
	SECTION LINE
	DELIMITED COMPACT BOUNDARY
	NATIONAL, STATE, COUNTY OR CITY PROPERTY LINE
	MATCH LINE
	COUNTY SEAT
	TOWN CENTER
	CORPORATE LIMITS
T.L.	CIVIL TOWNSHIP, ROAD IN PLACE
	DETAIL MAP OR INSET
1867	ELEVATION ABOVE SEA LEVEL
	MOUNTAIN RANGE, BUTTE OR MESA
	SMALL MONUMENT
	MARSH OR SWAMP LANDS
	DRAINAGE DITCH
	IRRIGATION DITCH
	LAKE, RESERVOIR OR POND WITH DAM
	ROAD OVER DAM
	DRY LAKE SUBJECT TO FLOOD
	SMALL BRIDGES CLOSELY SPACED
	HIGHWAY BRIDGE, OVER 20 ft IN LENGTH
	GENERAL BRIDGE, LONG CROSSING
	ARCH BRIDGE
	TRUSS BRIDGE, W-Wood S-Steel C-Concrete
	CONCRETE DIP OR FORD
	FORD ROAD ESTABLISHED
	INTERMITTENT STREAM
	NARROW STREAM
	DOCK, PIER OR LANDING
	NAVIGABLE STREAM WITH LOCK & DAM
	WIDE STREAM OR RIVER Direction of flow indicated
	TRIANGULATION STATION
NS 1000	I.D. NUMBER

	RAILROAD, ANY NUMBER OF TRACKS
	RAILROAD WITH STATIONS INDICATED
	GRADE CROSSING
	UNDERPASS, R R ABOVE
	OVERPASS, R R BELOW
	RAILROAD ON STREET
	MILITARY FIELD
	AIRPORT WITH COMPLETE FACILITIES
	AIRPORT WITH LIMITED FACILITIES
	LANDING STRIP, PRIVATE FIELD
	AIRPORT GENERAL OUTLINE OF FIELD, RUNWAYS SHOWN IN APPROXIMATE POSITION
	ROADSIDE PARK Picnic Grounds
	PLAYGROUNDS
	BATHING BEACH OR SWIMMING POOL
	SCENIC SITE
	MOTEL
	CAMP OR LODGE, Permanent Site With Buildings
SP	SMALL PARK SP-State CP-County MP-Municipal
	FOREST RANGER STATION
	OBSERVATION OR LOOKOUT TOWER
	CAMP SITE
	FISH HATCHERY
C	GOLF COURSE OR COUNTRY CLUB
A	ATHLETIC FIELD OR AMUSEMENT PARK
	FAIRGROUNDS, RACE COURSE
	DWELLING
8	NUMBER OF DWELLINGS CLOSELY SPACED
	COMBINED BUSINESS AND DWELLING
	POST OFFICE
	POST OFFICE COMBINATIONS
	SEASONAL DWELLINGS
	CHURCH OR OTHER RELIGIOUS INSTITUTION
	CEMETERY
	CHURCH WITH CEMETERY ADJACENT
	REST HOME
	HOSPITAL
	SMALL BUSINESS
	INDUSTRY
	SAW MILL
	MINE SHAFT OR DRIFT
	OIL OR GAS FIELD
	GAUGING OR PUMPING STATION
	WAREHOUSE
	GRAVEL PIT
	QUARRY
	SCHOOL
	TOWN HALL, LODGE OR COMMUNITY HALL
	COUNTY FARM
	DRIVE IN THEATER
	CORRECTIONAL INSTITUTION
	HIGHWAY GARAGE
D	JUNK YARDS & DUMPS A-Automobile B-Scrap Building Material D-Refuse, Garbage or Trash Dump F-Sanitary Fill G-Other
S	SEWAGE DISPOSAL PLANT
W	WATER SUPPLY STAND PIPE
	POWER PLANT
	BOOSTER STATION
	POWER SUB STATION
KOMA	TELEVISION OR RADIO STATION
	MILITARY INSTALLATION

ALL DATA CURRENT TO
DATE OF INVENTORY
MARCH 1980

ORIGINAL DRAFTING BY M.A DEC. 1980
STATE SYSTEM REVISED TO JAN. 1983

GENERAL HIGHWAY MAP
CLEVELAND COUNTY
OKLAHOMA

PREPARED BY THE

OKLAHOMA DEPARTMENT OF TRANSPORTATION
PLANNING DIVISION

IN COOPERATION WITH THE

U.S. DEPARTMENT OF TRANSPORTATION
FEDERAL HIGHWAY ADMINISTRATION